WHAT PEOPLE ARE SAYING ABOUT THE WRITINGS OF LILIAN B. YEOMA...

T0286106

I cheerfully recommend this incredible work to you, knowing that it will transform your understanding of healing and healing ministry. We need this more than ever, with the lack of teaching on this important topic that is all too common in many churches today. Take advantage of this treasure that has been unearthed once again, and make sure to let others know so that we can see John 14:12 fulfilled, where we are doing the same works that Jesus did! It's time to awaken!

DANIEL AMSTUTZ
Director of Worship Arts and The Healing School
Charis Bible College and Andrew Wommack Ministries
Woodland Park, Colorado

As a fairly new believer in the mid-1970s, I began to grasp truths on the subject of divine healing. I recognized the importance not only for every believer but also for the healing ministry that I began to see in my own life. I began to search for writings on the subject of divine healing. Amongst those books were the writings of Dr. Lilian B. Yeomans. Her writings were an amazing blessing to my life—the chapters on "The Praise Cure," the writings about Galatians 3:13, as well as many others.

Dr. Yeomans' writings for many years now have been one of my normal textbooks that I go to on a regular basis. I'm thrilled to see the further truths from the life and ministry of Dr. Yeomans in this book. I believe these truths will be a great help to all of us as we launch further into the greatest outpouring of divine healing the world has ever seen through the ministry of Jesus the Healer.

MARK BRAZEE
Pastor World Outreach Church
Tulsa, Oklahoma

Dr. Kenneth E. Hagin was instrumental in getting Dr. Yeomans' books back into print when I was his editor of publications from 1970 to 1980. He highly valued her teachings.

Long before establishing Rhema Bible Training Center in Tulsa, he traveled in ministry for years, always carrying with him a small green Samsonite suitcase. Inside, along with his Bible and notebooks, were Dr. Lilian B. Yeomans' writings on healing and *The Life of Faith* by Mrs. C. Nuzum. He read these over and over. I can think of no higher recommendation than this one by this prince with God, Dr. Kenneth E. Hagin.

One of Dr. Hagin's fortes was divine healing. And he knew Dr. Yeomans' teachings to be among the highest and best.

DR. BILLYE BRIM
Billye Brim Ministries
Branson, Missouri

Lilian Yeomans practiced medicine throughout Canada as well as the northern regions of Canada, which included a time serving the Cree Indian tribes. As Lilian's desire to see people healthy and recover from every malady grew, she left the practice of medicine and became a missionary of healing to the whole man: spirit, soul, and body. Many testimonies of healings and miracles followed Lilian from place to place! She later connected with Aimee Semple McPhearson's ministry and taught classes on healing in McPhearson's school of ministry.

Lilian's writings, based on her hands-on experience with the healing ministry as well as her own recovery story from severe drug addiction, will motivate the reader to both experience healing and become an instrument of healing to others through the person of Jesus Christ.

BILLY BURKE
Billy Burke World Outreach
Tampa, Florida

Lilian B. Yeomans firmly grounds the doctrine of healing in scripture. With personal experience of God's healing power in her own life, Lilian compassionately and effectively ministered divine healing to others, making her books a deep reservoir of both sound doctrine and practical experience. The rediscovery of more of Lilian B. Yeomans' writings opens a valuable treasure to this generation's earnest students of divine healing, as well as to those wanting to receive healing.

PATSY CAMENETI
Pastor, Rhema Family Church
Brisbane, Australia
Cameneti Ministries

As far back as I can remember, I have heard the name Lilian B. Yeomans in our household. When I was in Bible school, we, as believers desiring to understand divine healing, minister it to others and receive it for ourselves, were required to study the work of Dr. Lilian B. Yeomans.

That's why I am excited for you to discover this courageous woman's journey and discoveries that made her into a divine healing expert. Inside, you will discover not only her story but the truth about sickness and disease, methods of healing, and, most importantly, what the Word says about healing, including biblical examples as well as promises.

There is no better person to edit and compile these great works than my friend, Kaye Hoole Mountz. Kaye works with the Holy Spirit to arrange His words in the most powerful ways.

Healing School is the perfect title for this work; it is a textbook for a lifelong journey to be healed, stay healed, and share the healing power of Jesus with others.

KELLIE COPELAND
Author and Host of *Kellie on the Victory Channel*
Fort Worth, Texas

In 1985, I was curled up on my couch reading a sermon by Lilian B. Yeomans on the subject of divine healing. I remember it well. I often read her sermons, but that day I had a particular interest in her teachings because I had been experiencing some lingering physical symptoms. But on that day, just while reading her sermons, I tangibly felt the power of God strike that part of my body and instantly every symptom left! The revelation her sermons held imparted a spirit of faith into me, and the power of God met that faith.

Then again, about 15 years later, I was going through a particular test that had lasted for over a year. One day, I said to God, "I've done everything I know to do, but I'm not progressing as I should. I'm missing it somewhere." Then God spoke three words to me, "The Praise Cure"— the title of a Lilian B. Yeomans' sermon. That was my answer. I again pulled out that sermon, fed on it, and immediately began doing as she had taught. Within one week, I was on the other side of that trial—the test was over!

The sermons of Lilian B. Yeomans hold divine answers! When faced with opposition and life's challenges, we need to have answers from God and know how to apply them. This is an outstanding feature of the teachings of Lilian B. Yeomans—answers for everyday life! Divine answers to live on!

For 40 years, her sermons have been a staple in my spiritual diet, for they impart the spirit of faith. I feed on them over and over again. So, it is a great joy to have an expanded collection of her sermons in this treasured book.

I so appreciate that Kaye Hoole Mountz and Harrison House have taken the time and effort to reach back into the treasure trove of forgotten writings to once again steward these truths on divine healing that are so deeply needed in every generation.

PASTOR NANCY DUFRESNE
Dufresne Ministries
Murrieta, California

Jesus Christ is the same yesterday, today, and forever. And so too His healing message. You will be empowered by these teachings by Dr. Yeomans to heal and be healed in Jesus' name.

BECKY DVORAK
Healing Evangelist
Glendale, Arizona

The subject of divine healing has been my passion for over 20 years and as an avid learner and reader, the writings of Dr. Lilian B. Yeomans have been some that I have consumed. The fact that she came from the medical field before entering the healing ministry has always been something that has further intrigued me about her ministry and the truths she brings out in her teachings. In *Healing School*, we are once again given tremendous insights into God's healing power and His will concerning healing. *Healing School* is another timeless book by Dr. Lilian B. Yeomans that will go into my library and continue to be used for future reference!

CHAD GONZALES
President of Chad Gonzales Ministries
Founder of The Healing Academy

The books of Lilian B. Yeomans are truly inspiring and insightful. As you read her writings, you will truly begin to understand the meaning of "having done all, to stand." You will gain insight into reading the Word, believing the Word, and speaking the Word. So many miracles happened in her quest to see people healed and whole.

PAT HARRISON
Co-founder of Harrison House Publishers
Co-founder of Faith Christian Fellowship International
Tulsa, Oklahoma

I had the benefit of reading Dr. Yeomans' books on healing some 40 years ago.

I was struck with the clarity and strength of persuasion with which she declared the unchanging healing truths of God's Word.

Having been delivered from death and tormenting bondage herself, she experienced firsthand how nothing is too hard for Him.

At some point, everyone will need faith for healing: either for yourself, a loved one, or a friend. These gems are a great addition to your spiritual arsenal, to feed your faith before you need it.

I recommend them highly.

Pastor Keith Moore
Faith Life Church
Branson, Missouri, and Sarasota, Florida

In this book, Dr. Lilian B. Yeomans' collection of classic teachings and works meticulously convey her deep and genuine relationship with Jesus Christ as her Savior. Even though Dr. Yeomans' medical background was as a practicing physician, suffering with her own morphine addiction, she describes meeting God firsthand as her healer. While her own personal story is captivating, the insight written about what Dr. Yeomans called the "Praise Cure" is the most compelling example of the price Jesus paid when He went to the cross so that we could experience God's healing power. I highly recommend this book and encourage you to draw all you can from each chapter.

Dr. Richard Roberts
CEO, Oral Roberts Ministries
Tulsa, Oklahoma

Healing School is a remarkable gift to the body of Christ, both stirring and inspiring. As I began to read, I was greatly encouraged by Dr. Yeomans' faith and personal testimonies. This precious resource brings us profound teachings of a pioneering figure in the faith community and is an invaluable resource for anyone wanting to grow in the area of divine healing.

Readers are invited to become students of Dr. Yeomans' healing school, offering them the opportunity to engage with the book in the same way as those who were part of her original schools, answering questions and being stirred by her teachings. When asked to peruse the manuscript, I found myself unable to put it down as it continued to encourage and inspire me. My prayer is that, as you read *Healing School*, you too will be encouraged and provoked to accomplish greater works in Christ.

KATHERINE RUONALA
Senior Leader, Glory City Church
Brisbane, Australia

In 1986, I stumbled on a little booklet titled *The Great Physician* by an author of whom I was not familiar, Dr. Lilian B. Yeomans. It was a short little book with only 72 pages, so I surmised it would be a quick read. If it wasn't helpful, I thought I wouldn't have wasted much time. Little did I know that Dr. Yeomans' personal story and amazing insights into healing and deliverance would have such a dramatic impact upon my life and ministry. Her personal testimony of deliverance and healing ignited within me a quest to pursue and learn about God's divine healing power available to humanity today.

Dr Yeomans' insight on divine healing is not merely theoretical; it is built on a foundation of personal experience, derived from her encounters with the power of God and the revelation of His Word. Almost 40 years later, that little booklet remains at arm's length of my desk and has served as a valuable resource throughout my ministry. *Healing School*, a compilation of some of Dr. Yeomans' writings and teachings, is a must for every person pursuing divine healing.

EDDIE TURNER
Pastor, Teacher, Author
Cookeville, Tennessee

Dr. Lilian B. Yeomans'
HEALING
SCHOOL

Classic Teachings & Works
Unpublished Since the 1930s

COMPILED BY
KAYE HOOLE MOUNTZ

Published by Harrison House Publishers
Shippensburg, PA 17257

ISBN 13 TP: 978-1-6675-0335-6
ISBN 13 eBook: 978-1-6675-0336-3

For Worldwide Distribution, Printed in the U.S.A.
4 5 6 7 8 / 28 27 26 25 24

Note from the Publisher

Editorial content, medical terminology, statistics, and financial numbers are presented as the author wrote them. We have updated grammar, punctuation, and spelling to modern standards for reader convenience.

Dr. Lilian B. Yeomans, like many other ministers of her era, was often negative regarding medical treatment and medicines. We, at Harrison House Publishers, believe the medical field has come a long way in the past century, but God is still the ultimate source of healing then and now. When it comes to medical treatment and medicines, we encourage readers to follow the leading of the Holy Spirit.

ACKNOWLEDGMENTS

It wasn't long after working with **Brad Herman,** while he served as Harrison House Publisher, that it became obvious how much he loves books. His voracious reading habits rival those of anyone I know, and he's especially partial to books that share life-changing messages grounded in God's Word. Upon discovering writings by Dr. Yeomans, unpublished since the 1930s, we discussed her captivating teachings back and forth until it became obvious they had to be curated into a book. Brad fanned the flames of this project in every way—even down to personally computerizing old documents.

In the early stage of research, **Pastor Eddie Turner** is the first person to introduce me to the Flowers Pentecostal Heritage Center (FPHC) in Springfield, Missouri. He told me that a visit to the archives would provide a never-ending resource of all things Pentecostal. He could not have been more correct in pointing me to a treasure trove of spiritual heritage.

During my time at FPHC, I crossed paths with **Darrin J. Rodgers,** the director of the center and also the editor of the Assemblies of God *Heritage* magazine. Through Darrin, I became acquainted with his wife, **Desiree Rodgers,** who has graciously allowed us to republish her biography of Dr. Yeomans. Her article showcases extensive research, painting an all-encompassing biographical sketch.

At FPHC, I also met **Glenn Gohr,** reference archivist, who became an invaluable resource and friend. I quickly learned that if Mr. Gohr didn't know exactly where to put his finger on an item—no matter its position among towering file stacks or vaulted materials—it probably didn't exist or he would soon be on the phone tracking it down. The gentleman himself is a walking, talking Pentecostal resource.

While stymied one day in search of a particular Dr. Yeomans' resource, I was ever grateful that expert Pentecostal revival historian, **Joseph Martin,** came to my rescue. He *only* searched 120,000 e-books and articles in the cloud to get me an answer.

Finally, a very sincere thank you to my husband, **Matthew Mountz,** and my oldest daughter, **Nicole Mountz.** Both accompanied me to Springfield, Missouri, helping to tirelessly research, organize, and copy teaching from a bygone era, still brimming with anointing to impact lives today.

CONTENTS

FOREWORD

BY ANNETTE CAPPS

I absolutely fell in love with Dr Lilian Yeoman's writings in the early days of my ministry. The depth of her relationship with God and her understanding of His provision for our healing imparted something to me that is unlike any other author. Almost 50 years later, her books are still on my nightstand and read regularly. Although the pages are yellowed and falling out, these books are some of my most valued possessions (pictures below).

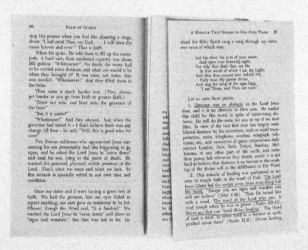

It is difficult to explain what makes her teaching so alive. I find myself not just immersed in the theory or theology of divine healing but in a living flow of the Master's touch.

That is why I was excited to receive the news that there were more of her writings to be released in this book. Brother Kenneth E. Hagin first introduced me to her writings on divine healing, and after reading the first one, I bought all her books that I could find at the time. In them, I recognized what my father, Charles Capps, called a "specialist ministry"—a ministry of healing.

Having received such a wonderful deliverance herself, Dr. Yeomans dedicated not only her medical training but her spiritual experience to healing the sick.

As you read these lessons on healing, you will sense the utter consecration to unveil the heart of God to heal His people. I ask you to open your heart to receive this revelation of love and the anointing on the Word that flows from this book.

INTRODUCTION

BY KAYE HOOLE MOUNTZ

Lilian Barbara Yeomans, M.D., devoted her life to fighting against sickness and disease—first as a medical doctor, then with far more powerful weapons as a leading divine healing evangelist of the 20th century. It has been a privilege to compile this curated selection of her sermons, still brimming with the anointing of God to impact lives today. Many of these messages have not been republished since the 1920s and 1930s when she originally taught them.

To help you navigate this collection, it's divided into three parts:

- Part 1 offers a **comprehensive six-volume exploration of "Divine Healing in the Scriptures."** These sermons were originally taught as a correspondence course by Dr. Yeomans at the Lighthouse of International Foursquare Evangelism (L.I.F.E), established in 1923 by Aimee Semple McPherson in Los Angeles, California. Although these sermons have been previously published under various titles, **our selection includes additional material Dr. Yeomans prepared for her healing school students, encompassing a practical method for studying, chapter outlines, and thought-provoking study questions.**

- Part 2 **showcases a book from Dr. Yeomans' literary repertoire titled *Resurrection Rays,* unpublished since its 1930 inception.** It focuses on resurrection rays, streaming straight from Heaven above, a token of God's love and healing power for you.

- Part 3 encompasses **timeless teachings from Dr. Yeomans regarding divine healing, most originally circulated in tract form circa the 1920s.**

On pages 7-23, we present an all-encompassing biographical sketch of Dr. Yeomans' life that offers extensive research.

On a more personal note, Dr. Yeomans' teachings have captured my heart and profoundly impacted my life since I began reading them while in Bible school in the early 1980s. She powerfully articulates her messages with boldness and precision, so much so that her in-depth study of God's Word and time spent in the presence of God are obvious and flowing with revelation. Yet Dr. Yeomans' teaching brings even more to the reader! Her sermons are underscored with practical insight—no doubt, a result of her delving into God's Word to personally receive healing and work one-to-one with countless others to do the same.

Dr. Yeomans' explanation of how she approached God's Word to take hold of her healing also best sums up the foundation of her teaching overall: "Not to while away a lonely hour; not to admire its literary excellencies I read The Book. *No, I read it for my very life!* I said, 'Now I have tried everything that willpower and medical science and suggestions and all the rest can do, and there is absolutely no hope for me unless it lies between the covers of This Book. I knew it was God's Book.'"

There—in God's Book—is where she found help, hope, and healing and led others to find the same. It's no wonder Dr. Yeomans had a reputation for shouting *"Hal-le-lu-jah!"* In fact, it was humorously written across her picture in the 1931 L.I.F.E. Bible School yearbook (picture on page 5).

In 1913, Lilian Yeomans and her sister, Amy, inherited property which they turned into a "faith home," ministering God's Word to those beyond medical help. Her medical background along with her daily encounters with sick people—who soon became healed people—provides those who read after her a powerful window into ministering divine healing to others.

Even at the age of 79, Dr. Yeomans still preached more than 100 sermons a year. And she would be happy to know that her sermons are preaching today. Her timeless sermons still carry the power of God. May the scriptural truths on the pages that follow carry health and healing to *you*. Dr. Yeomans would encourage you to, "Make Heaven ring with *your testimony* to His loving kindness, tender mercy, and faithfulness! Extol His great name!"

"Hal-le-lu-jah!"

ENCOUNTERING THE GREAT PHYSICIAN: THE LIFE AND MINISTRY OF DR. LILIAN B. YEOMANS

BY DESIREE D. RODGERS

Lilian B. Yeomans (1861-1942), a successful Canadian medical doctor, became addicted to morphine and nearly died. Out of desperation, in 1898 she turned to God and experienced a remarkable healing. Her encounter with the living God lit a fire in her heart, transforming her from the inside out. Yeomans went on to become one of the most prominent female Pentecostals of her era.

An educated woman leader in a movement deemed by some to be anti-intellectual and a medical doctor who believed wholeheartedly in divine healing, Yeomans plowed through obstacles and cultivated the faith of thousands. Becoming first a lay preacher, then a prominent healing evangelist, author, and educator, Yeomans interacted with leading Pentecostals such as Andrew H. Argue, Carrie Judd Montgomery, and Aimee Semple McPherson. Her speaking and writing made her a household name among Pentecostals in the 1920s and 1930s, and her books became best sellers.

Though Yeomans' testimony transcends time, her incredible life journey has been largely overlooked in recent decades. Her story highlights the human plight of one who worked tirelessly in the service of others, but neglected to care for her own physical and spiritual well-being. And were it not for the grace of God, that would have been the end of the story.

Early Life

On June 23, 1861, just a few months after the start of the American Civil War, a little girl was born in Madoc, Ontario, Canada, to Augustus A. and Amelia (LeSueur) Yeomans. Her father was of Puritan ancestry, and her mother was of respectable parentage. They were married just one year when nineteen-year-old Amelia gave birth to Lilian Barbara.[1] Lilian's father supported his young family as a surgeon for the United States Army during the Civil War.[2] Little is known about Lilian's childhood and early adolescence; however, in 1863, while the Civil War was still raging, a sister, Charlotte Amelia (Amy), was added to the family.[3] Charlotte would become Lilian's lifelong companion and coworker, first in the medical profession, and then in the soul profession.

Lilian was raised in a nominal Anglican family and recalled learning to keep the Ten Commandments from an early age.[4] However, learning the Law did not make a Christian of Lilian, but merely made her more aware of her spiritual hunger.[5] Her mother was dressing her for church in a frilly white dress one particular Sunday when she recognized herself to be a sinner. She later recalled this event in vivid detail: "the awful thought of my black heart inside of my white dress so overwhelmed me that I burst into a storm of weeping and cried, 'I am lost! I am lost!'" Her mother, who did not yet have a personal relationship with Jesus, replied, "I only wish you hadn't found it out when you had your best dress on."[6]

As a young adult, Lilian followed in her father's footsteps, furthering her education through medical training at the Toronto Medical School.[7] In 1880, after a year of study, her father, Augustus Yeomans, passed away.[8] Plagued by an ailment for many years, his sudden death was medically attributed to an overdose of the chloral he took to relieve his symptoms.[9] Lilian would later struggle with this same drug. By September 1880, Lilian's mother Amelia had matriculated into the Department of Medicine at the University of Michigan Ann Arbor as a junior at the age of 38.[10] Owing perhaps to the cultural pressures against women doctors in Canada at that time, or perhaps because she lacked the shelter of her father's own medical career and influence, Lilian also transferred to the University of Michigan Ann Arbor in the fall of 1881.[11]

As she studied, Lilian distanced herself from her Christian roots. Functionally an agnostic, she disliked her Christian classmates. She later noted that Christians are supposed to be "the salt of the earth," and that her Christlike classmates "made me smart, for I was sinner and I knew it."[12] Lilian graduated from the University of Michigan Department of Medicine in 1882.[13]

Following graduation, Lilian pursued a medical career. On September 20, 1882, she received her license to practice medicine from the Manitoba College of Physicians and Surgeons.[14] When her mother Amelia graduated and joined Lilian in Winnipeg the following year, it was a rapidly expanding city at the center of the Western Canadian economic boom.[15] Lilian had been working as the city's first female doctor, but the pair soon opened up a joint practice in Winnipeg.[16] Serving in general medical practice, they specialized in midwifery and women's and children's health.[17] By April 1886, Lilian was also working at a maternity hospital.[18] Lilian's sister, Amy Charlotte, graduated as a trained nurse from Cook County Hospital in 1885 and joined her mother and sister.[19] All three ladies were active in a local choral society and Mrs. Yeomans was also involved in social and humanitarian work in the city's poorer sections; an activity which probably also involved her daughters.[20]

Between social responsibilities, family obligations, and a growing medical practice, Lilian began to have difficulty sleeping.[21] To manage her daily stress and insomnia she began to dabble with sulphate of morphine and chloral hydrate.[22] She would later recall, "I was engaged in very strenuous work, practicing medicine and surgery," and that it was only "occasionally … in the times of excessive strain from anxiety or overwork" that she resorted to drugs "to steady my nerves and enable me to sleep."[23]

Though she explained the origin of her vulnerability to the addiction, she did not excuse herself for "daring to trifle even for a moment with such a destructive agent."[24] In order to satisfy her craving for drugs, she began to steadily raise her dose. Her *occasional* usage quickly turned into a life controlling habit. How did a medical doctor who knew the dangers of narcotics find herself an addict? Lilian wrote, "I can only reply in the words of the old Latin prayer: 'Mea culpa, mea culpa, mea maxima culpa'—'Through my fault, through my fault, through my most grievous fault.'"[25] Although raised in the church, she had only recently made a confession of faith.[26] Whether through ignorance or self-reliance, she did not take the stress of her situation to her Lord, but instead self-medicated.[27]

As if in an attempt to warn others of the dangerous and subtle way in which addictions can creep into the life of a believer, Dr. Yeomans wrote, "I was following [God] afar off ... it's a dangerous thing to follow afar off."[28] So subtle was the transfer of power between the user and the used, Lilian recounts, "I thought I was toying with the drug but one day I made the startling discovery that the drug, or rather the demon power [in] back of the drug, was playing with me."[29]

Her abuse of prescription drugs grew so severe that she found herself regularly taking morphine in doses up to "fifty times the normal dose for an adult man."[30] This she combined with chloral hydrate which she described as "a most deadly drug used by criminals in the concoction of the so-called 'knockout drops.'"[31] Of this, she took up to twenty-four times the recommended dosage.[32] That the dosage alone did not kill her was a miracle.[33] The drugs became so necessary to her existence that giving them up seemed out of the question.[34]

However, knowing they were destroying her, she desperately tried to quit.[35] On numerous occasions she disposed of huge amounts of the deadly narcotics.[36] "I believe I made at least 57 desperate attempts to rid myself of the horrible incubus," she would later write.[37]

IS HELP POSSIBLE?

Recognizing that she needed help beyond her own capacity, Lilian cried out to God. She saw the healing power of God manifest in the Bible, yet for her to "accept it" seemed about as attainable as it would be for her "to walk on air."[38] No matter how much she prayed, God did not seem to deliver her. She later attributed this lack of deliverance to a lack of faith in the "simple statement of the Word of God."[39] "I shut the door and prevented the power of God from operating unhindered in my body," she surmised.[40]

Consulting multiple physicians, she received opinions and suggestions, but none that could free her from the bondage to her addiction.[41] Quitting on her own wasn't working, so Lilian turned to various other cures and treatments, including the then-famous "Keely Gold Cure."[42] This treatment left her so broken mentally and physically that she had to enter a Sanatorium for Nervous Diseases, where for three weeks she was cared for by a specialist as well as her physician mother.[43]

Her relationship with God became more and more distant until she found herself dabbling in what she labeled "Christian Science, falsely so-called."[44] She even traveled to New York City to meet with leaders from that movement.[45] Immersing herself in Mary Baker Eddy's *Science and Health*, she determined that if Christian Science could set her free, she would follow it wholeheartedly.[46]

Reflecting on her experiment with Christian Science, Lilian wrote, "I was so determined to be HEALED that I tried to shut my eyes to its [Science and Health's] blasphemous heresies and swallow it 'holus-bolus.'"[47] Though the meetings and resources were not cheap, and neither was the New York housing, Lilian felt it was worth the investment.[48] Meeting one-on-one with a highly esteemed spiritual coach, Lilian remembered her Christian Science practitioner as a woman with perfectly arranged hair, and a temperament which was "placid as a summer sea."[49] The practitioner assured her:

> *There was absolutely no trouble about my morphine addiction,*
> *and the awful physical conditions, which had resulted*
> *therefrom; that it did not really exist, and would vanish like*
> *snow wreaths before the sun as soon as I freed my thought from*
> *its "self-imposed materiality and bondage" by absorbing enough*
> *of "Science and Health."*[50]

During the course of her treatments, rather than getting better, Lilian found herself worse. When her right arm became paralyzed, Lilian immediately went to her practitioner for help and found her not the least bit worried by this turn of events:

> *How could she be disturbed when she knew that not only had I*
> *no paralysis of the arm, but no arm to be paralyzed? She never*
> *turned so much as a silver hair.... Whether or not I had an arm,*
> *there was one thing I didn't have, and I was so sure of it that I*
> *didn't need to resort to Christian Science to tell me that I didn't*
> *have it, and that was money to stay on in New York.*[51]

Though she left New York for Winnipeg she hadn't given up on Christian Science, but was determined to continue her studies of the literature on her own.[52] Yet, God intervened in the form of an old friend, a long-time minister who visited her from abroad at this opportune moment.[53] This unnamed friend gently tried to convince her that the only place for her Christian Science book was in the kitchen stove.[54]

ENCOUNTERING THE HEALER

"If there is anything I did not try I have yet to learn what it is," wrote Dr. Yeomans of the completeness of her repeated attempts to free herself from addiction.[55] An unsuccessful attempt the previous year to wean herself from the drug addiction by "gradual reduction" resulted in hospitalization, after which Lilian awoke to find the drugs being injected intravenously.[56] It seemed that her body would not allow her to do without them; her heart and lungs would simply shut down when she did not receive her daily dose.[57] Her reaction to the removal of the drugs was so severe that her own sister, a nurse, described her "like a skeleton ... with a devil inside."[58] Though she did not appreciate this caricature, she admitted it was accurate.[59] Even her friends thought her condition a hopeless one and encouraged her not to attempt to give up the habit again.[60]

Weak as she was, Lilian spent a great deal of time in bed. Not ready to face eternity in her present spiritual condition, she began to read her Bible again. She did not just read it, but devoured its contents, finding solace and strength in its pages and in the clear small voice of the leading of the Holy Spirit.[61] She recalled saying, "Now I have tried everything that will-power and medical science and suggestion and all the rest can do, and there is absolutely no hope for me unless it lies between the covers of this Book."[62] As she read and pondered the word of God, she sensed the Holy Spirit speaking to her from Jeremiah 30: "I will break his yoke from off thy neck ... therefore fear thou not ... for I am with thee ... to save thee ... I will restore health unto thee, and I will heal thee of thy wounds ... and I will be your God."[63]

At first she thought this meant that she "must try again" to quit in her own strength, despite her weakened condition and previously failed attempts.[64] On the contrary, the Lord began to show her that to free herself of the addiction—"to get the victory"—was not her job, but God's.[65] Taking God at His word, Lilian began to tell her friends and family that she was delivered from the narcotics addiction.[66] Though they responded politely, it was clear that they thought she was out of her mind.[67] Even her mother had given up hope of her being cured.[68]

ZION DIVINE HEALING HOME

Deliverance came through a noted Australian faith healer, John Alexander Dowie, who had moved to America and established a city based on biblical principles. In the care of her sister Charlotte, the pair moved to Dowie's healing home on Michigan Avenue in Chicago, Illinois, in early

January 1898. Her mother did not join the pair on this trip, reportedly because she was engaged in lectures for the Women's Christian Temperance Union in Canada.[69] Lilian explained why she chose to go to Dowie's healing home for treatment: "It was not that I had lost confidence in the efficacy of means, but because it seemed to me, God told me very clearly that He would not deliver me from this by means."[70] Seemingly, the Lord wanted her to have a personal encounter with the healing power of His gracious hand.

The treatment at the healing home certainly did not use means, at least not those of the medical variety.[71] In fact, so strict were the standards by which it operated, that some questioned the safety of the home.[72] Upon Dr. Yeomans' arrival, all of her medications were confiscated, and she was left to face the ravages of the addiction without any transitional drugs.[73]

At times, Charlotte became frightened for her sister.[74] The withdrawals made her unable to retain any sort of food and at one point Charlotte believed her sister would simply die.[75] However, Charlotte also noticed that the grace of God was strong through those times, "It seemed to me as each symptom became unbearable to my patient, it was just smoothed over quietly; so that God let her have a certain amount, but just as she was able to stand it."[76]

At one of these low points, an unnamed individual encouraged Lilian to get up and go to church.[77] Believing the exertion would kill her, she began to make up her mind not to go, when the Holy Spirit spoke to her heart: "I sent him to tell you to go to the church. Arise."[78] With great effort, she stepped out in faith and *walked* to the church service accompanied by her sister, but noticed little change to her feeble condition.[79] Upon her return from the service, however, she began to feel better.[80] It was as if God used that simple act of faith as a catalyst for her healing. She later recalled, "From that time perfect victory through faith in the power of the name of Jesus was mine."[81]

FREE AT LAST!

Dr. Lilian B. Yeomans was age 36 on January 12, 1898, when she was freed from the demon drug addiction by the power of God.[82] And my how she did eat![83] Seven meals a day![84] Interestingly enough, her personal testimony in the book, *Healing from Heaven,* makes no mention of the Zion Divine Healing Home. Rather, it places the healing from the point at which she first began to earnestly search the Scriptures on her own.[85] Perhaps Dr. Yeomans (or her editors) chose not to include the Dowie reference in an attempt to distance her story from Dowie, who near the end of his life claimed to be Elijah the Restorer and fell into disrepute.[86]

Lilian certainly had a different approach to the medical profession than Dowie, who offered a scathing rebuke of doctors.[87] In at least one article, Lilian celebrated the healing God brought through faith as well as kindly remembering the hard-won achievements of physicians.[88] Recalling her own medical practice as well as that of her parents, she boldly stated: "No one could esteem more highly the noble work for humanity that has been done by the medical profession then I do."[89]

NEXT STEPS

After she left Dowie's healing home, Dr. Lilian Yeomans decided to give up the medical profession and make her life's work praying for the sick and sharing the gospel.[90] Lilian and her sister Charlotte became ordained with a Canadian Holiness association.[91] Moving north of Winnipeg to do missionary work among the Cree peoples, Lilian was the only doctor within 500 miles.[92] She began to be called upon to minister to physical needs as well as spiritual ones.[93]

Caring for the needs of Cree peoples as well as those of the Hudson Bay Company, she found herself in possession of the drugs she swore never to use again.[94] "I had to have morphine in my possession day and night," she recalled. When epidemics broke out among the Cree, the Canadian government demanded her services.[95] The intense pressure of being the sole doctor caring for so many, with the all too familiar drugs in her possession, could have been quite a temptation for the former morphine addict. However, God had healed Lilian of the craving so completely that she remarked, "I handled it constantly, but never wanted it. I felt, and feel, no more desire for it."[96]

During her work among the Cree, Lilian came to adopt a little girl of mixed Cree and Scotch blood named Tanis Anne Miller.[97] Lilian did not write much about her adopted daughter, but records indicate that Tanis stayed connected with the Yeomans family until well into adulthood.[98] By 1900 Lilian was already referring to herself as an "evangelist," however it is likely that the responsibility of a daughter prompted the 45-year-old to take Tanis and join her mother and sister in Calgary, Alberta, in 1906.[99] Lilian obtained a Civil Service job and apparently stayed in Calgary for the next 17 years.[100]

Though Lilian never married, according to historian Grant Wacker, this was not uncommon for influential female Pentecostal leaders of her time.[101] However, she did not have to serve God devoid of emotional and familial support, for her mother and sister were both active in the work of the Lord. At times, her mother was called upon to write of the miracles which God wrought by faith in His gracious provision, and her sister frequently accompanied her to Pentecostal meetings.[102]

SPIRIT BAPTISM

By 1907, though Lilian had completely given up the medical profession and was settled into her job in Calgary, she had not forgotten what the "Great Deliverer" had done for her.[103] Consequently, she held meetings to proclaim to others her "marvelous healing from the last stages of morphine addiction."[104] The morning of September 23 was a fairly typical one, and after her morning prayers she went to work.[105] When the workday ended, however, she had an atypical encounter with an old friend, a Mrs. Lockhart of Winnipeg. Lockhart had recently received the baptism in the Holy Spirit during the first Pentecostal outpouring in Manitoba, under the ministry of Andrew H. Argue.[106]

Lilian had heard of this recent outpouring, and her knowledge of the Bible coupled with the witness of her soul testified to the truth of her friend's experience.[107] The two prayed together before the evening service, but it was not until later that night, by Lilian's bedside, that she received her prayer language.[108] She described her experience with the Lord as "The most tremendous experience of my life up until that hour … truly this is The Rest … and this is The Refreshing!"[109]

Lilian became a fixture in the early Pentecostal movement in Calgary. She, along with her mother and sister, joined a small group of Pentecostals who met in homes for meetings. This group included Allan A. Swift, who went on to become a pastor, missionary and the first principal of Eastern Bible Institute in Green Lane, Pennsylvania. Swift later described this as "the original group who received the Pentecostal Baptism in Calgary in 1908."[110]

A 1959 history of Pentecostal Tabernacle of Calgary traced the congregation's roots to meetings held in Lilian's home in 1918.[111] She was also called upon to hold meetings with her sister in rural Alberta.[112] On one such occasion, Annie Douglas took Lilian and another woman to "a little Methodist church near Killarney, Manitoba." The three were invited to speak to the railroad workers near there. Douglas recalled, "Dr. Yeomans preached and I took the opening and after services."[113] Lilian later remembered God's work in the life of one young man who had recently run away from his faith and home to the railroad camp: "I realized what a hiding place we have in Him, as the boy found peace and rest and joy, though he was so far from loved ones."[114] Unfortunately, much of Lilian's ministry in the early Pentecostal movement was not documented and is now lost to history.

FROM CANADA TO CALIFORNIA

The Yeomans family eventually emigrated to California.[115] In San Francisco, Lilian and Charlotte were both engaged in full-time ministry, leading divine healing meetings, praying for the sick, and preaching at Glad Tidings Tabernacle and elsewhere.[116] By 1921 Lilian was also teaching at the Glad Tidings Bible Institute.[117] The pair obtained credentials with the Assemblies of God in 1922 as ordained evangelists.[118] Lilian did not limit her evangelism to San Francisco, but also ministered at the healing home of her friend, Carrie Judd Montgomery, the Home of Peace in Oakland, California.[119] As early as 1912, she had begun writing for Carrie's periodical, *Triumphs of Faith*.[120] Lilian and her family then moved to San Diego, where she likely served at the Berean Bible Institute in 1925.[121] The sojourn in San Diego was not long, for by 1926 she had moved to Manhattan Beach, located in southern Los Angeles County.

By 1927 she could be found teaching at Aimee Semple McPherson's Angelus Temple and L.I.F.E. Bible School.[122] For the next fourteen years she mentored pastoral and missionary candidates, teaching classes on church history and divine healing.[123] Known for giving all the praise and glory to God, the L.I.F.E. yearbook committee affectionately labeled her picture with a great big "Hal-le-lu-jah!"[124] Her ministry connection to McPherson would prove to be both a rewarding teaching platform and a source of tension between Lilian and her local Assemblies of God district.

Golden Years

Though settled in California, Lilian and Charlotte engaged in extensive evangelism outside of the Golden State. In the spring of 1927, the pair traveled through Minnesota, with local newspapers marking their arrival in Brainerd, Duluth, and Minneapolis.[125] Writing a letter to Assemblies of God General Superintendent W. T. Gaston, whom she had hoped to meet on her trip in the summer of 1929, Lilian detailed recent campaigns "in the East and Middle West, Wilmington, Baltimore, South Bend." She had expected to travel longer, but got "a rather nasty bang in an auto accident," which forced her to shorten her trip. [126]

Upon returning from this trip, she received a letter calling her to appear before the Southern California District to discuss the nature of her theological convictions and cooperative relationship with the Assemblies of God.[127] Perplexed about the nature of this meeting, she wrote immediately to Gaston: "Now as I have paid my dues, labored all year at Bible teaching and evangelism, etc., and lived in charity with all my brethren, I cannot see that I have left any room for doubt as to my desire to continue in fellowship."[128] She surmised that the only thing that the letter could be referencing was her being a professor at L.I.F.E Bible School. [129] Some members of the Assemblies questioned McPherson's adherence to Pentecostal distinctives and were further scandalized by her widely reported disappearance in 1926.[130]

Though Lilian declared her loyalty to the Assemblies of God, she also defended her calling to Angelus Temple. She even stated that she would consider relinquishing her credentials before giving up the opportunity to influence so many students.[131] Gaston encouraged her to avoid a reactionary decision by inviting her to write her district superintendent that she "would welcome advice and counsel from my brethren of the ministry" and that she was "seeking the glory of God in the greatest possible service."[132] The sound counsel and conciliatory tone seem to have provided sufficient impetus for Lilian to stay with the Assemblies of God, as she remained an active credential holder for more than ten additional years.[133]

WRITTEN WORK

So that others might never fall into the same snare, Dr. Yeomans frequently lectured and wrote about the subtleties of addiction.[134] She had a regular column in the *Pentecostal Evangel* and numerous articles in *Triumphs of Faith*.[135] Her first article for the *Evangel* was a serial on divine healing in 1923.[136] The miraculous power of God to heal and restore was to become the central feature of her written work. In addition to her numerous articles, Dr. Yeomans also authored six books published by Gospel Publishing House: *Healing From Heaven* (1926); *Resurrection Rays* (1930); *Divine Healing Diamonds* (1933); *Balm of Gilead* (1936); *The Royal Road to Health-Ville* (1938); and *The Hiding Place* (1940), as well as numerous tracts.[137] Historian James Opp declared that no other physician in the twentieth century wrote more prolifically about divine healing.[138] Like her periodicals, her books and tracts contain a combination of personal testimony, stories of faith, and theological instruction. Several of her published works, such as *Healing from Heaven,* originated first as lectures delivered in the classroom or the pulpit.[139]

True to her own Bible saturated healing, Lilian's writings are filled with Scripture quotations and biblical stories that illustrate her understanding of the healing work of God. Using her personal testimony as a launching point, she wrote of God's power to deliver from a whole variety of habits and diseases. Speaking directly to readers, she counseled: "You may not be in the morphine habit. I hope not. Perhaps you are in the habit of fretfulness or self-indulgence, though, and, if so, there is the same deliverance for you. Possibly you are in need of some physical deliverance.... I see in this Word all that is needed for our redemption."[140]

TAKE HAPPINESS FOR YOUR HEALTH AND OTHER THEOLOGICAL HELPS

Dr. Yeomans would frequently harken back to Old Testament themes to illustrate the care of God, the Heavenly Father, for His earthly children. She highlighted the faith narratives of Abraham, Joseph, and Moses; especially those stories which spoke of health or healing. Her theology of divine healing was trans-testamental, and it centered on the unconditional belief that God desired to heal everyone, *both* spiritually and physically.[141] Lilian noted the connection she saw between sin and sickness. To escape the law of sin and death one must embrace the "natural law" of God. She also saw a relationship between healing and faith, and this became a prominent motif in her writings. Responding to the question, "Can I prevent God's word from healing me?" Yeomans' wrote, "Certainly you can.... To get the action for any remedy you have to take that remedy according to directions."[142] Citing Matthew 9:29 and Hebrews 4:2, she observed that the proper way to take the "remedy" of God's word is to mix it with faith.[143]

A gifted author, she wove together exhortation, testimony, and humor to communicate her message. In her tract entitled "Moses' Medicine Chest," Dr. Yeomans reflected on how the Lord used Moses to keep the children of Israel healthy during their trek through the wilderness:

> *Moses, we know that those people you led out of Egypt were made of flesh and blood, just as we are. They had real hearts and real lungs, real glands and real gall ducts. And everybody in that expedition had an appendix! Yet all enjoyed perfect health and vigor. Oh, Moses, let us see inside that medicine chest!*[144]

Dr. Yeomans also believed that happiness and good humor were essential to physical health. She taught that being happy was "our duty" and that Scriptures exhorting believers to "Be glad and rejoice" (Joel 2:21) were commands of God.[145] Citing Deuteronomy 28:47, 48, 60, 61 she seemed to wonder how anyone who loved and served God could not be happy. Sickness was part of the curse, she posited, and must therefore be the punishment for not being happy with God's provision.[146] As universal as the laws of electricity or gravity, she wrote, "God's law for us is Holiness, Health, and Happiness. In absolute obedience to it, Jesus Christ, the Spotless Lamb, went about healing all that were sick, and diffusing joy and gladness."[147] She also found that release from oppression came through praising God. She exhorted others: "Make Heaven ring with your testimony to His loving kindness, tender mercy and faithfulness! Extol His great Name!"[148]

As Lilian's golden years progressed, long-time ministry companions became ill. When her own sister, Charlotte, stepped down from active ministry she wrote, "I cannot say how sorry I am to have her retire from the firing line even for a short period. However, she still prays and sings the wonderful songs God gives her and I believe her ministry is blessed of the Lord.... I believe she has work to her credit ... which will stand the fire that is to try every man's work."[149] It appears Lilian may have personally taken care of Charlotte until her death in 1939.[150] The depth of Lilian's connection to her constant companion and ministry partner may be felt in the posthumous tribute, "a succorer of many, and of myself also."[151]

Lilian seems to have lessened her ministry activities after the death of her sister, but she never officially retired. Rather, she continued preaching about the goodness of the Lord, both in person and in writing. In 1940, at the age of 79, Lilian Yeomans still claimed to have preached "approximately 100 times during the past year."[152]

Later in 1940, while evangelizing in the Midwest she succumbed to heat prostration and had to cut the trip short.[153] She lamented to the Lord, wondering why He did not simply take her "home."[154] As she prayed about this, the Lord showed her she still had work to do. But what sort of work might this be, at her age? Then she recalled how her old friend Carrie Judd Montgomery had encouraged her to have her sister's songs printed.[155] Consequently, Lilian assembled her last published booklet, *Gold of Ophir: Spiritual Songs Given Through Amy Yeomans*. Fewer than five months before her death, Lilian wrote the following on her final Assemblies of God annual ministerial questionnaire: "Have not preached during the past year ... resting and writing ... enabled to do work for the Lord by means of correspondence."[156]

In spite of her failing health, she requested prayer that "God may fit me for return to active work."[157] Dr. Lilian B. Yeomans reported for active duty in Heaven on December 10, 1942. Joining her sister Charlotte, she was buried at Forest Lawn Memorial Park in Glendale, California.[158] The *Pentecostal Evangel* honored her legacy by reprinting her testimony, noting: "Many who have been won for Christ and healed through her ministry will rise up and call her blessed. Prov. 31:28."[159]

LEGACY

A morphine addiction brought successful medical doctor Lilian B. Yeomans face to face with her personal limitations. Arriving at the end of her own strength she discovered the freedom and redemption found only though the healing power of God. This experience was so transformational that she could not keep it to herself. Working first bi-vocationally, and then as a full-time minister, Lilian devoted the second half of her life to testifying of "the Great Deliverer I had found."[160] An ordained evangelist with the Assemblies of God, an inspiring educator, and a gifted author of numerous books and articles, Lilian worked closely with other leading Pentecostals.

Though her ministry was a success, and her work testifies to the diligence with which she carried out her call, she did not take credit for her achievements. Author Jodie Loutzenhiser captured the essence of Lilian's life and ministry: "She did not just say, 'To God be the Glory,' she lived it!"[161] Though Lilian B. Yeomans has passed into eternity, her legacy lives on through her written work. May the testimony of her life call a new generation to boldly proclaim the freedom and redemption found in a wholehearted pursuit of God.

DESIREE D. RODGERS is pursuing a Ph.D. in Biblical Interpretation and Theology from AGTS and is an ordained minister with the Assemblies of God. She resides with her husband, Darrin Rodgers, in Springfield, Missouri.

"O send out thy light and thy truth; let them lead me."

Foursquare
Correspondence Courses
of the
Lighthouse of International
Foursquare Evangelism

President
Aimee Semple McPherson

⤳

DIVINE HEALING
IN THE SCRIPTURES

Volume II

by
LILIAN B. YEOMANS, M. D.

⤳

Lighthouse of International
Foursquare Evangelism
CORRESPONDENCE DEPARTMENT

1100 Glendale Boulevard   Los Angeles, California

PART 1

DIVINE HEALING IN THE SCRIPTURES

Dr. Lilian B. Yeomans taught the following six correspondence courses at The Lighthouse of International Foursquare Evangelism (L.I.F.E.) Bible School. This institution was founded by Aimee Semple McPherson in February 1923 in Los Angeles, California. Most of the course content can be found in earlier Dr. Yeomans' books. However, the material presented here preserves Dr. Yeomans' original teachings and includes her study methodology, chapter outlines for review, and the questions she specifically prepared for her healing school students.

VOLUME 1

METHOD OF STUDY

1. The method of teaching our correspondence courses is by syllabus. As long as the course continues, one of these will be sent you during the last week of each month.

2. Where the course involves consecutive study of any particular book of the Bible, read the book through, if possible, at one sitting. Endeavor to rid your mind of all previous conceptions and traditions, and thus leave yourself open to the reception of new impressions concerning it. When you have read it through in this way, then interrogate yourself as to the main idea gained from the reading. Repeat the experiment as often as you are able, each time acquiring some new fact of the truth. In this way you will gain a clear conception of the characteristic features of the book. Pursue the same method with each chapter in turn. By the time you have done this, you will have gained a clear conception of the whole, and will be able to think through the book even without the aid of the text before you. Many who are untrained in study will find help from this suggestion. Avoid loose reading! Train yourself to "observe exactly; state correctly; express cogently." Harness your wandering thoughts! Compel attention to the thing in hand, and you will soon be benefitted and greatly gratified by the results of your study.

3.   Be systematic in your study. Make up your mind how many hours a week you can devote to your Bible Study. Then hold to that decision rigidly. Aim high! Do not be afraid of work. The mines are full of precious ore which faithful study and the aid of the Spirit will enable you to bring to the light of understanding.

4.   Memorize thoroughly the main ideas, the characteristic, the key verses.

5.   Help in your study may be secured from the use of a good Concordance—Cruden's or Walker's; also from a Bible Dictionary—Smith's or Davis'; or Fausset's Bible Cyclopaedia.

6.   Examinations will be monthly. At the close of each month of study the student who has been drilling himself on the questions following each section of the study will now proceed to take his examination. This he should do in the following manner:

   (a) He will write out all the answers to the questions given at the end of each lesson. It will be unnecessary to write out the questions; simply number the answers.

   (b) He should write the above in duplicate, for he will forward one copy to the school and the other he will keep for himself. Get some sheets of carbon paper and thus make the two copies with the one writing.

   (c) Now close your books. Lift your heart in prayer that the Spirit may now bring to your remembrance that which you have faithfully studied during the preceding weeks. Then write your answers. Write briefly and inclusively. The instructor can easily tell whether you really know the answer or are only guessing at it.

(d) This is an honor system. We trust you as a Christian man or woman to take your examination as honestly as if you were seated under the eye of an instructor. "Thou God seest me."

(e) Take as long a time as you wish for your examination. But in the meantime, do not open your books.

7. Now enclose and mail your list of answers to the school. By this time, you will have received your syllabus for the following month's study; hence, you can continue without interruption.

8. Upon receipt of your examination paper by the school it will be examined and graded, but not returned to you. Instead, there will be sent you a complete list of answers, which you may compare with your own copy. This list of answers will also be accompanied by the grade secured in your examination. No doubt it will prove interesting to compare the answers with your own; and also to compare the grade awarded you with that which you would give yourself.

9. An average grade of at least 75% must be obtained to entitle you to the certificate of the correspondence school.

10. Enclose postage, if possible, with your examination papers for the sending of the list of answers and your grade.

11. "Study to shew thyself approved unto God, a workman that needeth not to be ashamed, rightly dividing the word of truth" (2 Tim. 2:15).

How?

1. As a diligent workman Study!
2. As a faithful workman. Rightly dividing!
3. As an approved workman. Approved of God!

FOREWORD

These teachings, a reprint of lectures on divine healing originally given to students in the classroom, are now issued in this form in compliance with numerous requests. They are called *Healing from Heaven*, because they tell of eternal life brought down to man by the Son of God. To all who accept healing as freely as it is given, it means that they may become conquerors here and now over sin and sickness. "The law of the Spirit of life in Christ Jesus hath made me free from the law of sin and death" (Rom. 8:2). Disease is death begun, a death process.

I once called on a doctor at his office, by invitation, to talk over the teaching of the scriptures on healing. In taking my seat, I accidentally knocked some bottles off a shelf beside me. Laughingly apologizing for the mischance, I said: "Perhaps I shall knock them all down before I get through." The words were prophetic, for after taking a few "doses" of Healing from Heaven out of the word, the doctor felt no further need for earthly remedies either for himself or for others; but devoted the remainder of his life to presenting the claims of the Great Physician, Jehovah-rapha, who has never lost a case.

Trusting that many others may be induced to "taste and see that the Lord is good," this message is prayerfully sent forth.

—Dr. Lilian B. Yeomans

CHAPTER I

HOW I FOUND HEALING

Out of the depths have I cried unto thee, O Lord. Lord, hear my voice:w Let thine ears be attentive to the voice of my supplications. If thou, Lord, shouldest mark iniquities, O Lord, who shall stand? But there is forgiveness with thee, that thou mayest be feared. I wait for the Lord, my soul doth wait, and in his word do I hope. My soul waiteth for the Lord more than they that watch for the morning; I say, more than they that watch for the morning. Let Israel hope in the Lord: for with the Lord there is mercy, and with him there is plenteous redemption. And he shall redeem Israel from all his iniquities."
(Psalm 130)

Out of the depths He lifted me! Abyss calls to abyss; deep answers to deep! Only those who know what it is to be bound as I was, captive to the mighty, the prey of the terrible, will be able to understand how great was the deliverance which God wrought in me when, twenty-eight years ago, He set me completely free from the degrading bondage of the morphine and chloral habits to which I had been a slave for years.

Sitting in darkness and in the shadow of death, bound in affliction and iron, I cried unto the Lord in my trouble, and He saved me out of my distress, brought me out of darkness, and the shadow of death, and brake my bands asunder. Do you not think that I have reason to praise God and glorify with every breath our all-conquering Jesus?

I shall begin at the beginning of the sad story with the glad ending and say that if anyone asks me how I contracted the morphine habit I can only confess: "Through my fault, through my fault, through my most grievous fault."

I had been saved several years before, but, like Peter at one stage of his career, I was following afar off when I fell into this snare. It is a dangerous thing to follow afar off; I have proved that to my cost.

Of course, it is needless to say that nothing was further from my thought than becoming a "drug addict," or "dope fiend," as they are styled today; but I was engaged in very strenuous work, practicing medicine and surgery, and in times of excessive strain from anxiety or over-work, I occasionally resorted to morphine, singly or in combination with other drugs, to steady my nerves and enable me to sleep.

Knowing as I did the awful power of this habit-inducing drug to enslave and destroy its victims, and with practical demonstrations of it before my eyes every day among the most brilliant members of the medical profession, I was utterly inexcusable for daring to trifle even for a moment with such a destructive agent. I am a graduate of the University of Michigan, Department of Medicine, regular school, Ann Arbor, Michigan. And, alas! I thought I was only toying with the drug, but one day I made the startling discovery that the drug, or rather the demon power back of the drug, was playing with me. The blood-thirsty tiger that had devoured so many victims had me in his grasp.

Of the anguish of my soul the day I had to acknowledge to myself that morphine was the master and I the slave, I can even now hardly bear to speak.

I have this fault to find with many testimonies of healing; that the individual, in telling of his healing, fails to make it clear that he really suffered from the disease from which he professes to have been cured. It may be quite evident that he believes he so suffered, but that is worlds away from the point at issue.

Testimonies of this character are quite valueless from a scientific standpoint, therefore to avoid falling into this error, I desire to leave no shadow of doubt on the mind of anyone that I was a veritable victim of morphinomania.

My ordinary dose of the drug varied from 10 to 14 grains a day. I thus took regularly about 50 times the dose for an adult man. I also took chloral hydrate, a most deadly drug used by criminals in the concoction of the so-called "knock-out drops," taking 120 grains, in two doses of 60 grains each, at an interval of one hour, each night at bed time. The safe dose of chloral is only about five grains, so I regularly took about 24 times what would be prescribed by a doctor. But in my opinion, there is no safe dose.

I took the morphine by mouth, in the form of the sulphate, in Parke, Davis & Co.'s 1/2 grain tablets, which I imported wholesale for my personal use I was living in Canada at this time.

While some have taken larger doses than this, I find it hard to believe that anyone was ever more completely enthralled by the drug than I was. I could, by desperate efforts—only God knows how desperate they were to diminish the dose somewhat, but I always reached a minimum beyond which it was impossible to carry the reduction.

To ask me whether I had taken the drug on any particular day was as needless as to inquire whether I had inhaled atmospheric air; one seemed as necessary to my existence as the other.

When by tremendous exercise of willpower I abstained from it for twenty-four hours, my condition was truly pitiable; trembling with weakness, my whole body bathed in cold sweat, heart palpitating and fluttering, respiration irregular, my stomach unable to retain even so much as a drop of water, intestines racked with pain and tortured with persistent diarrhea, I was unable to stand erect, to articulate clearly, or even to sign my own name. I could not think connectedly; my mind was filled with horrid imaginings and awful forebodings; and, worst of all, my whole being was possessed with the specific, irresistible, indescribable craving for the drug. No one who has not felt it can imagine what it is. Every cell of your body seems to be shrieking for it. It established a periodicity for itself in my case, and I found that at five o'clock every afternoon.

I HAD TO HAVE IT

The demand for it was imperative and could not be denied. I believe I should have known the time by the call, if I had been in mid-ocean without watch or clock.

Say what you may about willpower, for my part I am satisfied that no human determination can withstand the morphine demon when once his rule is established. His diabolical power is superhuman; but, thank God! One has said, "I have given you power over all the power of the enemy," and divine power is to be had for the asking and receiving.

I did not succumb, however, without many fierce struggles. I believe I made at least fifty-seven desperate attempts to rid myself of the horrible incubus. Over and over again I threw away large quantities of the drugs, determined that I would never touch them again even if I died as the result of abstaining from them. I must have wasted a small fortune in this way. I tried all the substitutes recommended by the medical profession. I consulted many physicians, some of them men of national reputation. I can never forget the tender consideration which I received at the hands of some of these, but they were powerless to break by fetters. I got so far away from God that I actually tried Christian Science, falsely so called. I also took the then famous Keeley Gold Cure. If there is anything I did not try, I have yet to learn what it is.

I left the Gold Cure Institute in a crazed condition, and then was transferred to a Sanatorium for Nervous Diseases and placed under the care of a famous specialist. From this institution I emerged still taking morphine and chloral, as the doctors would not allow me to dispense with them, partly because of my physical condition, and more perhaps because of my unbalanced mental state, which always became aggravated when I no longer used them. Of the suffering these efforts to free myself cost me I would rather not speak.

I was a perfect wreck mentally and physically. "Like a skeleton with a devil inside," one of my nurses said; and I think her description, if not very flattering, was accurate enough. My friends had lost all hope of ever seeing me delivered, and, far from urging me to give up the drugs, advised me to take them as the only means of preserving the little reason that remained to me. They expected my wretched life to come to an early close, and really could not desire to see so miserable an existence prolonged.

Perhaps many of us know "The Raven," that weird poem of Edgar Allan Poe's. The author, though he has been called the prince of American poets, perished miserably at a very early age, as the result of addictions such as mine. In this poem, he represents himself as opening his door to a black raven, a foul bird of prey who once admitted resists all efforts to eject him, but perching himself on a marble bust over the entrance gazes at him with the eyes of a demon. Each time he is commanded to depart he croaks out the ominous word "Nevermore!"

The poet cries to him:

> "... *Take thy beak from out my heart,*
> *And thy form from off my door."*
> *Quote the raven, "Nevermore."*
> *And the raven never flitting,*
> *Still is sitting, still is sitting,*
> *On the pallid bust of Pallas,*
> *Just above my chamber door;*
> *And his eyes have all the seeming*
> *Of a demon's that is dreaming;*

And his shadow from my heart,
And his form from off my door,
Shall be lifted—nevermore!"

The poem is a parable in which the writer tells of his cruel and hopeless bondage to evil habits. It used to haunt me when I, too, was bound; and again and again, Satan whispered to my tortured brain the awful word, "Nevermore!"

Though I dreamed night and day of freedom, the dream seemed impossible of realization. I said, "It will take something stronger than death to deliver me; for the hold of the hideous thing is far deeper than my physical being." And I was right, for it took the law of the Spirit of life in Christ Jesus which makes us free from the law of sin and death.

Do you ask, "Did you not pray?" Yes, I came to the place where I did nothing else. I prayed, and prayed, and prayed and prayed. Night after night I walked up and down our long drawing rooms calling on God, and sometimes almost literally tearing the hair out of my head. And you say "And you weren't healed after that?" No, I wasn't healed because I didn't believe the simple statement of the word of God; rather, my healing could not be manifested because of my unbelief. I shut the door and prevented the power of God from operating unhindered in my body.

"And why did you not have faith?" Simply because I did not have light enough to take it. It is a gift and has to be appropriated. And moreover, God's method of bestowing it is through his word. "Faith cometh"—note that it cometh—"by hearing, and hearing by the word of God" (Rom. 10:17).

I was getting very weak now and spent hour after hour in bed, and God in his mercy kept me much alone, so that he could talk to me. At last, I drew my neglected Bible to me and plunged into it with full purpose of heart to get all there was for me, to do all that God told me to, to believe all He said, and praise God! the insoluble problem was solved, the impossible was achieved, the deliverance was wrought! There is no trouble about it when God can get us to meet His conditions of repentance and faith. When God says faith, He means Faith. It is well to know that.

If anyone should ask by what special scripture I was healed, I feel as though I could almost say I was healed by the whole Book. For it is there in Job, the oldest book of the Bible which has as clear teaching on healing in the atonement as the word contains (Job 33:24); and in Genesis where God makes man as He wants him, in His own image and likeness, even to his physical being free from every disability; and in Exodus, where the chosen people marched out. You will read about it in Psalm 105:37, "and there was not one feeble person among their tribes." Think of it! What a glorious procession!

How did they do it? Through the wonder working power of the blood of the Passover Lamb. And Leviticus with its leper cleansing ceremony where, when the leper hadn't a sound spot in his whole body, he was healed by the blood of the bird slain over running water caught in an earthen vessel; a picture of Christ, who through the eternal Spirit offered Himself without spot to God; in Numbers, where every recorded case of sickness is dealt with by supernatural means, prayer, sacrifice and atonement; in Deuteronomy, where God explicitly promises to take away all sickness from His obedient people; but I cannot quote further. Suffice it to say that I found the Bible one mass of healing for the entire man, three thirds, not two thirds as I had mistakenly supposed; and when His words were found, I did eat them. And they did their work. They never fail.

I knew I was healed, that I couldn't help being healed because God was faithful, and I almost lost interest in my symptoms, I was so certain of the truth. The drugs went. I didn't know for nineteen years after my healing what became of them. I thought maybe God would send an angel to take them away and I was sort of watching for him, but the first thing I knew they were gone. And that wouldn't have helped much, but something else was gone. The specific, irresistible, indescribable craving produced by demon power was gone. The hideous black bird of prey that croaked "Nevermore!" had flown never to return. I had no more use for morphine and chloral than for "Rough on Rats," had no room for them or any other drugs in my physical economy. My appetite became so excellent that I had to eat about seven meals a day, and I had no room for drugs. And, needless to say, my soul was filled with his praises, and is still filled.

"My soul doth magnify the Lord, and my spirit hath rejoiced in God my Saviour" (Luke 1:46- 47).

And the best of all is that this healing was no happy accident, no special miracle on my behalf, but the working out in me of God's will for all of us, perfect soundness by faith in the name of Jesus of Nazareth. So far as I know the field, God's work is being done today principally by men and women who have been raised from physical as well as spiritual death; people who were given up to die by the medical faculty. I believe I could give off-hand the names of one hundred such.

And there are still vacancies in the ranks of the army of the King. If you are afflicted, step out and receive healing, and then get to work.

I was in Chicago immediately after my healing and went one day to the Women's Temple to the noonday prayer meeting. I don't know how it is now, but it used to be a sort of rallying place for Christian workers; they came from the Moody Institute and from many missions and churches. When I walked in, I found the preacher talking of the awful snares in which people who trifle with narcotic drugs, including tobacco, get entangled. He warned them to give them up entirely if they were tampering with them. And then he sat down. I knew from experience that they couldn't give them up unless they took Jesus, and so, prompted by the Holy Spirit, I rose and asked if I might say a word.

It was not parliamentary for me to do this, but God was in it, and I got leave. Then I said, "I am glad for the good advice our brother has given us. I want to tell you how to do it, and I am speaking from the depths of experience." And I told my story. I think many of them didn't believe in divine healing before I told it, but I don't believe there was one that didn't believe in it after I had finished. I was so happy, like some caged thing set free, that they couldn't help rejoicing with me, and spontaneously they rose to their feet and in one great burst of praise sang:

> *All hail the power of Jesus' Name,*
> *Let angels prostrate fall;*
> *Bring forth the royal diadem,*
> *And crown him Lord of all.*

Chapter 2

God's Will as Revealed in His Creative Work

And God saw everything that he had made, and, behold, it was very good.
Genesis 1:31

I believe that one of the greatest hindrances to healing is the absence of certain definite knowledge as to God's will. There is lurking in most of us a feeling that He may not be willing, that we have to persuade Him to heal us.

People often say "I know that He is able; He has power if he only will"; like the leper in Matthew 8, who said to Jesus, "If thou wilt, thou canst make me clean."

Many of us have been taught to pray, "If it be thy will, heal me." That wasn't the way David prayed. He cried in the 2nd verse of the 6th Psalm, "Have mercy upon me, O Lord; for I am weak: O Lord, heal me; for my bones are vexed." He was evidently very ill indeed, and the excruciating pains in the bones of which he complained, may have been due to his extreme debility; for he goes on, in the 4th and 5th verses imploring God to deliver him from impending death, and then adds, in the 9th verse, "The Lord hath heard my supplication; the Lord will receive my prayer."

There were neither ifs nor buts in that prayer. The prophet Jeremiah, too, had no doubt about God's will as to healing, for he cried, "Heal me, O Lord, and I shall be healed; save me, and I shall be saved" (Jer. 7:14).

And we, God's people of this day, should be as free from doubt regarding our Father's will for our bodies as were they; for it is clearly revealed in the Word as His will concerning the salvation of our souls.

In a sense the whole Bible is a revelation, not only of His willingness to heal our spiritual ailments, but our physical ones also. One of His covenant names is "the Lord that healeth" (Jehovah-rapha); and He is also the Lord that changeth not, the changeless, healing, health-bestowing, life-giving Lord, undisputed sovereign over all the powers of the universe.

Jesus is the express image of the Father, the perfect expression of God and His holy will, so that He could say, "He that hath seen me hath seen my Father also." He who declared that His works were not His own, but the Father's that sent Him, healed ALL who came to Him, never refusing a single individual. You cannot find a case where He said: "It is not my will to heal you;" or "It is necessary for you to suffer for disciplinary purposes." His answer was always, "I will," and this fact forever settles for us God's will in regard to sickness.

Of course, it has to be according to our faith, for faith is the hand that receives the gift, and God can only fill it to overflowing. I remember I once wanted to give a wee child some goodies, and I asked him to hold out his hands, and, oh, how sorry I was that they were so tiny. Let us pray God to enlarge our grasp of faith, for we are not straitened in Him, but in our own bowels, as the apostle puts it.

As the whole Bible is a revelation of God's willingness to heal and keep our bodies, as well as to save and keep our souls and spirits, we shall begin at the very beginning and ascertain what the first chapter of Genesis has to teach us about the matter.

There we find God's will clearly revealed in His creative work. God created man the way He wanted him, did He not? Did He make him with any disability, or disease, or tendency thereto? Was he deformed in any way; one leg shorter than the other, for instance? one shoulder higher than the other? or a squint in one eye?

No, we read that God said: "Let us make man in our image, after our likeness" (Gen. 1:26). Wasn't that wonderful? Doesn't it thrill you? It ought to.

God had created many beautiful and wonderful things before this; the sun, the moon, the stars, noble trees, exquisitely beautiful plants and blossoms, sea monsters, fish and land animals, some of them of surpassing strength, others were models of grace and beauty, but when it came to His masterpiece, man, He did not fashion him after any of these patterns; no, the model after which man was framed was a divine one. God said, "Let us make man in our image, after our likeness," and, after the work was done, God saw it, and "behold it was very good."

Man then, prior to the fall, was in some sense, in the image of God, even as to his physical constitution. And there is no doubt that, at the present time, we have no adequate idea of what a glorious being he was. Strong, beautiful, perfectly proportioned, magnificent, he stood forth a majestic and worthy head of creation.

Even to this day, though sadly defaced and marred by sin and its results, the human body bears the impress of the divine image and superscription as surely as the coin they handed to Jesus bore that of Caesar. I shall never forget the first time I saw a human brain. I was only a young girl, a medical student, worldly, utterly forgetful of my Creator in the days of my youth, but I can truly say that a feeling akin to holy awe filled me when I beheld it in all its wondrous complexity and beauty. Yes; those pearly gray, glistening convolutions seemed to me the most beautiful things I had ever seen, and when I realized that they were the home of thought, parts of the organ through which the most intricate processes of reasoning were carried out, the marvel of it well-nigh stunned me. I could have fallen on my knees, young heathen though I was, before this mystery and its author, the writing and superscription were so evidently divine.

In studying the anatomy of the human body, there are always two things that impress the careful observer. One is the perfection of the plan on which it is constructed down to the minutest cell, the marvelous adaptation of each part of the organism to its proper function; the wonderful cooperation between different organs and systems of organs, the perfect coordination of all the various parts and tissues to a common end.

The other thing that impresses one is the imperfections that meet you at every point. The trail of disease, or a tendency thereto, is over the whole organism, producing debility, and sometimes structural changes resulting in deformity. Evidences of disease of some kind, hereditary or otherwise, are apparent upon close examination of almost any human body, though these are of course much more marked in some cases than others.

Yet, while this is true, the plan of the whole, and the marvelous manner in which it is carried out, is so eloquent of infinite and divine wisdom that we instinctively take our shoes from off our feet, and veil our faces as we reverently view God's handiwork.

A great scientist once said these words in commenting on the facts that I have just stated:

> *I cannot understand how the consummate Artist who formed and painted a rose could also create a worm to gnaw at its fragrant heart, and cause its pink, flushed, velvet petals to turn the color of decay; neither can I understand how the Creator of such a glorious being as Man can bring into existence a foul and voracious thing like a cancer to prey upon that masterpiece of beauty and perfection, the human body.*

No; apart from God's Word, we are in Egyptian darkness regarding this problem of the ages; but the moment we accept the divine revelation it is as clear as noonday. God created man, the head of a new order of beings, perfect in spirit, soul and body, free from all deformity and disease, a reflection of the beauty and glories of his Creator. And "whatsoever God doeth, it shall be forever" (Eccl. 3:14). So this is His eternal purpose concerning us.

The marring of God's masterpiece, man, in spirit, soul and body, is the work of that malign being called Satan, which he effected by leading him to transgress God's law, thus introducing sin, with all its disastrous results, into the world.

Once a man gets out of line with God's will, he is open to all sorts of Satanic power which, entering him, defiles, deforms and ultimately destroys every part of his threefold being. "The thief cometh not, but for to steal, and to kill, and to destroy: I am come that they might have life, and that they might have it more abundantly" (John 10:10).

But our refuge is in God, and He will not fail us. His eternal purpose that we should be perfect as our heavenly Father is perfect, revealed in His creative work as well as being explicitly stated in the text of the Word, remains unchanged; and He has made provision for its fulfilment in you and me, for Jesus Christ was manifested to destroy the works of the devil (1 John 3:8); whether sin, sickness, or death, so that we may be preserved blameless in spirit, soul, and body, unto His glorious appearing.

"Faithful is he that calleth you, who also will do it" (1 Thess. 5:24).

In closing let me quote a few words on this subject from a recent writer, Dr. F. W. Riale, who has received much illumination on the Word regarding our bodies:

> *We are to reckon ourselves dead unto sin and alive unto God, and he will, as in the great faith of Abraham reckon this unto us in a most glorious righteousness. We are to feel that all sickness, like all sin, goes down forever in this great faith conflict. He forgiveth all our sins and healeth all our diseases.*
>
> *We are to cast all our diseases on the same Lord we cast all our sins upon. His Spirit coming in must banish all as far as the east is from the west. The life of God in the soul of man must mean that the diseases of men go like the sins of men in the fire of the divine life and the divine love.... Believe in thy heart that God will most surely accomplish that which He has promised*

to those who believe, and thou shalt be gloriously saved from all the diseases that man falls heir to. … The kingdom of heaven, where sin and sickness are doomed and downed forever, is at hand. It is now. Only believe this and thou wilt see the glory of God in thy life.

BRIEF OUTLINE OF CHAPTER 2

From the foregoing teaching, we derive the following brief outline on the will of God regarding our bodies, as revealed in His creative work:

1.   The first man was created in the image and likeness of God. This image is found in the tri-unity of man, and chiefly in his moral nature. But even his body reflected the glory of his Creator, and was pronounced "very good" (Gen. 1:26-27, 31).

2.   The fact that man was inspected by his Maker after creation and pronounced "very good," leaves no room for debility, disease or deformity.

3.   Perfect health was the normal and only condition before the Fall.

QUESTIONS ON CHAPTER 2

1.   How is the will of God concerning the physical condition of man
     revealed in His creative work? Give references.

     _____

     _____

     _____

     _____

     _____

     _____

     _____

2.   What was the normal and only physical condition before the Fall?

     _____

     _____

     _____

     _____

     _____

     _____

3.   What model did God follow in the forming of man, His masterpiece?

     _____

     _____

     _____

     _____

     _____

_____

_____

4.   What two things specially impress us as we study the human body?

_____

_____

_____

_____

_____

_____

5.   What caused the marring of God's masterpiece, spiritually and physically? Give references on both points.

_____

_____

_____

_____

_____

_____

6.   How does getting out of line with God's purpose lay us open to the inroads of disease? Prove from the scriptures.

_____

_____

_____

_____

_____

_____

_____

7. How may we be preserved "blameless" in spirit, soul and body? Give reference.

_____

_____

_____

_____

_____

_____

Chapter 3

The Source of Sickness

One fine morning, I was called by telegram to a certain rural settlement where I found a terrible state of affairs. It was a beautiful and very rich farming district. A number of people, including some of their very finest young men, were smitten by an awful scourge, a malignant type of typhoid fever. One magnificent specimen of young manhood, a boy of about seventeen, perfectly proportioned, with an intellectual head, a noble face, the oldest son of his father who was one of the wealthiest men in the vicinity, was in the article of death and perfectly unconscious when I arrived.

Needless to say, I did what I could, ministered to the sick ones according to the best methods then in vogue, but do you think I stopped with that?

You know I did not. I should have been guilty of criminal negligence if I had not taken steps to have the source of the infection discovered, with the view of shutting it off absolutely, and so stamping out the deadly disease.

And the last time I visited that beautiful place I found a great change. The farmers had completely altered their manner of life. The water supply was now free from taint, and the most sanitary methods prevailed in their homes, stables and dairies; so that their connection with the source of the epidemic was shut off, and I never heard of any more typhoid fever in that district. I don't think they ever had any more.

Do you understand the parable? I am sure you do. We have learned from our study of God's creative work that it is His will that His masterpiece, man, should be, as he was created, in the image of God; "very good," free from all deformity, disability and disease. This is God's eternal purpose regarding man, for "whatsoever God doeth, it shall be forever" (Eccl. 3:14). That being the case, let us ask what is the source of all the disease that we see about us, that is working alas! in some of our homes, and even in our bodies.

And let us make the inquiry with the view of shutting off our connection with the source of the evil, if it be possible, so that we may stand perfect and complete in all the will of God as it is revealed in His Word, our "whole spirit and soul and body, preserved blameless unto the coming of our Lord Jesus Christ" (1 Thess. 5:23).

It was the best thing that ever happened to those farmers when they discovered that the typhoid was due to dead hogs in the water supply, for they could get rid of them, and keep rid of them for all time to come, and so get rid, and stay rid of typhoid. If they had gone on drinking dead hog soup, they would have gone on having typhoid, but they didn't have to go on drinking it for there was plenty of pure, sparkling water, free from all germs, to be had for the taking. And I believe that God will enable me to point out in His Word to all who will listen in faith, first, the source of sickness; and second, how it may be absolutely shut off; and how we may drink of the water of life freely, instead of the contaminated well of earth, which, like the water supply in the typhoid infested district, contain the water of death.

Let us go back then to the book of Genesis, and we shall find in the third chapter and the first verse, Satan, the source of sin and sickness, making his initial attack on man in the words, addressed to our first mother Eve, "Yea, hath God said?"

Satan was compelled to attack God's Word, to question the authenticity of the divine revelation; for so long as man rests on the Word of God, he is perfectly invincible, impregnable, immovable.

"They that trust in the Lord shall be as Mount Zion, which cannot be removed, but abideth forever" (Ps. 125:1).

Satan cannot touch them. Rather, they are the most serious menace to all satanic devices, plans, plots and schemes; for to them has been given power over all the power of the enemy.

There is not a reinforcement which the prince of darkness can order up from the profoundest depths of his dark domain for which those who believe God's Word are not more than a match; not a poison gas manufactured in hell which the breath of God will not dissipate; not a fiery dart which the shield of faith will not quench; not a pestilence which the precious blood, boldly displayed on the lintel and door posts of our dwellings, will not avert.

"No weapon that is formed against thee shall prosper" (Isa. 54:17). So whether it be shot, or shell, gas, liquid fire, bombs, tanks, submarines, airplanes, artillery, cavalry or infantry, pestilence, famine, earthquake, lightning, or malicious tongues, we are perfectly safe as long as we are abiding in the Word of God.

Satan must dislodge us from our refuge in the secret place of the Most High before he can so much as touch us. Hence his introductory remark to our mother Eve:

"Yea." He always propitiates, conciliates, agrees with us as much as possible, avoids antagonizing us unnecessarily, "Yea, hath God said?"

> *"Hath God said!" was hatched in hell,*
> *Hear the serpent speak that word;*
> *Every soul that ever fell,*
> *Entertained that thought of God.*
> *God hath said; Yes, God hath said.*
> *God hath said; Yes, search the Word,*
> *For what God hath said is al—*
> *All you need and more and more;*

Here is most abundant store.
God hath said; Yes, God hath said.
God hath said, Lo! It is done.
What remains for us but praise?
While he conquers in the fight,
Praise the Holiest in the height.
God hath said; Yes, God hath said.

Yes, "God who at sundry times and in divers manners spake in time past unto the fathers by the prophets, hath in these last days spoken unto us by his Son" (Heb. 1:1-2).

God hath said, and here in the Bible is what He said; and if we will but abide in that Word, and treat any suggestion that would cast even the remotest doubt on the authenticity of this revelation, or its living truth in every part of it to us at this moment, as from the author of lies, continuous victory is ours.

My sister had a fearful physical test some time ago. For hours she coughed almost continuously. I have never heard anyone cough as she did. It was nerve-racking to hear her, and constitution-racking to her to do it. She coughed till the whites of her eyes were scarlet from extravasated blood. Her cough was so violent that you would think she would burst in her effort to get her breath. I was kneeling beside her bed in the small hours of the morning taking victory. I reviewed the whole situation in the light of God's Word. Under that illumination, I saw clearly that victory was hers. I took it, as it were, from the hands of God.

It seemed a concrete thing, round in shape, and smooth to feel. The rotundity denoted, no doubt, the completeness of our redemption in Christ Jesus; the smoothness, the gentleness of God in all His dealings with us. It was pleasant to the touch. I knew that if she would take it into her hands and hold it there Satan would fly, and that she would breathe as deeply, quietly, and easily as ever in her life.

I so pressed it upon her by prayer and exhortation that twice she took it and held it lightly; but no sooner did she do this than Satan came as a roaring lion and bellowed in her very face; and in her fear, caused by the agonizing sense of suffocation which the enemy was allowed to put upon her, she let it slip from her nerveless grasp, and was at his mercy. And he has none.

The Lord gave her the scripture, "Your adversary the devil, as a roaring lion, walketh about, seeking whom he may devour: whom resist, steadfast in the faith" (1 Peter 5:8-9), for he may not devour those who rest on God's Word. If we resist the devil, James says, he will flee from us. So if he roars, you resist steadfast in faith in the Word. If he roars more, resist him more. If he keeps on roaring, keep on resisting. The louder he roars, the more vigorously you are to resist, and you will have the joy of seeing him flee before you as did she.

But alas! Eve did not resist, but allowed Satan to instill doubt which matured into unbelief, and developed into disobedience, sin, sickness, and sorrow until death entered into the world.

Then God gave them the promise of a Savior, and responded to the faith in that promise by bestowing on them redemption in type. He clothed them with garments not made by themselves, but which cost the lives of innocent victims. These were placed on them by God's own hands and enveloped them, spirit, soul, and body in a covering of blood.

Here we have a beautiful picture of the redemption which is ours in Christ Jesus. Note that it takes in the body. God clothed them, enveloped their physical beings, as well as their souls and spirits, in a righteousness provided by sacrifice.

Jesus took the death penalty which we had earned and gave us his life, eternal life, instead. Hence, apprehension of Jesus Christ in all His offices, by simple faith, brings perfect peace, and thank God! "Tis everlasting peace, sure as Jehovah's throne."

But you say, "I don't understand how the death of an innocent victim on my behalf can bring me peace."

No, we don't understand, that is true; but, fortunately, we don't need to understand, but only to believe, and that we can do.

This much we know, because God tells us so in His Word, that, under His holy law, which will never be altered or diminished in its requirements by so much as a jot or tittle, "the wages of sin is death." That death, which is not only the disintegration, and ultimate dissolution of the body by the processes which we call disease or decay, but also the separation of the spirit from God, you and I have justly earned, and God must pay us our wages. Must do so, I say, in conformity with the constitution of His being, which is, in its very essence, righteousness and holiness. If I am sovereign of the realm under an absolute form of government, and I owe you certain wages and emoluments, I must in common justice pay them. On the other hand, if under the constitution of the realm I owe you the death penalty, I must inflict it, or cease to be just and right before men and the tribunal of my own conscience.

God owes us something, and that something is death, and He must pay the debt. He will pay it in full; "the soul that sinneth, it shall die"! But Jesus Christ, who had no sin laid to His charge, ran in between the human race and the death penalty, and bore it for us; so that God, having made His Son suffer the full penalty for sin, can justly pardon us.

Now He only requires of us that we acquiesce in this wonderful plan of redemption, that we let ourselves be clothed. Don't come all dressed up in filthy rags of self-righteousness, but be arrayed, body, soul, and spirit in the righteousness (rightness) of Christ. This is divine healing and divine health. Never forget that it comes only through the shed blood.

This teaching is not popular at present, but what matters a great deal more, it is true, for it is based on God's Word.

In closing, let me tell you a little true story I once read. I wish I could remember the name of the book in which I saw it but it escapes me.

A great English artist was once seized with a divine hunger for a clearer vision of the Christ. He said, "If I could see Him in his beauty, I could paint Him and make others see Him too." He thought if he could live where Jesus lived while on earth, breathe the same air, look on the same stars that shone upon the Holy One he might get the vision. So, he left everything; friends, home, fellow artists, studios, the applause of the multitude, and lived for years in a tiny tent in the awful solitudes that surround the shipless Dead Sea. He was, like Paul, in peril of robbers, but nothing daunted him as day after day he turned the leaves of his Bible. At last, the Holy Spirit brought to him the words, "The Lord hath laid upon him the iniquity of us all," and he caught up his brush to paint the Crucifixion, the spotless Lamb of God nailed to the tree. No, he could not touch brush to canvas, it seemed too sacred. He turned to the types and shadows of the sacrifice, the high priest robed in garments of glory and beauty, the great Day of Atonement, the priest entering the holiest of all, not without blood, the people outside prostrate on the pavement. No; that was not it.

Again, he turns to his Bible and a figure starts out from amidst the shadows, the figure of the scapegoat. It is led forward; the sins of the people are confessed and laid upon it; the scarlet fillet is tied around its neck ("though your sins be scarlet"), and as the doomed beast 'neath its crushing load of guilt is led forth to the wilderness, the high priest turns to the people with words of absolution and comfort, "Ye are clean"; and they return to their homes to enjoy the Sabbath rest, free from condemnation and doom, for it is God who has freed them from the burden of sin. But the doomed beast goes its lonely way far from the haunts of men. The moment chosen by the artist for his picture is the sunset hour. The animal is very near its end. Its strength is spent. The white lime soil is blood-marked from its wounded feet. It is crushed beneath its invisible load. Dying of starvation, parched with thirst, tottering with feebleness, eyes glazing, in its dumb distress it bears the curse that the guilty Israelites

59

may go free and rejoice in His glorious liberty. This is a very faint picture of what this great redemption, for spirit, soul, and body, cost the Lord Jesus Christ. Surely, we are bought with a price; therefore, let us glorify God in our bodies and in our spirits, which are His.

Art critics were much disappointed in the picture, for the offense of the cross has not ceased. But while it is foolishness to them that perish, to us who believe the cross of Christ is the power of God unto salvation, our only hope, our only plea, our sole glory.

And in that crushing load our sicknesses, as well as our sins, were borne, and not only that, but the cross cast into the bitter waters of life, as at Marah, makes them sweet and we need no longer drink of poisoned springs, for the Lamb will lead us to fountains of living waters.

So, we can get rid of sickness and stay rid of it through the awe of the Spirit of life in Christ Jesus:

> *Banished my sickness, those Stripes did heal,*
> *Because the work on Calvary is finished;*
> *Now in my body His life I feel,*
> *Because the work on Calvary is finished.*

BRIEF OUTLINE OF CHAPTER 3

Assimilate thoroughly:

1. By Adam's one act of disobedience sin entered Eden and the entire human race fell under the curse (Gen. 2:17; 3-19; Rom. 5:12-14).

2. Sickness entered the world as a consequence of sin, and forms part of the curse resulting from sin (Deut. 28-15, 18, 21-22, 27-29, 35, 58-61).

3. God gave to Adam and Eve the promise of a Savior (Gen. 3:15).

4. Under the type of a garment God promised Redemption. This garment was

   a. Not made by man himself.

   b. Procured through the death of an innocent victim.

   c. Placed upon them by the hand of God.

   d. Designed to cover spirit, soul, and body (Gen. 3:21).

   e. Intended to be coextensive with the reign of sin, and equally adequate for the salvation of the soul and the healing of the body.

QUESTIONS ON CHAPTER 3

1. How did sin enter the world? Give references and explain.

_____

_____

_____

_____

_____

_____

2. How did sickness come into existence? Give reference and explain.

_____

_____

_____

_____

_____

_____

_____

3. Explain the relation between sin and sickness. References.

_____

_____

_____

_____

_____

_____

_____

4. What one remedy did God provide for sin?

_____

_____

_____

_____

_____

_____

_____

5. What is God's provision for sickness?

_____

_____

_____

_____

_____

_____

_____

6.   Explain God's method of applying the remedy for sin.

_____

_____

_____

_____

_____

_____

_____

7.   How may the remedy be applied so as to secure healing from sickness?

_____

_____

_____

_____

_____

_____

_____

8.   What would be the best thing to do when Satan "roars" symptoms at you? (1 Pet.5:8-9).

_____

_____

_____

_____

_____

_____

_____

9.   How may one remain healthy?

_____

_____

_____

_____

_____

_____

10. Can we continue in sin and remain free from disease? Prove from scripture.

_____

_____

_____

_____

_____

_____

_____

CHAPTER 4

SAFETY FIRST

Let us go back in thought to the time when the children of Israel were in bondage in the wonderful old land of Egypt. For truly it was a wonderful land, a mighty empire, a surpassing civilization. It is an interesting fact that we really knew very little about it until the beginning of the nineteenth century; for until then the most learned men in the world had utterly failed in their strenuous efforts to read the elaborate system of Egyptian hieroglyphics, the writing of the priests, a sort of sign language.

So, we had nothing to go upon regarding Egypt except the comparatively meager information in the Bible, and the statements of Greek historians; and the latter cannot be depended upon very much, for the writers themselves did not understand the ancient Egyptians.

But in the year 1799, a French officer discovered a stone at a place in Egypt called Rosetta, called from the locality where it was found, the "Rosetta Stone." It had upon it inscriptions in Egyptian hieroglyphics, Greek, and the language of the Egyptian common people, called "demotic," and it was soon discovered that the Greek was a translation of the hieroglyphics and also of the demotic, so the mystery was a mystery no longer.

When it became known that the Egyptian hieroglyphics had been deciphered, interest in everything Egyptian was greatly stimulated. Money was poured out like water for excavation and exploration in Egypt, and the country was filled with people bent on unraveling the long and jealously guarded secrets of the land of the Sphinx and the pyramids. And the results attained have well repaid the expenditure of money and energy. For, as I said at the outset, it was a wonderful land.

Among other things, the ancient Egyptians possessed a most perfect system of embalming, the secret of which is now lost to the world. But though this has not been rediscovered, we know much, very much about them in many ways, and no doubt our store of knowledge will be greatly augmented when the results of the recent opening of King Tutankhamen's tomb are made known to the public. Even now, all the great nations of the world have in their official museums collections of Egyptian articles, books, furniture, works of art, tools, ladies' toilet articles, yes, they had them even away back in the times of the Pharaohs and Ptolemies—games and toys. We know of their religion with its elaborate ritualistic worship, and their bible called most appropriately, "The Book of the Dead." We have also learned that 4,000 years before Christ, they believed in the resurrection of the body and expended tremendous sums in mummifying human bodies because they expected the souls to rejoin them some day.

For my part, I wouldn't want the finest mummy that was ever mummified for a resurrection body. Would you? No. I want one made like unto His glorious body.

I know from personal experience that the Egyptians must have been engineers of no mean skill, for I am witness to the difficulty the best engineers in America encountered, some thirty years or so ago, in removing the obelisk, which had been brought by ship from Alexandria, Egypt, from the dock to Central Park where it now stands. I cannot at this moment recall its height, but it is an immense thing, and all in one piece, and it certainly made very slow progress along the narrow streets of lower New York.

Now why am I writing so much about Egypt? Why lay such emphasis on its wonders? Simply to bring out clearly that, with all its wisdom, learning, glory and beauty, God had but one use for Egypt, so far as His children were concerned, and that was to get them out of it. "I loved him, and called my son out of Egypt" (Hosea 11:1).

Egypt is a type of the world, and it is a wonderful old world. It has all sorts of ingenious and beautiful things in it, but, like Egypt, it is one vast tomb. Its bible is a "Book of the Dead," for all who belong to it are dead in trespasses and sins. And so far as we are concerned, there is only one thing for us to do, and that is to come out of it, "Come out from among them and be ye separate...touch not the unclean thing" (2 Cor. 6:17).

In the chapters of Exodus preceding the 11th, we find that God has been dealing with the Egyptians by means of awful judgments to make them let His people go, but all in vain. The heart of Pharaoh is obdurate, and God has come to the end of His long-suffering; and the final, awful judgment, the destruction of all the firstborn of Egypt, by means of a pestilence unheard of in virulence and fatality, is impending.

In the first verse of the 11th chapter of Exodus, we find the Lord saying to Moses, "Yet will I bring one plague more upon Pharaoh, and upon Egypt." These terrible words signed the death warrant of Egypt's firstborn, chief of all their strength. "And Moses said, Thus saith the Lord, About midnight will I go out into the midst of Egypt; and all the firstborn in the land of Egypt shall die, from the firstborn of Pharaoh that sitteth upon his throne, even unto the firstborn of the maidservant that is behind the mill... And there shall be a great cry throughout all the land of Egypt, such as there was none like it, nor shall be like it any more" (Ex. 11:4-6).

This was to be the final plague; death in every house. Truly it was a terrible epidemic!

"But against any of the children of Israel shall not a dog move his tongue, against man or beast; that ye may know how that the Lord doth put a difference between the Egyptians and Israel" (Ex. 11:7).

The Lord puts a difference between His people and those who are strangers to Him as were the Egyptians, and the difference is the difference between life and death.

He draws a line, on one side of which is life; life more abundant; life for spirit, soul, and body; on the other side is death; death for spirit, soul, and body, the second death.

The Egyptians may have been as fair, or fairer than the descendants of the Israelites. They may have been as good, from a human stand-point, or better than the offspring of Jacob; nevertheless, throughout the length and breadth of Egypt, from the king on his throne to the menial behind the mill, there was nothing but death; while in the dwellings of the Israelites there were peace and security, and the sound of those who kept a holy solemnity unto the Lord as they feasted on the Passover Lamb.

What made the difference? What did the Israelites have that the Egyptians lacked?

Note that before God's clock struck the hour of doom, there was a pause during which absolute safety, perfect immunity from disease and death, was provided for all who would avail themselves of it, Israelites and Gentiles alike. For there was a "mixed multitude" that went out with the children of Israel, by the institution of the Passover, type of the atoning work of Jesus Christ, the Sacrifice of the spotless Lamb of God of Jesus Christ, the Sacrifice of the spotless Lamb

Further, note that there was one, and only one protection against this death-dealing epidemic, and that was the blood.

The one thing that the Israelites had that the Egyptians lacked was the blood upon their dwellings.

The firstborn of Israel, as well as those of the Egyptians, were secure only through the blood. "When I see the blood, I will pass over you, and the plague shall not be upon you" (Ex. 12:13).

All that the Egyptian physician could do, and they could do a great deal, was in vain. The history of medicine shows us that they had a most elaborate system of medicine and surgery. In an ancient graveyard dating back to 1500 B. C., skeletons were exhumed on which all sorts of delicate and difficult surgical work had been performed, while from the Ebers papyrus it is evident that the ancient Egyptians prior to and contemporaneous with Moses performed many surgical operations, including the removal of tumors, and operations on the eye, in which department of surgery they were particularly well versed. Skulls on which trephining has been performed have been unearthed dating back as far as B.C. 2800.

Egyptian surgeons, who were also the priests and undertakers, were so skillful in their manipulation of the dead body that they removed the entire brain through the nasal orifices after death, in connection with the process of embalming. In this way they could avoid making the least change in the contour of the face which might have been occasioned if an incision had been made.

As to medicine they had an extensive pharmacopoeia, including castor oil and opium, two of the remedies that are most used today. They also used inhalations, potions, snuffs, fumigations, salves, clysters, injections, and poultices. They also seem to have had some quack medicines, or something very like them, for we read of a famous powder called "The Powder of the Three Great Men"; while another bore the title, "Powder recommended by five Great Physicians." They were enthusiastic about elimination and fasting in the treatment of disease, just as many doctors are today, and they had meat inspected and water boiled if they thought them impure.

Yes, the physicians and surgeons of Egypt were doubtless capable and clever; but, confronted with the deadly plague which slew the firstborn of Egypt, they were as helpless as infants. No doubt a consultation of the best medical men in the empire was hurriedly called by the royal physician whose business it was to watch over the health of the heir to the throne; but before they could assemble, he had passed forever beyond their reach. A gasp, a gurgle, a convulsive struggle for breath, bulging eyes, a livid hue about the lips, a stiffening of the muscles in the death agony, and the lineal descendant of all the Pharaohs was as dead as the son of the poor servant behind the mill.

Medical science is strictly limited in its possibilities and the best doctors are the first to confess this. The list of incurable diseases is long, very long, and even in the case of diseases that are classed as curable, the result of treatment is often palliative rather than curative. One of America's foremost physicians, now dead, said: "Back of all disease lies a cause which no remedy can reach."

The cause we know from the Word of God is sin; and for sin and its outworkings in the body in disease, debility and deformity, there is but one remedy, and that remedy is the blood of Jesus Christ, the Lamb of God.

To this all-efficacious remedy, and to it alone, the Israelites owed their immunity at the time of the awful visitation in Egypt, and, thank God! it has never lost its power.

During the recent epidemic of Spanish influenza which baffled our modern physicians almost as much, or quite as much, as the plague which destroyed the firstborn of Egypt baffled those of ancient Egypt, thousands of God's people were rendered perfectly immune by getting under the shelter of the blood and staying there.

When the fell destroyer was literally raging in the town in which we lived, my sister said by faith in the power of the blood to all with whom she came in contact, "Here is one house on which you will never see an influenza placard, for the blood is here, and God will not see it dishonored." And God made her boast in the Lord good; for though we were freely exposed to the disease, I myself never refusing to minister to the afflicted ones, our whole family enjoyed perfect immunity from it.

It was to the blood, then, and to the blood alone, that the Israelites were indebted for their deliverance. Carefully note these four essential points with regard to it:

1.   It had to be shed. The lamb must be slain. "Without shedding the blood is no remission" (Heb. 9:22). "I determined not to know anything among you, save Jesus Christ, and him crucified" (1 Cor. 2:2).

2.   The blood had to be applied. "Through faith in his blood" (Rom. 3:25).

3.   The blood had to be applied openly before three worlds. "Lintel and door post," i.e., public confession of Christ crucified.

4.   The blood had to be continually upon them. "Ye shall strike the lintel and the two side posts with the blood and none of you shall go out at the door of his house until the morning" (Ex. 12:22).

The whole man—spirit, soul, and body—was thus continually sheltered behind the blood. So, we must ever abide under the shadow of the cross, and the result will be perfect physical as well as spiritual victory.

I have titled this chapter "Safety First," and surely no slogan was ever more popular than this, and deservedly so, for what good is anything else if we lack safety? The lesson which we are learning from the book of Exodus is that there is no safety apart from the blood. Would to God that this truth might be burned into our very souls in these days of awful apostasy; so that we might cry to those who are prating of "safety," while denying the blood that bought them. "There is no safety except in the bleeding side of the Man of Calvary." We should shun, as we would vipers, all the literature put out by so-called "Modernists," though they are as ancient as the devil himself, or the cults that trample underfoot the blood of the Son of God shed for our redemption if we would really and truly put "Safety First."

The end of this thrilling story we have been reading in Exodus is found in the following words from the 37th verse of the 105th Psalm: "He brought them forth...and there was not one feeble person among their tribes."

What a refreshing sight! A mighty nation, including thousands of aged men and women, tiny children and young mothers, and not one feeble among them all. Every frame erect and stalwart, every skin clear, every eye bright and shining, every man, woman and child fit for the day's march, their strength as their day.

No wonder the fear and dread of them fell upon the surrounding nations and peoples as they marched along. No wonder Balaam had to confess "God is with him... he hath as it were the strength of an unicorn" (Num. 23:21-22).

We are told that the things that happened to them were for an ensample unto us upon whom the ends of the world are come. But God has provided "some better thing for us;" for they dwelt in types and shadows while we have the substance; theirs were half lights while we have the full radiance of the outpoured Holy Ghost who is come to lead us into all truth, to teach us all things. But what kind of a battle front do we present as compared with theirs?

We are passing in procession down the aisles of the ages as truly as did they: we are being reviewed by a mighty host of witnesses including the heroes of faith of previous dispensations. Does not the thought come to you at times that we present but a sorry spectacle as compared with the Israelites? How many of us are limping along while others actually have to be carried on stretchers? What is the matter with us? Have we one promise less than they? Does not every assurance of physical health and healing which was made to them apply equally to us?

No one who believes the Word of God can answer this question other than affirmatively. God says, "I am the Lord that healeth thee" (Ex. 15:26). "My Word shall be health to all your flesh" (Prov. 4:22), and He also said, "I am the Lord: I change not" (Mal.3:6).

The covenant of healing (see Ex. 15:26) which secured to them absolute immunity from disease conditioned upon their obedience to God's statutes is ours, and the condition need not affright us, for by the obedience of One many are made righteous. Christ is the end of the law for righteousness to every one that believeth; and the righteousness of the law is fulfilled in us who walk not after the flesh but after the Spirit. Therefore, not healing only, but absolute immunity from disease is ours in Christ Jesus as we walk in the obedience of faith.

That is what the world is looking for today. Chinese families are said to pay their doctors to keep them well, and the income of the family doctor ceases from that particular family if anyone in the house becomes sick.

Western medical science is reaching out into the field of prophylactic, or preventive medicine also, and I do not desire to belittle anything that may have been accomplished; but this I do say, that immunity from disease which is the dream, the unrealized ideal of medical science, is realizable by any simple child of God who will take his stand on the promises of God, and not stagger at them through unbelief.

God wants us to be living epistles. This word is to be written in our very flesh, in a language that all can read, for he is the health of our countenance (Ps. 42:11); and the very heathen will have to say, "The Lord hath done great things for them" (Ps. 126:2). Thus will they seek unto the Lord our God.

BRIEF OUTLINE OF CHAPTER 4

1. Sickness and death came as a judgment on all the firstborn in Egypt (Ex. 11:5).

2. Even the firstborn of Israel could not escape by their own merits or efforts (Ex. 12:13).

3. A perfect sacrifice had to be offered (Ex. 12:5-6).

4. The blood had to be sprinkled upon the dwellings (Ex. 12:7).

5. Only those who remained behind the shelter of the blood were protected from the destroyer (Ex. 12:13, 22-23).

6. While resting behind the blood, they feasted on the flesh of the Passover lamb (Ex. 12:8-11).

7. All pointed to the sacrifice of the Lamb of God as our only hope for pardon and healing (1 Cor. 5:7-8; 1 Pet. 1:18-19; 2:24; John 6:51-58).

QUESTIONS ON CHAPTER 4

1. Could the firstborn of Israel escape the fatal epidemic because they were Israelites, or because of their merits?

_____

_____

_____

_____

_____

_____

2. What was demanded?

_____

_____

_____

_____

_____

_____

_____

3.   How was immunity from the plague secured?

_____

_____

_____

_____

_____

_____

4.   Give scriptures to show that the Passover pointed to the Lamb of God slain as our only hope of healing and pardon.

_____

_____

_____

_____

_____

_____

5.   What does the history of medicine tell us of medicine and surgery in Egypt prior to and at the date of the Exodus?

_____

_____

_____

_____

_____

_____

_____

6. Upon what did Moses, who was versed in all the learning of the Egyptians, teach the people of God to depend? Give references.

_____

_____

_____

_____

_____

_____

7. What was the physical condition of God's people when they left Egypt?

_____

_____

_____

_____

_____

_____

CHAPTER 5

A WONDERFUL TREE

The Lord shewed him a tree.
(Exodus 15:25)

O ur last chapter dealt with the institution of the Passover and of the triumphant march of the Israelites out of the Egyptian bondage under which they had groaned for upwards of 400 years, in connection with which marvelous things, absolutely without parallel in history either sacred or profane, transpired. With a high hand, an outstretched arm, and mighty signs and wonders God delivered them; and they made their exit from the land of the Pharaohs where they had been so long in thralldom, laden with the treasures of their former masters. For we read in the 35th verse of the 12th chapter of Exodus that, according to the word of Moses, they "borrowed" from the Egyptians jewels of gold, and jewels of silver, as well as raiment.

I once heard a learned Jewish convert to Christianity tell of an incident in relation to this text which I have found most instructive, as illustrating how people who know nothing about it will venture to criticize the Word of God.

He had dropped into a meeting of Socialists in a hall in London, England, just as a speaker was saying, "The God of the Christians! The God of the Christians is a thief, a robber. In the 12th chapter of Exodus, we read that He directed the Israelites on their departure from Egypt to 'borrow' jewels of silver, jewels of gold and raiment, which they could never return. And they obeyed Him and spoiled the Egyptians."

The Jewish convert rose and asked to speak, and when the right was accorded Him, he said: "I think, my friend, that you should know something more about the Bible and its author, God, before you undertake to criticize it. I am a Hebrew, that book is written in my mother tongue. The word in the original is not *'borrow'* but *'ask'* (that is the marginal reading in the Bible), and the real meaning of the word is 'demand.' Surely you who profess to be so anxious to see all men righteously dealt with, ought to be the last to object to this. Demand recompense for all your centuries of toil, for your labor, your sweat, your blood, the lives which the cruel lash of the slave master have cost. And this is what they did."

Well, to resume the wonderful tale, the children of Israel were led out and, by God's itinerary brought to the Red Sea at a point where they were walled in by perpendicular rocks, while the horses and chariots of Pharaoh were heard in full pursuit in their rear. At God's command they marched forward and the Red Sea which also heard His voice promptly piled itself upon either side so that they passed dryshod through colossal walls of water. They reached the other side and held a jubilee of triumph. Miriam led in the dance as the maidens played on the timbrels.

"Sound the loud timbrel o'er Egypt's dark sea, Jehovah hath triumphed, His people are free."

But alas! alas! alas! the echo of these strains of joy have hardly died away before they are replaced by murmuring against God. Can it be possible? Only a short time since these people were doubtless saying: "For my part, after what I have seen with my own eyes and heard with my own ears, I shall never forget the wonder of it! I can never doubt again.

No, not until the next time. Here we find them in the 23d verse of the 15th chapter of Exodus murmuring because the waters at Marah were bitter. You would think they would have reflected that the God who had delivered them, who had rolled back the Red Sea at their cry, could also remedy this trouble; but no! they murmured against Moses. When people are not right with God and want to murmur, but are afraid to find fault with Him, they are apt to attack His servants. So let us be careful if we find that tendency even in our hearts, much less bitter words on our lips. They had forgotten that it is through our needs that God reveals Himself to us.

Jehovah is distinctively the redemption name of God, and in His redemptive relation to man Jehovah has seven compound names which reveal Him as meeting fully every need of man from his lost estate to the glorious ending of a completed redemption. Physical healing can be clearly seen in each of the seven:

1. Jehovah-jireh. "The Lord will provide" (Gen. 22:14). Our first need was a perfect sacrifice, and that God provided by giving His Son, the spotless Lamb of God, to bear our sins and sicknesses on that cruel tree on the Hill of the Skull near Jerusalem.

2. Jehovah-rapha. "The Lord that healeth" (Ex. 15:26).

3. Jehovah-nissi. "The Lord our banner" (Ex. 17:8-15); the Lord who fights our battles for us when Satan would attack us, whether in soul or body.

4. Jehovah-shalom. "The Lord, our peace" (Judges 6:24). Only one who is in perfect health physically as well as spiritually and mentally can be kept in perfect peace, and Jesus offers Himself to us as peace for our triune beings, for "He is our peace" (Eph. 2:14).

5. Jehovah-ra-ah. "The Lord our shepherd" (Ps. 23:1). The physical well-being of the sheep is the shepherd's responsibility. He applies the healing balm from his horn of oil to the sores and bruises. So, Jesus, the Good Shepherd, heals those who are His.

6.   Jehovah-tsidkenu. "The Lord our righteousness" (Jer. 23:6). Righteousness or "rightness" for spirit, soul, and body; all three of which God teaches us to pray may be preserved blameless unto the coming of our Lord Jesus Christ.

7.   Jehovah-shammah. "The Lord is present" (Ezek. 48:35). The same Jesus who healed all who were oppressed by the devil is with us today.

And when the Israelites were brought face to face with the bitter waters of Marah, God was there to reveal Himself to them under a new name to meet the new need, "The Lord that healeth," (present tense), who always heals (present, continuous healing). Truly life, of which water is a type as it forms the great bulk of all living things, is embittered at its very fountain head. The tiny baby is hardly born into the world before the anxious mother is enquiring whether it is strong, or if it shows any evidence of this or that hereditary disease, or any tendency thereto; and the saddest thing of all is that every baby has some inherited morbid predisposition, if not an actual disease, when it arrives on this sphere.

And the Lord showed Moses a tree! Oh, for a fresh, God-given vision of that tree and the fruit that it bears! Truly, as it is put in the Song of Solomon, we can sit down under its shadow with great delight, and its fruit is sweet to our taste.

There is a substance known in chemistry that is about 700 times sweeter than sugar. It was discovered accidentally by a chemist when he was experimenting with coal-tar products. He had been called to dinner, and washing his hands in the laboratory as usual, he changed his coat and sat down at the table. Taking a sip of tea, he was disgusted to find it sweeter than the sweetest syrup he had ever tasted. He was about to remonstrate with his wife, but took a bite of bread first to take the cloying taste of the sweetness out of his mouth. To his amazement the bread tasted like the richest cake. The thought occurred to him, "Is it possible that I am sweet?" He put his thumb in his mouth to suck it like a baby, and it was as though he had a sugar plum in his mouth. To his wife's surprise he jumped up and ran to the laboratory where he carefully examined the contents of every test tube and crucible. At last, he found the compound he had accidentally produced when boiling some chemicals together, the vapor from which had gotten into his throat, on his lips, and into his very lungs, so that he was all sweetness.

When we see this tree in the light which the Holy Ghost sheds upon it through the Word, everything becomes sweet:

> *Never further than thy cross,*
> *Never higher than thy feet;*
> *There earth's richest things are dross,*
> *There, earth's bitterest things are sweet.*

Yes, everything is sweet to us for we are ourselves sweet; nay, rather we are sweetness, if Jesus, who is the Word of God, and is sweeter than honey and the honeycomb, is dwelling and reigning within us; for it is no longer I, but Christ who dwelleth in me. That was a wonderful tree that God showed Moses, and it bears wonderful fruit.

When Jesus, Moses, and Elias met in the glory of the Mount of Transfiguration, there was no theme so fitting for their discourse as the decease which Jesus was to accomplish at Jerusalem. For that death was the greatest achievement that this world has ever witnessed, the only act of sacrifice acceptable to God that has ever been performed by a human being since the Fall, for Jesus was true man as well as very God of very God. For all the righteous acts of the saints are necessarily performed in the power of that one sacrifice of Himself, by which he hath forever perfected them that are sanctified, and are, as it were, an integral part of that accomplishment. On that tree we find pardon and peace, healing and health, victory over death and hell; for by His death on that tree, Jesus conquered death and Him that hath the power of death. "Bowed to the grave, destroyed it so, and death, by dying, slew."

That tree was most fittingly set up on Calvary (Latin, Calvarium, the place of the skull), the very zenith of Satan's power; for what more fully shows the depth of man's fall than the transformation of the beautiful human countenance, radiant with intelligence, and glowing with emotion, bearing the impress of the divine image upon its lineaments, into a ghastly, grinning, gruesome skull?

This, then, is the tree that God showed Moses, which, when cast into the waters, made them sweet. In a book which I have been reading, it is stated that the waters in the vicinity of Marah are still bitter from excess of alkali salts, but that the fount which was healed by the branch can still be distinguished from the others by its comparative sweetness. Notice that the tree had to be cast into the waters; that is, the atoning merits of Christ have to be applied to our own particular case of sin, sickness, or both, as the case may be, by our own personal faith.

I am told that in the public library at Boston, Mass., Sargent, one of the greatest modern artists, has brought out most beautifully and clearly in his mural decoration, "The Dogma of Redemption," the truth of our deliverance from sin, sickness and death through the sacrifice of Christ.

In the picture Jesus hangs on the cross, and on either side of Him are our first parents, Adam and Eve, each holding in their hands golden chalices in which they are catching drops of the precious blood which flows from his pierced hands. Above the cross are the words "Dying for the Sins of the World"; and beneath the whole the inscription, "He came to redeem our bodies and to cleanse our hearts." In all the work, there is a strong line of demarcation between celestial and terrestrial, but the uplifted cross breaks through this and lets Heaven and earth run into one. Praise God! That is what the cross does for us. The cross itself is upheld by angels whose faces are radiant with bliss, as though they comprehended the final, fullest, most glorious purpose of God in the supreme sacrifice and could not contain their joy. And the instruments of agony; the scourge, the hammer, the spear are all held in the hands of angels who are bathed with the rest of the scene in unutterable glory.

May God in His mercy show us the Tree, and when we see it may we apply it to our hearts and lives, our spirits, souls and bodies, so that we may become the very sweetness of Jesus. "There he made for them a statute and an ordinance, and there he proved them!"

The Word of God always proves, or tests us. Some people say, "I will try God's promises for healing." No, you won't; they will try you. God's promises are tried, purified seven times, forever settled. You are the one that is on trial. God is not on trial. His truth reaches to the heavens and His faithfulness to the clouds. He made this statute and ordinance and they have never been repealed. He sealed them with His covenant, and forevermore He is Jehovah-rapha, the Lord that healeth. They are conditional upon our diligent hearkening and faithful obedience. But before He made these conditions, He showed us the Tree.

That tree cast into our lives will remove every trace of the bitterness of sin and rebellion from our natures, and make us sweet with the heavenly sweetness of our Lord. Then we can claim absolute immunity from all the sickness which is brought by God in His righteous judgments on the Egyptians.

The great poet Dante has placed in his poem "Inferno," over the portal of hell, the well-known words, "All hope abandon, ye who enter here." But entering as little children into the kingdom of Heaven through faith in a crucified Savior, we read in golden letters, "All fear abandon, ye who enter here." For He hath redeemed us from all evil and will preserve us blameless in spirit, soul, and body unto His glorious coming.

BRIEF OUTLINE OF CHAPTER 5

"I the Lord am healing thee" (Ex. 15:26). (Dr. Young's translation.)

1.   "There he proved them" (Ex. 15:25). This was a test for God's people. It is also a test for the people of today, for it will show whether we really believe God.

2.   This, the so-called "covenant of healing" (Ex. 15:26), is the first definite promise of bodily healing in the Bible.

3.   As this covenant of healing is much older than the law of Moses, it could not have been abrogated by the passing away of Mosaic institutions (Gal. 3:17).

4.   It was renewed to the Israelites (Ex. 23:25; Deut. 7:15).

5.   Claimed by Solomon as part of God's covenant with His people (1 Kings 8:23, 37-39, 45; 2 Chron. 6:14, 28-30).

6.   Renewed by the prophets (Isa. 33:24; 35:3-6, 38; 53:4-5; Jer. 17:14; 30;17).

7.   It tests God's people because it is conditioned upon diligent hearkening and obedience (Ex. 15:26).

8.   It is all ours in Christ, who is made unto us righteousness, holiness and wholeness (1 Cor. 1:30).

QUESTIONS ON CHAPTER 5

1.   Where do you find the first definite promise of physical healing in the Bible?

_____

_____

_____

_____

_____

_____

_____

2.   How do you know that it was not superseded by the passing away
      of the Law?

_____

_____

_____

_____

_____

_____

3.   Give references showing it was twice renewed to the Israelites.

_____

_____

_____

_____

_____

_____

4.   Give at least two references showing its renewal by the prophets.

_____

_____

_____

_____

_____

_____

_____

5.   Upon what is it conditioned and how can the conditions be met?

_____

_____

_____

_____

_____

_____

_____

6.   Of what may the bitter waters of Marah be regarded as a type?

_____

_____

_____

_____

_____

_____

_____

7.   Mention some ways in which human life is embittered at its fountainhead.

_____

_____

_____

_____

_____

_____

_____

8. How does the application of the "Wonderful Tree" to those bitter waters sweeten them? Give references.

_____

_____

_____

_____

_____

_____

9. How does the covenant of healing prove and test us?

_____

_____

_____

_____

_____

10. Can anyone "try" divine healing? If not, why not? Give references.

_____

_____

_____

_____

_____

_____

_____

11.   Who is on trial when confronted with the Word of God?

_____

_____

_____

_____

_____

_____

_____

_____

CHAPTER 6

THE PRAISE CURE

Bless the Lord, O my soul: and all that is within me, bless his holy name. Bless the Lord, O my soul, and forget not all his benefits: Who forgiveth all thine iniquities; who healeth all thy diseases; Who redeemeth thy life from destruction; who crowneth thee with lovingkindness and tender mercies; Who satisfieth thy mouth with good things; so that thy youth is renewed like the eagle's. The Lord executeth righteousness and judgment for all that are oppressed. He made known his ways unto Moses, his acts unto the children of Israel.
(Psalm 103:1-7)

I have administered a good many cures, seen a good many administered, and heard about a good many more. I remember a friend of mine telling me of one she took, but whatever the results may have been they were certainly not lasting, as she repeated it every year. She complained, moreover, that it was very unpleasant.

"It was horribly expensive as well," she continued, "but as I had plenty of money in those days, that didn't matter so much; but the unpleasantness of it, I shall never forget."

"What was there so unpleasant about it?" I inquired.

"Well to begin with I had to go to Austria for it, for only there is a certain kind of mineral water to be found which my doctor says my constitution needs. It is horribly nasty; tastes like sulphur matches and rotten eggs. When I got there, I was put in a little attic room and had to be thankful to get it, the place was so crowded. It was a room such that I would not dare to ask anyone in America to sleep in, not even a tramp. Then we were awakened in the morning, at five o'clock, by a sort of clapper which made a very loud and grating noise. At the very first stroke we had to leap up."

"Why such haste?"

"Because if we didn't get up immediately we would be late, and that meant no breakfast. That was part of the cure!"

"Oh, I understand. I suppose then you hastily took your bath and ran down to a well-prepared meal."

"That's all you know about it," she replied. "There was no bathroom, and already blue with cold I had to wash in a hand basin in ice water. Honestly, I have sometimes found a thin film of ice on the water in the jug. Then I had to dress as quickly as ever I could in all my outdoor things, including heavy walking boots, and putting on a warm wrap, I dashed downstairs to join the procession on the way to breakfast."

"Why, where was the breakfast?"

"Oh, miles and miles away. That was part of the cure. The road was very rough. I think that was part of the cure, too, to shake up your liver."

"Well, I suppose you arrived at last and went into a building where they had a huge open fireplace with great logs burning in it, and sat down in front of its grateful warmth to a substantial German breakfast all steaming hot."

"That shows all you know about it. No! When we reached our destination, we were at a sort of fountain surrounded by a platform which was always slippery and damp. There we formed in line and at last reached the man who dispensed the water. When you gave your name, he turned to a sort of file he had to see how many glasses you had to drink, then handed them to you, one by one, watching to see that you consumed the last drop of each. Then, and not till then, he handed you a ticket that entitled you to breakfast, and you made a mad rush with the rest of the patients to a sort of garden, only it had no flowers in it, just some discouraged shrubs. There we found some small tables (for we always took our meals in the open air if possible, that being part of the cure) on which were rolls of some kind of black bread. But I tell you they tasted good, and the only trouble was the rolls were so small."

"But you could eat plenty of them, I suppose," I interjected.

"Maybe you're a doctor, but it's plain to me that you know nothing about cures," my friend said almost contemptuously. "No, we were allowed only two rolls at the most; some patients got only one, all the time they were there. Once in a great while some of us got an egg each, or a very thin slice of cold meat with our roll, but that was only by the doctor's special order. Then we had a cup of very weak coffee made with milk. It was hot and was the only warm thing we encountered from the time we got up until dinner time. They usually had some very thin soup for dinner, and two kinds of vegetables, very small helpings, and some days a tiny, tiny bit of meat or fish. No dessert, excepting on gala days, an apple. Supper wasn't worth mentioning, and often I was deprived of it altogether. It was considered a great cure and you had to apply months beforehand to be sure of getting in; and counting your traveling expenses, doctors' bills and board, it came very high."

That's one kind of a cure, and there have been and are many others; for example the grape cure, where patients are allowed to eat all the ripe grapes they can get outside of, but nothing else of any kind; the barefoot cure, where they go barefoot; and the hot mud cure—no, they don't have to eat it, only wallow in it, etc., etc. I am far from saying that nothing is accomplished by these and other kindred methods, but I do say that the cure of which I am going to speak is the only sure cure. It is the most expensive one ever known, but the price was paid by another, for it was purchased, not with corruptible things, as silver and gold. "but with the precious blood of Christ, as of a lamb without blemish and without spot" (1 Peter 1:19). And the poorest may enjoy its fullest benefits.

I call it the Praise Cure because it is most readily applied by simply singing yourself into it. "Enter into his gates with thanksgiving, and into his courts with praise: be thankful unto him, and bless his name" (Ps. 100:4). You know you can sing yourself and shout yourself into and through things that you can't get into or through in any other way.

There was an old man, a Presbyterian elder, who was terribly opposed to anybody making a noise over his religion. He thought religion should be like the newest style of typewriters, absolutely noiseless, with a guarantee to that effect. He had one daughter, however, a most saintly girl, who had so much glory in her soul that she occasionally bubbled over. He labored with her to no effect, for it seemed as though she could not help it, though she hated to grieve her old daddy. At last, one day the old man came to the end of his well-spent life, and as he felt himself entering the valley of the shadow of death, he had a glimpse of the glory that is to be revealed. To the amazement of all his family, he gave one shout of great joy and called for his shouting girl, "Come along, daughter, and help me shout my way through clear home to glory." And that is exactly what she did, though the tears were streaming down her face meanwhile.

We can stand on God's Word for salvation and healing after we have met God's conditions and grounded every weapon of rebellion, and we can praise our way through to perfect manifested victory. This I call the Praise Cure, and it never fails when the praise is the outflow of a heart resting on God's unchanging Word.

There was a missionary from China, staying at Mrs. Carrie Judd Montgomery's, Beulah Heights, Oakland, Calif., not very long ago. I forget her name for the moment, but she had the most wonderful healing of smallpox while on the field, just by the application of the Praise Cure.

She fearlessly nursed a sister missionary who had the disease though she had not been vaccinated. Standing on God's promise that no plague should come nigh her dwelling, when a very bad case of confluent small-pox—that was what it looked like to the doctors—came out on her, and she did not know what to do; she asked the Lord, and He told her to sing and praise Him for His faithfulness to His Word. They took her, shut her up and told her to lie quiet, but she declared if she didn't praise God the very stones would cry out. So, she sang and sang, and praised and praised. The doctor said he feared for her life, that the case was serious, and awful complications threatening, yet she praised and praised and sang and sang. He said she was evidently delirious, but having so little help that he couldn't restrain her, she sang and sang, and praised and praised. They told her that if by any chance she recovered, she would be disfigured for life, but she sang and praised louder than ever.

They asked, "Why do you praise so much?"

She answered: "Because I have so many pocks on me. God shows me I must praise Him for each one separately." And she kept right at it.

The Lord had shown her a vision of two baskets, one containing her praising, half full; and the other, in which was her testing, full. He told her that the praise basket must be filled so that it would out-balance the other, so she kept at it. Her songs and shouts were so Spirit-filled that they were contagious, and the nurses who were Christians couldn't resist join-ing in, so they kept the place ringing. At last, the Lord showed her that the praise basket was full and overflowing. She saw it sink, and the test-ing basket rise in the air, and in a moment, as it seemed, the eruption and all attendant symptoms vanished, leaving no trace in the way of so much as a single scar.

Perhaps that may seem almost too much to believe by some, but I can from my own personal experience furnish a case where the smallpox eruption disappeared instantaneously in answer to believing prayer and the application of the Praise Cure.

One evening we were about to open the meeting at a mission where I was then working, when a man ran hastily into the hall and asked to have a few moments private conversation with me. I led the way to the prayer room. He said:

"Dr. Yeomans, my wife has just broken out all over with smallpox!"

"How do you know that it is smallpox?" I inquired.

"Why, we had a doctor who said so, and he told us not to stir from the house as he was going down to get the health doctor and have the place placarded 'SMALLPOX' without a moment's delay. But as soon as he had left the house my wife said: 'Run down to the mission. They will just be beginning the meeting. Get Dr. Yeomans to pray, and I am sure God will clear this plague off my skin and out of my blood.'"

So right on the spot we applied the Praise Cure, and the brother ran home to find his wife without a single trace of the disease. A little later the doctor returned with the health doctor and was unmercifully joshed by the latter for reporting a case of smallpox when there wasn't a pock in sight, nor any symptom of disease.

"Where is your smallpox?" the health officer inquired. "Well, where is it? It was here when I left."

"Well, where is it now?" inquired the health doctor, and with some jokes as to the probable character of the beverages in which his colleague had been indulging, he left the place without further comment.

Yes, the Praise Cure works every time. It is not unpleasant; rather it is delightful. The cost of it has been met for us by another, and it is available this moment to each and every one of us.

Are you ready to begin it? The last clause of the 8th verse of the 1st chapter of the 1st epistle of Peter tells us exactly how to begin. Listen! "Believing, ye rejoice with joy unspeakable and full of glory."

Just believe what God says concerning what Jesus has done for you, body, soul, and spirit. Think about it, talk about it, sing about it, shout about it, and the Praise Cure has begun. You are not to take it once a year, but all the time. "I will bless the Lord at all times: his praise shall continually be in my mouth" (Ps. 34:1). The Psalms, that book of praise inspired by the Holy Ghost, which has been used by the people of God in all ages, which Jesus Himself used, are full of this Praise Cure. Just observe the first verses of the 103rd Psalm:

"Bless the Lord, O my soul: and all that is s within me, bless his holy name. Bless the Lord, O my soul, and forget not all his benefits: who forgiveth all thine iniquities; who healeth all thy diseases; who redeemeth thy life from destruction; who crowneth thee with lovingkindness and tender mercies; who satisfieth thy mouth with good things; so that thy youth is renewed like the eagle's" (verses 1-5).

I personally knew a man who was dying of acute tuberculosis of the lungs, who praised himself into perfect, rugged health that lasted a lifetime, in the words of that third verse. Begin now. You can't afford to postpone it by so much as a moment. Tread the young lions under your feet by the praise of faith. It has never failed and never will.

Sometimes people say, "That's true, and I feel better already, but when Jesus spoke the word when He was here in person the symptoms always disappeared instantly, and mine haven't disappeared, or have only partly disappeared, so I can't be healed."

The scriptural answer to this difficulty is that the symptoms did not always disappear immediately, even when Jesus was here in person.

The nobleman's son, referred to in the 4th chapter of John's Gospel, began to amend, get better, improve, convalesce. "At the seventh hour the fever left him."

The healing of the blind man at Bethsaida, related in the 8th chapter of Mark's Gospel, is not only markedly gradual, but in three distinct, separate stages.

First, Jesus took him by the hand and led him out of Bethsaida, which city he had abandoned to judgment. (See Mark 8:23; Matt. 11:21-24.)

Second, Jesus began the healing with an anointing of spittle, after which He asked the man if he saw anything. The man replied that he saw men as trees walking; or, in other words, that he had a degree of distorted vision.

If the man who now possessed enough sight to enable him to blunder around had departed and told people that Jesus had healed him, but that he could only see to get around and had no use of his eyes for work that required clear vision, I believe he would have done just what many thousands of people who come to be prayed with for healing are doing today. Those to whom he told his story would have said, "Well, that's the kind of work Jesus of Nazareth does, is it? It's a wonder He didn't make a good job of it while He was at it." But that wouldn't have been Jesus' fault, would it? And it isn't His fault if you have not perfect soundness in the presence of all this hour. If you are in the second stage, press through to the third one. For in it the man received perfect sight and saw every man clearly. Notice Jesus made him look up (vs. 25), and that one look of faith to the Lamb of God brought perfect restoration of his sight.

Let us look into His face and praise Him for the fulness of the redemption He has purchased for us; for it is a wonderful cure, the Praise Cure, and the only unfailing one that has ever been discovered or ever will be discovered.

BRIEF OUTLINE OF CHAPTER 6

The Psalms of David are the God-given, Holy Ghost inspired Prayer Book and Hymn Book of Israel. Truth is revealed here in simple form and familiar terms. Songs constantly used in worship are a most valuable means of impressing truths on the minds of those using them. (See Deut. 31:28-30; Deut. 32:1-2.) We are commanded to teach one another in spiritual songs (Col. 3:16).

The Psalms teach that:

1. Immunity from sickness is God's will for His people (Ps. 105:37; Ps. 91:9-10).

2. In case of sickness, it is to God that His people are to turn (Ps. 107:20; 30:2).

3. Healing is a part of redemption, a link in the seven-fold chain (Ps. 103:1-7):

    (1) Forgiveness, verse 3

    (2) Healing, verse 3

    (3) Redemption, verse 4

    (4) Crowning, verse 4

    (5) Satisfaction, verse 5

    (6) Deliverance, verse 6

    (7) Revelation, verse 7

QUESTIONS ON CHAPTER 6

1. What is the general teaching of the Psalms in regard to the Lord for the body?

_____

_____

_____

_____

_____

_____

2. Give a reference showing that immunity from sickness is God's will for His people.

_____

_____

_____

_____

_____

_____

_____

3. In case of sickness to whom is Israel taught to turn in this book? Give references.

_____

_____

_____

_____

_____

_____

_____

4. Is there a sure cure given in the Psalms for any and every disease? If so, where?

_____

_____

_____

_____

_____

_____

_____

5. What do you understand by the "praise cure"?

_____

_____

_____

_____

_____

_____

_____

6.   How often is it to be taken? Reference.

_____

_____

_____

_____

_____

_____

7.   Describe exactly in scriptural language how to take it.

_____

_____

_____

_____

_____

_____

_____

_____

_____

_____

_____

_____

_____

CHAPTER 7

MIRIAM'S MISTAKE OR DIVINE HEALING AND THE USE OF THE TONGUE

Miriam, mighty woman of God that she was, is spoken of in the prophecy of Micah as one of the divinely appointed leaders of Israel. Hers was the alert intelligence and watchful affection that God employed to secure for Moses, her brother, the shelter of his father's rooftree; the pillowing of his infant head upon his mother's bosom, with all that these things implied of godly training, and instruction in the ways of the Lord. When the daughter of Pharaoh drew him out of the water in the rustic little ark in which his mother had placed him, was she in despair? Never; it was in faith, for we find her on the Faith Honor Roll of the 11th of Hebrews, where we are informed that she and the child's father "were not afraid of the king's commandment." They had no need to be, for they were trusting in the King of Kings in whose hand Pharaoh's breath was.

It was Miriam's bright eyes that watched the frail little basket with its precious contents, as it drifted hither and thither in the breezes that rippled the surface of the Nile. It was Miriam's insight that recognized the softening of the proud Princess' heart toward the helpless babe, who did all a baby three months old could do to plead his cause. "Behold, the babe wept." And who had the courage to step boldly forward and suggest a Hebrew nurse for him? It was in Miriam's tender arms that the young hero was borne home in loving triumph. How Miriam loved him in that hour! Every woman who is a real woman knows what I am talking about! The only wonder is how she refrained from hugging him to death before she got him home.

As he grew to manhood, and revealed such splendid powers which were carefully developed and matured under the very best teaching that the advanced civilization of Egypt could provide; and as he became mighty in word and deed, her love doubtless grew with his growth, and intensified with his development.

We next find her leading the hosts of Israelitish women after the Red Sea crossing, where God brought His people through dryshod; and where the Egyptians who attempted to follow them went to the bottom like so many stones.

It was she who led the inspired song, known ever since as "Miriam's Song."

> Sing ye to the Lord, for he hath triumphed gloriously;
> The horse and his rider hath he thrown into the sea.

But this wonderful woman, wonderful because of the marvelous way in which God used her to affect his purposes, and to put his plans into execution, made a terrible mistake. She committed an awful sin which cost her and the leaders of God's people untold suffering, besides holding back the onward march of the Lord's host for seven full days. As a result of this sin, she became a leper, white as snow. In other words, she was afflicted with the most hopeless, most loathsome of all diseases, the disease that so devours and disfigures the human form and visage that often no resemblance to humanity remains.

"O tell us without delay what this terrible sin was, so that with all our might we may resist any temptation that might have a tendency to lead us in the same direction; tell us that we may watch against it with constant prayer," does some one say?

To be sure that we get it exactly right, I shall read it out of the word of God; "And Miriam and Aaron spake against Moses because of the Ethiopian woman whom he had married; for he had married an Ethiopian woman. And they said, 'Hath the Lord indeed spoken only by Moses? Hath he not spoken also by us? And the Lord heard it'" (Num. 12:1-2).

"The Lord heard it." It is a good thing to remember that He who planted the ear can hear. We are apt to forget it at times.

The Lord heard them talking against Moses because of the Ethiopian woman whom he had married, for the scripture plainly states that he had married an Ethiopian woman.

I think I can see how Miriam's very love for her brother, mighty man of God that he was, one of the outstanding figures of all time, with her pride in the achievements of the one whom she under God had rescued from a watery grave, tempted her to commit this sin.

"How could he ever have married her?" she must have asked herself again and again.

Each time she looked at her sister-in-law, no doubt she seemed more alien, and altogether more unsuitable for the position to which she had been elevated. Indications are not lacking in the scriptures that there were things about Moses' wife, quite apart from her foreign appearance, that would make it very difficult for Miriam to understand how a man who lived in such close and intimate communion with God could have selected her for a life companion. But then she did not have to understand why Moses did so; to his own master he stood or fell; but she did need to mind her own business and keep her mouth shut.

As the Holy Spirit says in 1 Thessalonians 4:11, "Study to be quiet and to do your own business, and to work with your own hands, as we commanded you."

Miriam had her own God-appointed work to do, part of which was to accord to Moses every particle of authority and preeminence which God had seen fit to bestow upon him; and to do it ungrudgingly and whole-heartedly; and to command and exhort those under her control or influence to do the same.

Instead of attending strictly and quietly to her own business, she became Moses' harsh critic, and evidently induced Aaron to follow her evil example. For this she was dealt with by God as the prime offender. "And the Lord heard it…And the Lord spake suddenly .. And the Lord came down in the pillar of the cloud, and stood in the door of the tabernacle," and defended his servant, and said, "Wherefore.. were ye not afraid to speak against thy servant?" (Num. 12:4-8). And the cloud departed and behold Miriam had become leprous. And Aaron recognized the awful disease which had seized her its clutches and turned imploringly to Moses crying to him to forgive, and not to let her be "as one dead, of whom the flesh is half consumed when he cometh out of his mother's womb" (Num. 12:12).

And what did Moses, the ex-Egyptian prince and physician do? He took out his medicine chest. Do you recall what is to be found there? No Egyptian remedies, whether pills, powders, poultices, or tinctures. Not even so much as a dose of castor oil for the thousands of babies he had under his jurisdiction; no opium to relieve pain, though they had plenty of opium in Egypt, and Moses knew all about it. But he also knew of something as much better than castor oil and opium as the heavens are higher than the earth.

And it was well for Miriam that Moses' medicine chest was not filled from Egyptian drugstores, for there was nothing in such remedies, and there never has been anything in any collection of remedies concocted by human hands, and devised by human brains, that could touch a case like Miriam's. But the remedy, the one remedy of Moses' medicine chest exactly met her need, and cleansed her from the foul virus of leprosy that had infected every cell of her body to the very corpuscles of her blood and the marrow of her bones. And it never fails to cure any person who honestly takes it, for it is the word of the living God and cannot fail.

That word was the covenant of healing. You will find it in the 15th chapter of Exodus and the 26th verse, the concluding words of which are, "I am the Lord that healeth thee." Thank God, He is the one who changes not (Heb. 13:8).

And Moses cried unto the Lord, saying, "Heal her now, O God, I beseech thee."

There was no "if it be thy will." It was not necessary to prefix any such conditional phrase to His prayer; nay, rather it would have been an affront to Him who is the true and living God to have done so; for had He not revealed Himself under His covenant name of the "Lord that healeth"? Praise God, His name is still the same, and they that know His name will put their trust in Him.

Miriam and Aaron had sinned, but when God gave His people the covenant of healing for all diseases, and even of immunity from attacks of sickness, conditioned upon their obedience to His statutes and commands, He showed Moses a tree and Moses never forgot the sight. It was in type the tree of the cross which bore such precious fruit for us through the dying agonies of our Lord, even the salvation of our souls and the healing of our bodies. And remembering that sight Moses had courage and faith to call confidently upon God for his sister's deliverance. And there could be but one answer to that prayer. Since it was in accordance with God's will, Miriam was healed.

And now what is the lesson to be learned by us from this thrillingly interesting scripture incident? What is its practical bearing upon our lives here and now? Simply this: that we are under the care—spirit, soul, and body—of our Lord who is our Physician as well as our Savior. Rather, would it be correct to say that He is our Physician because He is our Savior and, must therefore, provide for the healing and preservation of our bodies, as well as for the deliverance and salvation of our souls. It behooves us, therefore, to study untiringly the laws of health which our Physician has placed in His Word for our instruction and guidance, and having learned them, to obey them implicitly, looking to Him for grace and strength. Only thus can we get well and stay well; but we can do it this way, for it is God who worketh in us to accomplish all His holy will in and through us.

Now one of the points on which we are repeatedly warned in the Bible in relation to our physical health and longevity, is in regard to the use we make of our tongue. In Proverbs 12:18, we read that "the tongue of the wise is health," i.e., health to the speaker and health to the listener.

We once had a neighbor, a very clever woman, an artist of no mean ability, and a woman of very keen sensibilities, though I am sorry to say, not a saved woman up to the last we knew of her. She was always talking about "vibrations" and always moving around in order to find a spot where the "vibrations" were good, life-giving, healing, strengthening, and soothing. There was no lack of money in her case, hence she was able to indulge all her whims. While she was living near us, she greatly felicitated herself upon the "waves" which she received from our house. I do not know whether to attach much importance to her views, but this I do know, that there are no such life-imparting, healing, strengthening and soothing "vibrations" as those which are set afloat by continually speaking as the oracles of God; letting your conversation be seasoned with salt, and your lips as a thread of scarlet.

When I find myself in the midst of such heavenly converse, immediately I am consciously uplifted, stimulated, strengthened, soothed and empowered, not only in spirit but in every vein, nerve, artery, muscle, and blood corpuscle. "The tongue of the wise is health" (Prov. 12:18). "He that keepeth his mouth keepeth his life" (Prov. 13:3). How can we keep our tongues, those unruly little members? Only by having our hearts kept by the indwelling Christ; for out of the fulness or abundance of the heart the mouth speaketh (Matt. 12:34).

"Death and life are in the power of the tongue" (Prov. 18:21). What does this mean? Just what it says. I believe it to be possible that a sin unto death may be committed with the tongue, and that when we come to pray for a person who has committed such a sin, the Holy Spirit will warn us to desist (1 John 5:16). Upon one occasion, I entered the room of a dying woman. She had double pneumonia, she was not young and was also very much overweight, which as you may know, is a very serious handicap in that disease. As I looked at her and thought how hopeless the case appeared, the Lord spoke to me as plainly I think as He ever did in my life, and said, "She has not committed a sin unto death; ask life for her." I did so, and she was healed.

On another occasion, a group of believers were gathered in our home to pray for the recovery of the Christian husband of one of our sisters. One of the brethren united with us for a short time, and if I am any judge, he is one of the strongest men on divine healing, if not the strongest, I have ever met. I have been able to watch his life for years amidst tremendous testings in his own family. After a few minutes he arose and walked quietly out of the room, making a sign for me to follow him. Once outside, he led the way to the front verandah, and carefully closing the door, uttered these words, no more and no less, "That is the chamber of death." Having said so he walked out, closing the gate behind him. He had no means of knowing anything conclusive about the condition of the patient whom he had not seen. But in a few short hours the man was dead. God had shown him not to pray for his recovery.

Longevity is associated with the proper use of the tongue in Psalm 34:12-13; where we are told that if we would see good days and long life we are to refrain our tongue from evil, and our lips from speaking guile. On the other hand, we are warned that, "There is that speaketh like the piercings of the sword" (Prov. 12:18). When we speak harsh words of any one, we may stab them, but we need to remember that we are transfixing our own vitals at the same time. We may not be conscious of it at the moment, but we shall realize it to our awful cost later, for God is not mocked. His Word is true, and means exactly what it says. "The words of a talebearer are as wounds, and they go down into the innermost parts of the belly" (Prov. 18:8).

How terrible are some of the diseases which are developed in the intimate structure of deep-seated organs! How mysterious their origin from the standpoint of medical science! How agonizing the suffering which often has to be endured! How hopeless the outlook from a human standpoint! I believe from the Bible that the origin of these is often in the misuse of the tongue, especially in carrying tales. May God deliver us all from this sin which doth so easily beset us! He will do so if we will yield wholly to Him. He will make the words of our mouths and the meditations of our hearts acceptable in His sight (Ps. 19:14), quickening and upbuilding to all who are brought under the range of our influence; for divine health is catching. I am glad of it, for in this dark world there are so many evil things like fear, sickness, and vice which are contagious.

You can let God so vitalize and energize you with His own life that it will stream through you to all about you. God wants men and women through whom He can "stream." Are you a candidate? Let this become your testimony: "I have rejoiced in the way of thy testimonies, as much as in all riches" (Ps. 119:14).

BRIEF OUTLINE OF CHAPTER 7

Note that out of the four cases of healing of disease recorded in the wilderness wanderings, the remedies for which were always spiritual and types of the cross, therefore not material, though Moses was a fully qualified Egyptian physician and surgeon, (Acts. 7:22) three were caused by misuse of the tongue, viz., Miriam (Num. 12); murmuring (Num. 16:41-50); speaking against God and Moses (Num. 21:4-9). Misuse of the tongue always indicates that the heart is not right, for out "of the abundance of the heart his mouth speaketh" (Luke 6:45).

The Word of God connects health and longevity with a right use of the tongue. It was created that with it we might glorify God. In Ps. 30:12, the psalmist calls his tongue his "glory." If some people were honest, they would call their tongue their "grouch."

> *"The tongue of the wise is health"* (Prov. 12:18).
>
> *"He that keepeth his mouth keepeth his life"* (Prov. 13:3).
>
> *"A wholesome tongue is a tree of life"* (Prov. 15:4).
>
> *"What man is he that desireth life, and loveth many days…* *keep thy tongue from evil, and thy lips from speaking guile"* (Ps. 34:12-13; 1 Pet. 3:10).
>
> *Misuse of the tongue is connected in the Bible with disease and death:*
>
> *"Death and life are in the power of the tongue"* (Prov. 18:21).
>
> *"There is that speaketh like the piercings of a sword"* (Prov. 12:18).
>
> *"The words of a talebearer are as wounds, and they go down into the innermost parts of the belly"* (Prov. 18:8).
>
> *"The tongue is … a world of iniquity… it defileth the whole body"* (James 3:6).

Our Lord Jesus Christ tells us that it is "not that which goeth into the mouth defileth a man; but that which cometh out of the mouth, this defileth a man" (Matt. 15:11).

Those who are appointed as was Miriam (Ex. 15:20, Micah 6:4) to speak in the name of the Lord are doubly responsible for the use they make of their tongues. For the priest's lips should "keep knowledge, and they should seek the law at his mouth; for he is the messenger of the Lord of hosts" (Mal. 2:7).

Our hearts should continually be lifted up to God in the prayer of Psalm 19:14, "Let the words of my mouth, and the meditation of my heart, be acceptable in thy sight, O Lord, my strength and my redeemer."

QUESTIONS ON CHAPTER 7

1. What sin brought upon Miriam the curse of leprosy? Explain.

_____
_____
_____
_____
_____
_____
_____

2. What sin caused the plague with the death of 14,700 persons as recorded in Numbers 16? Explain.

_____
_____
_____
_____
_____
_____
_____

3. What sin brought the judgment of the fiery serpents?

_____

_____

_____

_____

_____

_____

_____

4.   Of what was the brazen serpent a type? Explain.

_____

_____

_____

_____

_____

5.   What is the connection between health and longevity and the right use of the tongue according to the Scriptures? Give at least five references.

_____

_____

_____

_____

_____

_____

6. Give five references showing that misuse of the tongue is connected with disease and death.

_____

_____

_____

_____

_____

_____

7. What should be the attitude of those who like Miriam are appointed of God in respect to their influence and especially the use of the tongue? Give references, chapter and verse, then write them out.

_____

_____

_____

_____

_____

_____

_____

_____

CHAPTER 8

TIMOTHY'S WINE AND HEZEKIAH'S POULTICE

1 TIMOTHY 5:23
ISAIAH 38:1-5, 20-21

"Drink no longer water," (or "water only," marg.) but use a little wine for thy stomach's sake and thine often infirmities" (1 Tim. 5:23). It is wonderful how many people can quote this scripture more or less correctly. I remember hearing a preacher say that he had met those who couldn't quote another verse from the Bible but who were quite familiar with this one. I once had a seeker at the altar with whom I was dealing, and whose greatest weakness was a love for strong drink, say to me: "But doesn't the Bible say that Timothy was told by the apostle Paul to use a little wine for his stomach's sake?"

"Yes, to be sure Paul told Timothy to use a little wine for his stomach's sake, but that does not warrant you in using a great deal of whiskey to destroy your stomach and all the rest of your organs," I replied. And then I have had people quote it as their authority for using all sorts of drugs. Because Paul told Timothy to take a little wine, they felt free to take a great deal of quinine or some laxative, or favorite tonic, or aspirin, or Tanlac, or other patent medicine.

Of course, this matter is only part of a much larger question, viz.: "What is the attitude of the word of God toward man-made systems of healing?" But let us look into this question of Timothy's wine. I do not feel free to omit, in studying this passage, what the eminent Bible scholar Moffatt says of this verse, that it is "either a marginal gloss or misplaced." But as it occurs in the King James' and other versions in use among us, I shall consider it as belonging to the original text; and I believe that in it, Paul advised Timothy in regard to his diet, suggesting the substitution of the juice of the grape, which is most valuable from the standpoint of nutrition, for water as a beverage, just as I would counsel one of you to take cocoa or other nourishing drink with your meals instead of water only.

In the New Testament we are left perfectly free, under God, as to our diet; and as long as we eat and drink to His glory, we may consult our preferences as to the selection we make. Indeed, with a perfectly healthy person, and God makes us perfectly healthy if we trust Him, the tastes are an index of the requirements of the system and should be regarded as such. That God desires us to enjoy a variety of foods is evident from the fact that He has provided so many different kinds, each possessing some special property peculiar to itself and valuable to us. I believe that we should show our gratitude to Him, first by thanking Him for His lavish kindness in this regard; and second, by furnishing our tables with a varied diet so far as our means will permit. There is no doubt that such a diet makes for health and efficiency. Children should be trained from their earliest days to eat and enjoy varied diet, comprising as many different kinds of vegetables and fruits as are obtainable, as well as nuts, a little meat, milk, eggs, butter, cheese, cereals, whole wheat bread, etc.

With reference to Hezekiah's poultice. We note from careful study that His case was a perfectly hopeless one. God Himself had told him to set his house in order for he was going to die. The case had been analyzed by a distinguished Christian physician, author of a treatise on *Bible*

Diseased, and pronounced one of carbuncle, followed by general blood poisoning. A carbuncle is like a gigantic boil which involves the deeper tissues of the body. Hezekiah prayed and received God's promise of healing and was told that fifteen years would be added to his life. Isaiah then directed him to place a poultice of figs on the boil, but such an application could have no effect on the course of such a hopeless disease as carbuncle and general blood poisoning. It might have been used as a cleansing application. It used to be customary to cleanse ulcerating and discharging surfaces by applying large moist poultices of soft pultaceous material, such as bread and milk, linseed and charcoal, etc., but they had no curative properties. On the other hand, the order to place a lump of boiled figs on the boil or carbuncle may have been merely a test of Hezekiah's obedience, just as Naaman was ordered to dip seven times in Jordan. While on this point, allow me to quote the following from the *Sword of the Spirit.*

> *Any means ever used in the Bible had no healing virtue in them whatever, and as we have already said, were used only as a test of faith and obedience … When the children of Israel were bitten by the serpents in the wilderness, God told them the means by which they might be healed, which was for Moses to make a polished brass serpent and put it on a pole. One look at this serpent would bring pardon, cleansing, and healing to the bitten and dying Israelites. The serpent was preserved as a memorial of what God had done. A long time afterwards, in Hezekiah's time, they began to depend on the virtue supposed to be in the serpent. This brought a stern rebuke from Hezekiah, who ground the serpent to pieces and threw it away.*

Now let us consider the question referred to earlier in this chapter, "What is the attitude of the Word of God toward man-made systems of healing?"

Of the futility of turning to human physicians in sickness instead of to Him, God has given us three examples in the Bible: First, the illness and death of Ahaziah, king of Israel and son of Ahab, who enquired regarding his case of Baalzebub, god of Ekron, instead of the Lord God of Israel (2 Kings 1:2-4). Second, the illness and death of Asa, who sought not to the Lord, but to the physicians, and "slept with his fathers" (2 Chron. 16:12-13). I was talking with a doctor the other day about different schools of medicine, allopaths, homeopaths, naturopaths, etc., etc. He answered, "All the 'paths' lead but to the grave, so it doesn't matter much which 'path' you take." That was where Asa's physicians led him, that is certain. Third, the woman who suffered many things of many physicians, spending all she had, and was nothing helped but rather grew worse (Mark 5:25-26; Luke 8:43). It is worthy to note that Luke, himself a physician, does not speak of the woman having suffered many things of the medical fraternity, but being rather worse than better as the result of their ministrations; though he mentions that she had spent all she had upon them; but the most striking thing about the attitude of the Word of God towards human systems of healing is that they are ignored therein as though they were non-existent. In view of the fact that elaborate systems of medical science flourished during the periods covered by the sacred record, it would seem that no words could be more eloquent than the divine silence regarding them.

The distinguished scientist, Dr. Albert T. Buck, in his exhaustive work on the *History of Medical Science,* after speaking of the skill of ancient Egyptian physicians and surgeons, the many remedies including powders, inhalations, potions, snuffs, salves, fumigations, injections, etc., employed by them, their dietetic measures, eliminative treatment, and other therapies, adds:

The Israelites made small use of medicinal agents, dietetic measures and external applications. They placed their chief reliance on prayers, sacrifices and offerings.

No, the Israelites had no need for Egyptian remedies, efficacious though they may have been, for their God had promised that He would bring on them none of the diseases which He brought upon the Egyptians, for He is the Lord who healeth His people. The history of medical science reveals the fact that from prehistoric times men have fought with all the powers of intellect they possess against sickness; but noble as have been their efforts, for science has its martyrs as well as religion, and many have actually laid down their lives in the battle against disease, they have yielded very unsatisfactory results. Scientific men are themselves the witnesses of these things.

Note these words from the pen of H. A. Rowland, in the *American Journal of Science,* quoted by Dr. Fielding H. Garrison in his *History of Medicine*:

> *An only child, a beloved wife, lies on a bed of sickness. The physician says the disease is mortal; a minute plant called a microbe has obtained entrance into the body and is growing at the expense of the tissues, forming deadly poisons in the blood or destroying some vital organ. The physician looks on without being able to do anything. Daily he comes and notes the failing strength of the patient; daily the patient goes downward until he rests in his grave. But why has the physician allowed this? Can we doubt that there is a remedy that will kill the microbe? Why then has he not used it? He is employed to cure but has failed. His bill we cheerfully pay because he has done his best and given a chance of cure. The reason for his failure to cure is ignorance. The remedy is yet unknown. The physician is waiting for others to discover it, or is perhaps experimenting in a crude and unscientific manner to find it.*

And this sad confession is made after centuries and centuries of investigation, research and effort, during which the animal, vegetable, and mineral kingdoms have literally been ransacked for remedial agents. In the 16th century A. D., a Chinese doctor published a book on medicine in 52 volumes, and at that time the Chinese had eighteen hundred different drugs in their regular pharmacopoeia.

Some people go so far as to say that medical science is God's way of healing His people; that He enables men to discover remedies in order that we may utilize them. If that were the case, Moses, who was versed in all the learning of the Egyptians, including medical science, would have so taught the children of Israel instead of pointing them always and only to God the Lord as their physician. Also, if medical science were God's chosen way of meeting our need in sickness, it would not be so uncertain, unreliable, fluctuating, and changing, nor so diverse in its teaching.

In all periods of the world, there have been conflicting and rival schools of medicine as there are today. If the physician is God's way for me, I shall have to ascertain which physician, the regular, the homeopath, the eclectic, the osteopath, the chiropractor, the drugless, etc., etc. No, God's way of healing is One, even Christ Jesus the Lord, who is not only the Way, but also the Truth and the Life of spirit, soul, and body.

While we know that God always blesses men just as much as they will let Him bless them, and meets them just where they are, we have the plain statement of the Scriptures that the Lord Himself is the Healer of His people, and His glory will He not give to another.

The great French physician, Charcot, says: "The best inspirer of hope is the best physician"; and our physician is the God of Hope, for the Lord Jesus Christ is Himself our Hope (1 Tim. 1:1). So, in order to be true to God and His Word, it seems to me that we have to do as did His people of old and trust for our bodies as well as our souls to Him alone.

The Bible teaches that sin, sickness, and suffering actually exist, are real and not illusions of mortal mind as the Christian Scientists would have us believe, but that they are completely removed by God, in answer to believing prayer offered in the name of Jesus Christ, who Himself bore the full penalty of our sins in His body on the cross of Calvary. This truth which was fully and simply accepted in apostolic times and for hundreds of years afterwards, was later so mixed with prayers at the tombs of saints, the veneration of their relics, bones, clothing, and things of that kind, as to be almost lost to the Church. But at the time of the Reformation, it again came to light with the unearthing of the Scriptures and their diffusion among the people, when many notable healings took place. With every subsequent revival, the tide of divine healing has risen higher. Remarkable healings took place in the Quaker revival and in the meetings led by the Wesleys, under Drs. Simpson, Dowie, Cullis of Boston, and others; and now in connection with the last great outpouring of the Holy Spirit, the mighty tide of healing is rolling in with an irresistible flood of blessing.

In this connection, I shall quote some statements regarding a case of organic disease, tuberculosis of the lungs and spine, which was cured by the prayer of faith and anointing according to James 5:14, after all human means had been applied unsuccessfully. The truth of the case is vouched for by certificates furnished by the attending physicians, men eminent in their profession; by the *Elim Evangel* published in Belfast, Ireland; by Pentecostal leaders in Great Britain, among whom are Pastors George and Stephen Jeffreys of whom we all have heard.

Sister Edith Cuffley, the person who was healed, spoke as follows at a meeting in Elim Tabernacle, London:

> *I am led by God to let others know, especially those who are seeking divine healing, how very miraculously I was cured after being ill for four years and nine months … I was a sewing-machine operator by trade, consequently, my work was very heavy; especially so when the war broke out, and I had to work on soldiers' coats, tents, etc. … One day I collapsed while at work and had to be taken to the hospital. Two weeks later, I had a very bad hemorrhage of the lungs, and for two years, I lay in my own home in Kennington, having a nurse daily to attend to me with the doctor coming three times a week. During this*

time, the doctor tried to get me into a hospital or sanatorium, but admission was not obtainable as by this time I had become a bedridden case. Then I began to lose all use of my limbs and endured dreadful pain in my spine. The doctor found that the disease had traveled to the spine, and I was put under X-rays to make sure; and to my great sorrow it was found to be true. The pain became so great that my husband asked the doctor to try and get me away. The only place available was the Home for Incurables and Dying at Thames Ditton, where I lay from April 1919 till August 1920. Here my condition became very critical, and a spinal jacket was made with the hope that it might prove a support and enable me to sit up in bed. This however was quite useless, and when I was put into it the pain only increased. I got much worse, was put on a water bed, and given hypodermic injections of morphine, twice a day for eight months.

In August 1920, Mrs. Cuffley left the hospital in an apparently dying condition, her relatives yielding to her wish to be at home, though those in charge of the institution warned them that she would probably die on the way there. However, she did not die but lived to declare the wonderful works of God. It came about in this way. When in awful agony and almost departing this life, the Lord appeared to her in a most wonderful vision. She says:

It was as though the roof lifted and a most wonderful beam of light shone into my roof. Then I saw the Lord in all His glory, and this is what I heard: "Fear thou not, for I am with thee; be not dismayed, for I am thy God." Then I felt His touch on my arm, and heard His voice saying, "These are My words, take them, and believe them, and act upon them." The verses were James 5:14-15. Three times I heard these words repeated to me.

In response to her call, seven Christian brothers and sisters gathered in her room, and after prayer and reading of the Word, carried out implicitly every command in James 5:14-15, anointing her with oil in the name of the Lord, and praying the prayer of faith over her. Jesus again visited her in glory; she felt His hand on her head; her limbs were straightened out; and she felt a tingling, starting at her toes and reaching to her finger tips. The Lord spoke, saying, "Arise, and get up." She said, "O Lord, I cannot." He spoke the second time, "Arise and get up, now or never!" She said, "O Lord, I will have it now." Then she received power to obey His command, jump out of bed and walk around the room. Immediately she was perfectly restored to health, and said, "Give me something to eat." Her deformed body was absolutely straight, and she ate two eggs with bread and butter, and drank some tea with enjoyment. The next evening, she walked one mile to a meeting.

The following certificate was signed by her attending physician, P. Eugene Giuseppe, M. B., C. M., J. P., formerly Government Medical Officer, Trinidad, British West Indies, 180 Kennington Park Road, S. E. April 15, 1921.

> *I hereby certify that Edith May Cuffley has been under my professional care since December 1917, and before that date under my predecessor the late Dr. R. Foster Owen for several years. She was rendered unfit for work in June 1916 by reason of pulmonary tuberculosis which was followed by spinal tuberculosis. She was more or less prostrated from that time until the 4th of April last when she appears to have mysteriously recovered, having received no systematic treatment since her removal from a sanatorium in August 1920. For the last two years she has been crippled, bedridden, and believed to be incurable. In my opinion, she is now recovered and will soon be quite fit for work, and her cure can only be ascribed to her wonderful faith in prayer. (Signed.)*

The following notes are from the pen of Dr. A. T. Scofield, Specialist, of Harley Street, London:

> To my great pleasure I can record the case of Mrs. Cuffley of 40 Denmark Road, Camberwell, S. E. After careful examination, I must consider it a supernatural cure of organic disease. Mrs. Cuffley developed tubercle of the lung, had had hemorrhage, and lay in her bed for two years. X-rays showed advanced tubercle, and she was removed to the Home for Incurables and Dying at Thames Ditton. She lay in a spinal jacket and later on a water bed. ... She has been nearly eight months perfectly well, walking about all day, visiting the sick and poor. I examined her chest and spine and there was certainly no active disease.

God is sovereign and will instruct us when we come to Him as to the care of our bodies. "Whatsoever he saith unto you, do it" (John 2:5).

One of the most distinguished physicians ever produced by America, S. Weir Mitchell M. D., says that, "Back of each disease lies a cause which no drug can reach." As we learn from the Bible the cause of sickness is sin, and sin can be removed only by the precious blood of Jesus Christ.

QUESTIONS ON CHAPTER 8

1. Mention two examples in the Old Testament of the futility of trusting in the arm of flesh in sickness. Write out the references.

_____

_____

_____

_____

_____

_____

2. Can you refer to a similar case in the New Testament? Write out the reference.

_____

_____

_____

_____

_____

_____

3. What may have been the purpose of the poultice of figs?

_____

_____

_____

_____

_____

_____

4. Give your interpretation of 1 Timothy 5:23.

_____

_____

_____

_____

_____

5.   Give a brief account of the case of Asa, King of Judah.

_____

_____

_____

_____

_____

_____

_____

6.   Paraphrase the accounts of the woman with the issue of blood as recorded in Mark 5:25-34 and Luke 8:43-48, and give your own comment.

_____

_____

_____

_____

_____

_____

_____

7.   What is the most striking thing in the attitude of the Bible toward the human system of healing?

_____

_____

_____

_____

_____

_____

_____

_____

_____

CHAPTER 9

THE CONQUERED CURSE

DEUTERONOMY 28:1-2,8,15,18,
21-22,27-28,35,58-62; 29:22-23
GALATIANS 3:13

Christ redeemed me from the curse of the law As He hung on that shameful tree, And all that is worse is contained in the curse, And Jesus has set me free.

Refrain:

Not under the curse, not under the curse, Jesus has set me free; For sickness, I've health; for poverty, wealth, Since Jesus has ransomed me. Christ paid the price of the broken law, He paid the whole price for me; God saw not one spot, one blemish or blot, In the Lamb that was slain for me. Do not abide in the ancient days, Ere ever the Lamb was slain; Take that which was given as freely as heaven, And join in the glad refrain.

From the 28th chapter of Deuteronomy it is evident that disease, all disease, is included in the curse of the broken law. The following eleven diseases are specified as part of the penalty for disobedience to God's holy commands:

1. Blindness
2. Botch (perhaps leprosy)
3. Consumption
4. Emerods
5. Extreme burning (acute inflammation)
6. Fever
7. Inflammation
8. Itch (incurable form)
9. Madness
10. Pestilence
11. Scab

The Word further states: "Moreover he will bring upon thee all the diseases of Egypt, which thou wast afraid of; and they shall cleave unto thee. Also every sickness, and every plague, which is not written in the book of this law, them will the Lord bring upon thee, until thou be destroyed. And ye shall be left few in number, whereas ye were as the stars of heaven for multitude; because thou wouldest not obey the voice of the Lord thy God" (Deut. 28:60-62).

It is related that Frederick the Great of Prussia once said to his chaplain: "Prove to me in one word that the Bible is a divine revelation."

The chaplain instantly replied: "The Jew, your Majesty."

And surely nothing could be more stimulating to faith than a consideration of the unchanging faithfulness of God in fulfilling to His chosen people Israel each and every promise whether of blessing or cursing.

In a certain town in which I resided for some time there was a synagogue, only one, for it was not a large city. It was located in an obscure district, amidst unattractive surroundings, but was nevertheless a favorite place of pilgrimage for me. Not that I ever entered it, or took part in the worship that was held there, or even became acquainted with the worshipers. No, I only stood and gazed and gazed at the building; noted the date of its erection which was given in accordance with Jewish chronology; noted its name, "House of Jacob," and the inscription "O House of Jacob, come ye, and let us walk in the light of the Lord" (Isa. 2:5), and the strongly marked Hebrew facial characteristics of the attendants at the services. Once I caught a glimpse of a man robed in a talith or praying shawl. And as I looked the word found in the chapter we are studying, words uttered through human lips thousands of years ago, would chant itself in sad, solemn strains in the very depths of my spirit:

> *Because thou wouldest not obey ... ye shall be plucked from off the land wither thou goest to possess it ... The Lord shall scatter thee among all people from the one end of the earth even unto the other... And among these nations thou shalt find no ease, neither shall thy foot have rest: but the Lord shall give thee a trembling heart, and failing of eyes, and sorrow of mind: and thy life shall hang in doubt before thee: and thou shalt fear day and night, and shalt have none assurance of thy life* (Deut. 28: 62-66).

The reason I loved to gaze at the synagogue and the poor exiles from the Promised Land who worshiped there, was that I learned from their condition, scattered among strangers who despised them, the exactitude with which God fulfills His word, whether of blessing or doom. He permits us to see with our eyes, and hear with our ears, the literal fulfillment of many portions of this 28th chapter of Deuteronomy; and history records the fulfillment with the most marvelous accuracy of many other portions. Take for example verse 32: "Thy sons and thy daughters shall be given unto another people, and thine eyes shall look, and fail with longing for them all the day long: and there shall be no might in thine hand" (Deut. 28:32).

In Portugal and Spain, laws were actually in force at one time which permitted anyone who was so minded to seize Jewish children and bring them up as Roman Catholics. This was esteemed a very meritorious action and one not infrequently performed by believers in Roman Catholicism. In such cases the Jewish parents were without recourse, had "no might" in their hands, as the Bible foretold. Look also at verses 49-50: "The Lord shall bring a nation against thee from far…as swift as the eagle flieth; a nation whose tongue thou shalt not understand; a nation of fierce countenance, which shall not regard the person of the old, nor shew favour to the young."

Apparently, the Roman standard which bore the eagle is referred to here. Then no two languages could be more unlike than the Hebrew and Latin. The typical Roman countenance is cruel and stern. Indeed "Roman-nosed" has been almost synonymous with disagreeable. Also note verse 52: "He shall besiege thee in all thy gates." "He," first Nebuchadnezzar, later Titus, "And the Lord shall scatter thee among all people, from the one end of the earth even to the other…" (verse 64). This has been literally fulfilled.

A converted Hebrew, the Rev. Mr. Schor, recently traveled extensively showing the present condition of the Hebrew race by means of exhibits. These I carefully examined, finding among them photographs of Jews taken in all parts of the world: Chinese Jews, wearing robes and queues; African Jews, many of whom were almost, if not quite, black in color; Russian Jews; Polish Jews; English Jews, etc., all partaking more or less of the characteristics peculiar to the countries where they resided.

If you ever have any doubt as to whether God always means exactly what He says, read with me verse 68: "And the Lord shall bring thee into Egypt again with ships… and there shall ye be sold unto your enemies for bondmen and bondwomen, and no man shall buy you."

This actually happened after the taking of Jerusalem by Titus, after the Jews had filled the measure of their rebellion against God by crucifying his Son, their Messiah and our blessed Savior, for their young men were shipped to the Roman works in Egypt and there sold as slaves. So despicable were the Jews deemed at this time that Romans were actually ashamed to have them working for them even as slaves, which was doubtless one reason for their transportation to Egypt.

I wonder how many of us feel that these instances are sufficiently numerous to convince us that God means just what He says in this 28th chapter of Deuteronomy. How many think so? Well then, we may feel sure that every other promise we find here, whether of blessing or of cursing will be as exactly fulfilled as the ones which we have here examined. Hence, we shall consider more especially the passages relating to sickness and deliverance therefrom.

The children of Israel whom we have followed in their exodus from Egyptian bondage, across the Red Sea and through their wilderness wanderings, have now entered the Promised Land where they are immediately confronted with two alternatives, viz.,

1. The Blessing. This follows obedience to God's commandments, and embraces every part of their being and possessions, spirit, soul, body, children (fruit of their bodies), cattle, crops, etc. The blessing guaranteed them immunity from all disease. "Blessed shalt thou be in the city, and blessed shalt thou be in the field... The Lord shall command the blessing upon thee...in all that thou settest thy hand unto.... The Lord shall establish thee...and all the people of the earth...shall be afraid of thee. The Lord shall make thee plenteous in goods in the fruit of thy body and in the fruit of thy cattle, and in the fruit of thy ground.... The Lord shall open unto thee his good treasure.... The Lord shall make thee the head and not the tail" (Deut. 28:3, 8-13).

2. The Curse. This was consequent upon failure to obey, and included every form of sickness and disease which can attack humanity. In other words, disobedience to God's law men under the curse. God is the Lord who changes not (see Mal. 3:6). A life of holiness is essential

to a life of physical wholeness, and both are ours through faith in the Lamb of God and can be obtained in no other way. He was made a curse for us. While I am far from depreciating the efforts that are being made to stamp out sickness by scientific research, I say on the authority of God's Word that such efforts can be attended only with a very limited measure of success; for so long as sin exists, it will when it is finished bring forth death; and disease is death begun. The latest statistics show a greater mortality from cancer than ever before in the history of the human race in spite of all the work that has been done in millionaire-endowed laboratories.

Perhaps no more determined effort has ever been made by leaders among the medical fraternity than that which has been directed against the white plague, tuberculosis. I myself knew a most able man who spent eighteen years of his life in research work on this one disease alone. The results of his labors were contained in locked books, the contents of which were written in cipher. But in spite of his labors and others of the same kind, for of course he was only one of an army of scientific explorers and investigators, tuberculosis still claims its annual quota of victims. Even if tuberculosis could be completely stamped out, so long as sin remains it would inevitably be followed by sickness of some sort or another, for as has already been said "sin, when it is finished, bringeth forth death" (James 1:15), and disease is death begun.

Therefore, to be delivered from disease, we must come to the One who settled the sin-and-sickness question for us on the cross of Calvary by being made a curse for us, and looking to Him, the Lamb of God, sing with grateful hearts,

> *Not under the curse, not under the curse,*
> *Jesus has set me free,*
> *For sickness, I've health, for poverty, wealth,*
> *Since Jesus has ransomed me.*

At one time, I wondered why God saw fit to specify so many diseases in this chapter as part of the penalty for breaking His holy law, when it plainly states that all sickness, "every sickness, and every plague, which is not written in the book of this law" (Deut. 28:61), is included in the curse; but the Holy Ghost vouchsafed great light to me upon this point when dealing with persons afflicted with some of the diseases here specified. Take tuberculosis of the lungs, for instance, commonly called consumption. I thank God that I have personal knowledge of many marvelous healings of this well-nigh hopeless disease. I use the word advisedly, for while modern methods have undoubtedly done a great deal toward arresting its course in the earliest stages, there is still practically no prospect of recovery from advanced cases, except by faith in the work accomplished for soul and body on Calvary. I know no better way of dealing with such than by giving them the Word of God as it is found in Deuteronomy 28 in connection with some New Testament scriptures, more particularly Galatians 3:13 which states that "Christ hath redeemed us from the curse of the law."

I often hear the plaint, "There's no hope for me, Doctor; I have consumption; three physicians have pronounced it tuberculosis of the lungs. I have been X-rayed and all the rest. They say it is quite advanced, and the best I can expect is that my life may be prolonged somewhat if I am very faithful in following the instructions, they have given me and in taking their remedies."

To all of which I invariably reply, "Do you believe that the Bible is the Word of God, and absolutely true in every particular?

"Oh, yes, I know it is."

"Well then, the Word of God explicitly states that Christ Jesus healed you of consumption, mentioning the name of the very disease from which the doctors tell you that you are dying at this moment."

"Oh, where is it? I have never seen it in the Bible."

And then turning to Deuteronomy 28:22, I point out that consumption is a part of the curse of the broken law, from which curse Galatians 3:13 tells us that Christ has redeemed us by being made a curse for us or in our stead.

"Now repeat with me," I urge, "Christ hath redeemed me from the curse of the law, of which curse consumption is a part, hence Christ hath redeemed me from consumption." The seeker obeys, and over and over again with the Bible open before us at Deuteronomy 28:22 and Galatians 3:13 we say together, "Christ hath redeemed me from consumption." Thus, faith cometh by hearing the word of God and the mountain of disease is cast into the sea.

How thankful I am that God in His mercy and wisdom saw fit to include consumption, the great white plague, among the diseases specially mentioned in this category in Deuteronomy 28.

Let me relate in brief the history of a case that was healed by the Word of God through my sister's ministry in our own home in Calgary, Alberta, Canada. I may say that later this woman received the baptism of the Holy Ghost, and has been a true witness for Jesus on all lines ever since her deliverance some five years ago.

She is a trained nurse. Upon being pronounced tuberculous and made to live in a separate bungalow from the rest of the family, and eat of marked dishes, she became very interested in the things of God. She had been saved some years before and came to our home in the hope of getting nearer to Jesus in her spiritual life. She had no hope of being cured of the disease from which she was suffering, but wanted to be fully ready for the home call.

My sister was alone in the house when she called, and after a little conversation which served to reveal the needs of the seeker, the Bible in which the sick one implicitly believed was searched, especially regarding healing, the 28th chapter of Deuteronomy and other scriptures being brought to her notice with the result that she saw full salvation for her entire being, including her body. When she saw that all of this was perfectly secured when Jesus was made a curse for her on Calvary, she was immediately healed.

Sometime afterwards she was staying at the home of a prominent doctor who held her in high esteem. He had not known her prior to her healing. One day, just for fun, my sister called him up and asked him if he saw any signs of tuberculosis of the lungs about the nurse he had in his family.

"Certainly not!" he replied rather testily, and then he was told the wonderful story.

We are in constant touch with this nurse and hear from her at regular intervals and know well her life ever since her healing. It has been one of continual effort and sacrifice for others, a "poured out life," and there is never a hint of any recurrence of the dread disease from which she suffered when first we met her.

It is noteworthy that among the diseases enumerated as part of the curse of the broken law are found some of the most malignant and virulent from which humanity suffers. Botch, for instance, is said to mean leprosy. We shall go more fully into that when we consider Bible diseases. Then fevers are among the most dreadful scourges, especially in hot countries. Even in our own land some of them, such as typhus, typhoid, scarlet fever, smallpox, and other eruptive fevers, have a high mortality rate. Blindness is one of the most awful afflictions from which any one can suffer, being only surpassed by "madness"; while the scab, an incurable form of itch, evidently refers to some of those awful and intractable forms of skin disease with which we sometimes come in contact. How delightful to be able to say, on the authority of God's Word, "Christ has redeemed you from fever, whether it be typhus, typhoid, scarlet fever, or smallpox. I can give you chapter and verse for it."

"Christ has redeemed you from blindness too, for Deuteronomy 28:28 says it is included in the curse of the broken law, and Galatians 3:13

says that Christ redeemed you from the whole curse. Christ has redeemed you also from that hopeless skin disease. The Bible says so."

I remember going out to a rather remote settlement with an evangelistic party comprising several workers, only one of whom was a brother. The sisters were given a little house to live in, but the poor brother was taken to sleep with the game warden who had a terrible skin disease from which he was seeking healing. He told us next day how sorely tempted he had been to refuse to sleep with the man; but how could he permit himself to be afraid of contracting a disease which he was telling the other fellow was part of the curse from which Christ had redeemed him?

The devil said: "If you have to get into bed with him, keep all your clothes on, and you may escape contagion, though even then you will be taking terrible risks."

At first, he was going to accept this suggestion, but the Holy Spirit lifted up a standard and said: "Can't you trust Jesus?"

With that he said, "Yes, I can and do trust him." Undressing he jumped into bed and slept as peacefully as an infant on his mother's breast. And the brother with the skin disease was perfectly healed. He always called his trouble itch, though it wasn't itch at all, but something far more serious. I suppose it itched, it looked as though it would, and that was the reason he gave it the unpoetical name.

It seemed as though we would never hear the last of his healing. Sometime later we were holding meetings in a fine Methodist church, where the large congregation contained many well-to-do and refined persons. In opening the service one evening I called for testimonies. Of course, I meant nice, polite testimonies. Who should jump up but Johnnie Hourie the game warden. I didn't even know he was there as it was far from his home.

He simply convulsed the audience by the following testimony: "Well, praise the Lord! He healed me of the itch!"

You should have heard them laugh. But you couldn't doubt his testimony. He made it very plain that he had suffered tortures from which God had completely relieved him, and in consequence of which he was now bubbling over with gratitude.

How glorious to be able to tell every sick one, no matter what the disease from which they are suffering, that Christ has redeemed them from it, even if it is not specified by name in this wonderful 28th chapter of Deuteronomy. For we are told in verses 60 and 61 that all diseases, without a single exception, are included in the curse.

Oh, that we might sing with heart and voice, day and night:

I'm not under the curse, I'm not under the curse,
For Jesus has set me free;
For sickness I've health, for poverty, wealth,
Since Jesus has ransomed me.

QUESTIONS ON CHAPTER 9

1. How much is included in the curse of the broken law?

_____

_____

_____

_____

_____

_____

_____

2. Enumerate 10 diseases specified in Deuteronomy 28.

_____

_____

_____

_____

_____

_____

_____

3.   State some results of the disobedience of the Jews.

_____

_____

_____

_____

_____

_____

4.   How would you prove by the Jew the unchangeableness of God?

_____

_____

_____

_____

_____

_____

5.   Give 10 blessings resulting from obedience.

_____

_____

_____

_____

_____

_____

_____

6.　Give 10 results of the curse consequent upon disobedience.

_____

_____

_____

_____

_____

_____

7.　What scriptures would you quote to a seeker after healing?

_____

_____

_____

_____

_____

_____

8.　How inclusive is God's provision for healing?

_____

_____

_____

_____

_____

_____

_____

9.   What is God's purpose in specifying certain diseases?

_____

_____

_____

_____

_____

_____

10.   Should we trust God to the extent of neglecting ordinary precaution?

_____

_____

_____

_____

_____

_____

_____

CHAPTER 10

WHAT SOLOMON SAYS ABOUT DIVINE HEALING

The Psalms are an inspired manual of devotion, containing prayer, praise, worship, and adoration, and have been the songs of God's people in the house of their pilgrimage through all ages. They are still used in public worship in every branch of the church militant, and by means of these, we shall doubtless praise and worship God throughout eternity, for the Word of God lives and abides forever. They contain the clearest teaching regarding God's will for our physical health and well-being, and the provision which He has made to fulfill that will to all who will meet the conditions laid down.

When God wanted certain great truths indelibly impressed on the minds of the Israelites, He bade Moses write a song and teach it to them so that they in turn might teach it to their children and might never be forgotten out of the mouths of their seed (Deut. 32). In ancient times it was customary, especially prior to the invention of printing, to impart certain branches of learning by means of songs which the students committed to memory, and afterwards retained by frequent singing. One great student of human nature said, "Let me write the songs of a nation, and I shall wield a far greater power over it than the man who writes its philosophies and histories."

How profound then must have been the effect on the younger generation of Israelites of such teaching as that contained in the 107th Psalm! That magnificent, divinely inspired anthem of praise is said to have been used by thousands of voices on the subject of the origin of sickness, and of God's provision for delivering man from its power. Listen to these verses:

"Fools because of their transgression, and because of their iniquities, are afflicted" (Ps. 107:17).

That doesn't leave much room for doubt as to the close relationship between sin and sickness, does it? No; they are "Siamese twins" as the Bible teaches, and you can't take one into your house without having them both, any more than you could invite Mr. Chang to dinner and leave Mr. Eng at home.

"Their soul abhorreth all manner of meat; and they draw near unto the gates of death" (Ps. 107:18).

"Then they cry unto the Lord in their trouble, and he saveth them out of their distresses. He sent his word and healed them, and delivered them from their destructions" (Ps. 107:19-20).

Then follows the great Hallelujah Chorus sung by thousands of voices—one writer says there were probably twenty thousand.

"Oh that men would praise the Lord for His goodness, and for His wonderful works to the children of men! And let them sacrifice the sacrifices of thanksgiving, and declare his works with rejoicing" (Ps. 107:21-22).

Young Israelites who sang this and other magnificent psalms from their earliest days would be in no doubt as to God's will for their bodies, would they? I know some fortunate young people even in the present generation who have never heard a doctor telephoned for in case of sickness, but only the strains of the old hymn, "The great Physician now is near, the sympathizing Jesus," as saints gathered around to anoint the sick one with oil in the name of the Lord.

I know one little girl who had such an experience. In the first place she was a child of faith, for the physicians had said her mother would never have another child. She had all but lost her life with the first one. But when the mother accepted Jesus as her physician as well as her Savior, she trusted Him wholly, and only desired to leave herself in His dear hands when the little one was expected. But her husband, who was the principal dentist in the city, was determined to have doctor, nurse, and all the devices known to medical science. However, "prayer changes things!" Some women continued in prayer, in answer to which the little daughter arrived in the sweetest peace before either doctor or nurse could be brought in an automobile. This child developed a very active faith on her own part, so that when she was only three years old, she would climb up on a chair, get the oil bottle off the shelf, and come with it prepared to join in prayer for the afflicted one. One day some friends of her mother who did not know the Lord as the healer were staying in the house. One of them being suddenly taken ill, baby came as usual with the bottle of oil. But when the visitor showed some reluctance about receiving anointing according to the Scriptures, baby was very indignant and rapped her soundly on the head with the bottle.

Now as the Psalms are an inspired book of prayer and praise, the Proverbs of Solomon are an inspired manual of rules for daily living. God-given instructions, adapted to all times, countries, and individuals, and embracing all the practical details of our daily life are found therein. If the Psalms especially guide our thoughts, the Proverbs are intended to direct our actions. We are, therefore, not surprised to find here many passages showing clearly the close relation that exists between our spiritual walk and our physical condition. Likewise, the most definite instructions are vouchsafed to us as to how we must govern ourselves, so that we may enjoy perfect immunity from disease.

> *My son, attend to my words; incline thine ear unto my sayings. Let them not depart from thine eyes; keep them in the*

midst of thine heart. For they are life unto those that find them, and health to all their flesh. Keep thy heart with all diligence; for out of it are the issues of life (Prov. 4:20-23).

It is a very significant fact that there is not in this practical treatise any intimation that, in the event of sickness overtaking us, we are to resort to the physicians and apothecaries for aid. This is the more noteworthy in view of the fact that in the non-canonical, uninspired Wisdom Books, notably the Book of Wisdom, written probably between B. C. 217 and 40 A. D., and Ecclesiasticus which likely originated about the same time, we find people directed to resort to the physician in case of sickness. These books are accepted as canonical by the Roman Catholic Church, although they do not form part of the Hebrew canon of scripture. While not truly scriptural or inspired, they are yet valuable as showing what was actually believed and taught among the Jews of that period.

The author of the Book of Wisdom says: "It was neither herb, nor mollifying plaster that healed them, but thy Word, O Lord, which healeth all things" (Book of Wisdom 16:12). Nevertheless, he goes on to teach the descendants of these very people who had been healed by the power of God, and by that power alone, to resort to physicians in their illness. This was on account of their apostasy and spiritual degeneracy, due in part to their long sojourn amongst heathen to whom they had been subject, and with whom they had intermarried. As a result, they no longer had faith in the true and living God as their healer.

The author of the book called Ecclesiasticus goes further in this direction and says, "Honour the physician for the need thou hast in him… The Most High hath created medicines out of the earth and the wise man will not abhor them…The Most High hath given knowledge to men that He may be honored in His wonders. By these he shall cure and allay their pains, and of these the apothecary shall make sweet confections, and shall make up ointments of health, and of His works—the apothecary's—there shall be no end…Give place to the physician for the Lord created him;

and let him not depart from thee, for his works are necessary. For there is a time when thou must fall into their hands. He that sinneth in the sight of his Maker shall fall into the hands of the physician."

Compare these utterances with the instruction found in the book of Proverbs. The contrast as great as between light and darkness. In chapter 4:20-23, we are commanded to keep the Word of God before our eyes and ears, and hidden away in our hearts; and we are promised that if we faithfully do this it will be life to us and health to all our flesh, so that there would be no need of the ministrations of an earthly physician. What more excellent counsel could we find than that in Proverbs 3:5-8? "Trust in the Lord with all thine heart; and lean not unto thine own understanding. In all thy ways acknowledge him, and he shall direct thy paths. Be not wise in thine own eyes: fear the Lord, and depart from evil. It shall be health to thy navel, and marrow to thy bones."

These mysterious words, "health to thy navel," mean the complete cleansing of the system from all hereditary taint, as it is at this point known as the navel that the blood vessels supplying the child with oxygenated blood in prenatal life enter the body. Some people are hindered by the idea that they cannot be healed of hereditary diseases. But this is not the case, for Jesus healed all manner of sickness and all manner of disease (Matt. 4:23; 10:1). Among these was the man born blind. A young man once came to a preacher and said, "There is no hope for me: I am a down and out, a sodden drunkard. The doctors say that it is not only a sin with me but an hereditary disease from which I cannot escape. For three generations and perhaps longer my ancestors have been hopeless drunkards. They say that no power of will or anything else known to man is strong enough to break the chain of heredity and remove the transmitted vice from the system."

"I am far from attempting to minimize the awful power of a vicious heredity, my boy," said the preacher kindly, "but I am thankful to say that, strong as it is, powerful as is its influence in determining a man's character and destiny, I know of something infinitely stronger, and that is the blood of Jesus." The young man believed, came to the foot of the cross, and was saved and healed. Yes, the blood of Jesus is stronger than heredity.

Then we note the words, "marrow to our bones." This seems to promise the most profound physical well-being, as the marrow is one of the deepest tissues in the body, having as part of its function the nourishing of the skeleton, the solid structure which supports all the rest of the anatomy.

Again, in Proverbs 19:23, we read, "The fear of the Lord tendeth to life: and he that hath it shall abide satisfied; he shall not be visited with evil."

As pointed out in Chapter 7, about Miriam's mistake, the book of Proverbs abounds in warnings that if we use our organs of speech in talebearing and backbiting, we shall become the victims of dire disease; and on the other hand, we are told that the tongue of the wise is health, health to the speaker and health to the listener (Prov. 12:18).

The Queen of Sheba came from the ends of the earth to hear the wisdom of Solomon and to try him with hard questions, but he proved fully equal to the occasion and exceeded all the fame that had reached her. He answered all her hard questions, for the Word says, "He was wiser than all men" because God had given him a wise and an understanding heart (1 Kings 3:12, 4:31). Solomon says that the words of God if studied, believed in, and hidden in our hearts, is "health to all our flesh"; and there is not so much as a hint in the whole book of Proverbs of any necessity, under any circumstances, of employing any other agency, such as physician, surgeon, drugs or operative procedure. He further tells us that the taint of hereditary disease is removed by obedient faith, and real faith is always obedient. In addition, it promises us longevity as the result of keeping God's commandments. Thank God for the clear instruction in this practical treatise on right living and wise ways of conducting ourselves. But let us thank Him still more that one greater than Solomon is here to heal all who will come to Him.

I was strongly impressed with a case of healing I once witnessed, and I believe God would have me relate it for His glory. The sufferer was a Baptist minister. He had a very deep-seated abscess somewhere under his tongue. His throat and mouth were so swollen that he could hardly breathe. His tongue, purple and tremendously swollen, protruded out of his mouth so that he could not articulate a single word. They had a doctor who frankly stated that he could not do a single thing for him as he would not dare to operate until the acute inflammation and tremendous swelling had somewhat diminished. It did not seem as though the man could possibly survive long enough for any improvement to take place in his condition. So his wife asked the doctor for his bill, at the same time remarking, "I suppose you would be prepared to sign a death certificate for us, if necessary, as we desire to comply with the provisions of the Health Act"? The doctor answered in the affirmative, and added, "I don't like to take your money for the reason that I am unable to do anything. In any case, why be in such a hurry about paying me?"

"Well," said the wife, "we want to place the case unreservedly in the hands of the Lord, and we can't have two doctors on it at once." So the physician took his check and departed.

That evening I was sent for, and with a brother in the Lord we prayed for and anointed the patient. After we had done so, though there was no visible improvement in his condition, the Lord gave me very definitely the second verse of the fourth chapter of Malachi, "Unto you that fear my name shall the Sun of righteousness arise with healing in his wings: and ye shall go forth and grow up as calves of the stall." Only the Lord gave me another version of it, which I had seen somewhere and which reads, "Ye shall go forth and gambol as calves of the stall." That means to kick up your heels like a well-fed calf. I solemnly gave this scripture to the apparently dying man who was at the moment enduring the most excruciating agonies and to his wife who was utterly crushed under her load of anxiety. Then I went home, leaving the brother to stay all night with the patient.

At first the sick man walked up and down in his misery like a caged animal. He didn't cry or groan because he couldn't make a sound, but his torture was awful to witness. Then he sat down for a moment and taking the brother's hand wrote on it "Though he slay me…."

The brother said "Yes, I understand, but that isn't good enough. You must wax valiant in fight and put to flight the armies of the aliens. You must believe that Jesus heals you now. I shall sit down here beside you on the bed and take your head on my breast. Just believe with me for refreshing sleep, and it will come. God is faithful."

So the sick man obeyed and in a few moments he was fast asleep, the first sleep he had had for many days. The brother reached for the light and turned it low, and prayed with every breath. The patient slept for twenty minutes when suddenly the air of the room was filled with the most awful odor, as though it were the concentrated extract of graveyards. Turning up the light the brother found the patient and himself and the bed on which they were sitting literally deluged with the most awful mass of pus and blood, absolutely putrid in its character. What had happened? God had operated and had opened the deep-seated abscess that no surgeon dared touch, and drained it clean of its poisonous contents. From that hour the man was well.

Of course, he needed the most complete overhauling and cleaning. The bed and clothing had to be burned, but the little wife gladly undertook that part for her husband was free from pain and danger was a thing of the past. Some months later they moved to the outskirts of the city and there they purchased property. They used to come in to the services, but as they were several blocks from the street car, the man made a large sled on which to drag his wife to the car. One day he and his oldest boy were doing this. They were playing ponies, and the father kicked up his heels like a young horse, when the Lord brought to the wife's mind the words

He had given them from the fourth chapter of Malachi and asked, "What do you call that? Isn't he gamboling like a calf?"

She answered "Yes, Lord, he is. I praise You for Your faithfulness."

Now, let us wholly trust Him with our troubles, whether spiritual or physical, and prove Him wholly true.

BRIEF OUTLINE ON CHAPTER 10

In our chapter titled "The Praise Cure," we have already referred to the Psalms as the inspired hymn and prayer book of Israel. They also contain much valuable teaching regarding the will of God with reference to our physical condition (see Ps. 107:17-20).

But in the Proverbs, the sayings ascribed to the wise man, we find an inspired manual of rules for daily living adapted to all ages, countries, and individuals; embracing all practical details and abounding in definite instructions as to how we should live if we would enjoy not only immunity from sickness but abounding health and vigor (see Prov. 3:1-8; 4:20-23; 12:18, last clause; 13:3; 18:21, etc.).

It is most noteworthy that in this practical manual, we find no hint of turning to the physician for aid in the event of sickness. This is all the more significant in view of the fact that the uninspired and non-canonical books of wisdom, which resemble the book of Proverbs, but belong to a later period, abound in such references. The difference faithfully reflects the apostate period to which they belong.

Longevity is promised in the book of Proverbs (3:13) to the man who "findeth wisdom." We know that "the fear of the Lord is the beginning of wisdom" (Ps. 111:10). Hence, if we desire life and aspire to many days, we must "depart from evil, and do good" (Ps. 34:12, 14).

It is possible that Proverbs 3:8 refers to hereditary disease. But in any event, we know that Jesus healed all manner of disease and all manner of sickness among the people, including even hereditary ailments (see John 9).

QUESTIONS ON CHAPTER 10

1.   In its relation to God's people, how may the book of Proverbs be designated?

_____

_____

_____

_____

_____

_____

2.   Give two quotations showing what this practical manual has to say about health.

_____

_____

_____

_____

_____

_____

3.   What does Proverbs teach regarding longevity?

_____

_____

_____

_____

_____

_____

_____

4. Does Proverbs contain any intimation that human aid should be sought in healing?

_____

_____

_____

_____

_____

_____

5. How do the uninspired books of wisdom compare with Proverbs?

_____

_____

_____

_____

_____

6. Do these uninspired books agree with Exodus 15:26 and Malachi 3:6? Explain the reason for disagreement.

_____

_____

_____

_____

_____

_____

_____

7.   Do these uninspired books agree with the teaching of Isaiah concerning healing?

_____

_____

_____

_____

_____

8.   In the light of questions 6 and 7, do you find any present-day analogy?

_____

_____

_____

_____

_____

9.   Give your version of Proverbs 3:8. To what may it possibly refer?

_____

_____

10. What is stronger than hereditary disposition to disease?

_____

11. Give two cases of healing of hereditary disease by Jesus.

_____

CHAPTER 11

THE BIBLE OR CHRISTIAN SCIENCE—WHICH?

MATTHEW 7:21-23
1 JOHN 4:1-4
2 JOHN 7:11

The Bible or Christian Science—which shall it be? You cannot have both, for they are opposed to one another on all essential points as the following passages make perfectly clear.

"But I thought that Christian Scientists recognized the Bible and are diligent students of it," someone says.

They may read the text, especially portions of it and carry tents of it, a copy of it, along with *Science and Health with Key to the Scriptures,* but they do not receive it as the Word of God in truth, eternal, immutable, and forever settled in Heaven. For on page 139, lines 20 and 21, of their official textbook, we read: "A mortal and material sense stole into the divine record, with its own hue darkening to some extent the inspired pages." And of a statement of the Holy Ghost, in the 7th verse of the 2nd chapter of Genesis, "The Lord God formed man of the dust of the ground," Mrs. Eddy does not hesitate to say (you will find it in the third paragraph of page 524 of the *Key to the Scriptures*): "How could a material organization become the basis of man? ... Is this real or unreal? Is it the truth, or is it a lie? ... It must be a lie." (All quotations are from the edition of 1917.)

Much of Christian Science literature is vague and difficult to understand, but whenever anything essential is stated clearly, it is found to be absolutely antagonistic to the Scriptures.

Sometimes people ask, "What is the difference between Christian Science and divine healing as taught in the Bible?" To which the answer is, "They have nothing in common." The false philosophy on which Christian Science is founded, denies that Jesus Christ is come in the flesh, that His body was a real body, and it is, therefore, anti-Christian.

"The Bible teaches healing as coming to us through the atoning work of Christ on Calvary," but Christian Science does away with this altogether, for, according to Mrs. Eddy's teaching, "Since there is no sin, there can be no redemption."

"But do they not have healings?" I believe, from the Bible, that they do, for we are taught to expect to see miracles wrought by satanic power, especially toward the end of the age, but the infidelity which they teach is so fatal that I feel about their healings like a woman who sent a request for prayer for her son to a meeting I was holding in a Methodist church in Oakland. It was in writing and she said: "My son is terribly sick; there is no human hope, but I ask you to pray for his healing to the God with whom all things are possible. But let none but those who believe in the precious blood of the Lamb as our only approach to God, pray for my boy. Let no one who does not honor the blood touch my suffering boy by so much as a thought."

Dr. A. B. Simpson was one of the most well-balanced men spiritually I have ever met, and he says of Christian Science, "I would rather be sick all my life with every form of physical torment, than be healed by such a lie."

"Open confession is good for the soul," and I feel impelled to relate just here a bit of my personal experience, which I much prefer to keep to myself, and to say that if anyone ever tried to believe Christian Science, I was that person.

As I have already told you in a former chapter, I awakened one morning to the realization that I was in a hopeless quagmire of drug addiction, from which nothing human could extricate me. I had tried everything that medical science could suggest, had been discharged from the hospital as a patient they could not help, had taken the Gold Cure, and after spending practically all I had, impoverishing my poor mother, and other relatives as well, by my ceaseless efforts to find relief from some source, I turned to my neglected Bible and my interrupted prayer life and very soon the light on healing began to dawn upon me from the cross of Calvary.

As I felt a faint flutter of hope in my breast, where all had been for so long the stillness of despair, I turned to older Christians for encouragement, and not one crumb of comfort did they give me. Remember this was over 26 years ago. As I read and re-read the Bible, I saw more and more clearly that not only was provision made for our healing, but that we were ourselves commanded to go forth and, in the name of Jesus, lay hands on the sick and heal them. I said, "I will go to some of the believers I know and point these scriptures out to them, and ask them to pray with me that I may be healed," and I started on my weary rounds.

I was so desperate that I knew no shame in presenting my petition. No rebuff was stinging enough to make me desist. Some said, because they were ashamed to confess that they did not believe the Word of God: "We are too busy to deal with your case today. Some other time, at the prayer meeting perhaps, you might ask for prayer."

And I would reply, "Nothing you can possibly be doing is as important as complying with Jesus' last command to you to lay hands on the sick that they may recover. Pray with me right here and now, and I believe God will heal me."

But they would not and, at last, I said: "The Bible says, 'These signs shall follow them that believe,' and as they don't follow these professed Christians, evidently, they are not believers. It is said that they follow Christian Scientists, that they heal the sick, so they must be believers, and I will appeal to them." I went to New York City and got in touch with the then leaders of the work there.

Through the influence of a friend who stood very high in Christian Science circles, she was afterwards a prominent practitioner in Berlin, Prussia, I secured treatments from a most eminent Scientist, then practicing in New York. Of course, I paid a goodly sum for them, but it was a great favor to get them at any price, and I was made to feel that I was under the greatest obligations to all who had assisted me to do so.

Of course, I purchased all their literature, and, at the command of my practitioner, plunged up to the neck in *Science and Health,* reading it every waking moment, or nearly so, very rarely allowing myself a dip into Mrs. Eddy's *Miscellaneous Writings.* I was told that there was absolutely no trouble about my morphine addiction, and the awful physical conditions, which had resulted therefrom; that it did not really exist, and would vanish like snow wreaths before the sun as soon as I freed my thoughts from its "self-imposed materiality and bondage" by absorbing enough of *Science and Health.*

> *I had a fall, I broke my arm, wherever should I go?*
> *A Christian Science doctor shall dissipate my woe.*
> *I found a lady calm and sweet, for it was office hours,*
> *and she on absent treatments must concentrate her powers;*
> *You think she felt the broken bone? No, nothing half so tame,*

she looked into the distance and just denied the claim;

In mortal error you are swamped but truth you now shall see,

For as you have no arm to break, no arm can broken be.

Since all is good, and good is all, just voice the truth and say,

"My arm is strong, and sound, and whole. Ten dollars, please.
Good-day!"

I said, "Because, in light and truth you're plunged up to the
neck,

Just say, I have ten dollars now, and thank you for your check."

That sounded good to me, you may believe, and I simply devoured Mrs. Eddy's book. Although I did not know the Bible as I do now, I am conscious that I know very, very little about it yet, though I have been studying it ever since I felt something like the man (I regret that I cannot recall his name) whose experience I read some time ago, who was told by a woman friend that what he needed was to study *Science and Health with Key to the Scriptures* by Mrs. Mary Baker-Eddy.

"Why, I didn't know the Scriptures were locked, but if they are, it is a mighty lucky thing the lady found the key," he replied.

"Yes, it is the greatest blessing that had ever befallen humanity," said his friend.

And she was so enthusiastic that he finally consented to enter the Bible with her, she obligingly opening it with the wonderful "Key."

"Mother used to teach me the Bible, and it seems as if I would enjoy visiting some of the old rooms in it. Take me to the one where we learn about how God created man, and man disobeyed God and fell."

"Oh, this is a very wonderful book, and you must be prepared for some surprises, delightful ones all of them. That room you speak of is closed, for Mrs. Eddy discovered that God did not create man, 'for God and man coexist and are eternal' (page 336, line 30, *Science and Health*), and also that 'Whatever indicates the fall of man…is the Adam-dream… not begotten of the Father'" (page 282, lines 28-31).

"Lead me to the incarnation room where we are brought where we a face to face with the ineffable mystery of the Word made Flesh, the Holy Ghost coming upon the virgin, the power of the Highest overshadowing her, so that that Holy Thing was born of her, Christ Jesus, was true God and true man."

"Well, I must prepare you for changes there for, 'Those instructed in Christian Science have reached the glorious perception that...the virgin-mother conceived this idea of God and gave to her ideal the name of Jesus'" (page 29, lines 14-18, *Science and Health*).

"But if Jesus was only an 'idea' how could He say to His disciples after the resurrection—you will find it in the 24th chapter of Luke, and the 39th verse—'Behold my hands and my feet that it is I myself; handle me and see; for a spirit hath not flesh and bones, as ye see me have.'"

"Oh, don't let that trouble you at all. Mrs. Eddy explains it away beautifully. Just listen to these marvelous words of wisdom—you will find them on page 313, lines 26-29, of *Science and Health*—'To accommodate Himself to immature ideas of spiritual power...Jesus called the body, which by spiritual power He raised from the grave, flesh and bones.'"

"Well, if you don't mind, I think I will keep out of that room for there is a scripture that says, 'Every spirit that confesseth not that Jesus Christ is come in the flesh is not of God: and this is that spirit of antichrist ... Receive him not into your house, neither bid him God speed: for he that biddeth him God speed is partaker of his evil deeds' (1 John 4:3; 2 John 10-11). Take me to the room where Jesus Christ is evidently set forth crucified, His own self bearing our sins in His own body on the tree, by whose stripes we were healed, where the blood, which cleanses from all sin, and brings us nigh to God, by which we have boldness to enter into the holiest, is extolled."

"I cannot, for that room is closed forever to all believers in Christian Science."

"Closed? What do you mean? The Bible says in Hebrews 9:22, 'Without shedding of blood is no remission.'"

"Yes, but Mrs. Eddy has made the glorious discovery, which had much to do with the wonderfully rapid increase in our membership, that there is no need for remission of sin because there is none to be remitted. She has taught us the 'Nothingness of sickness and sin' (page 347, line 28), that 'sin, sickness and death' are 'a dream' (page 188, line 12). Isn't that a blessed release? Just believe it and see how comfortable you will feel!"

"I don't seem to get much comfort out of it for a scripture that mother taught me, 'If we say we have no sin, we deceive ourselves, and the truth is not in us' (1 John 1:8), will keep floating through my consciousness, try as I may to drown it. Perhaps I had better pray for light. The Bible says, 'Ask and ye shall receive'" (Matt. 7:7).

"To what purpose? We are taught in *Science and Health* that prayer to a personal God is a hindrance. On page 3, we find this question: 'Shall we ask the divine Principle ... to do His own work?'"

"So you are taught to think of God as a Principle merely. Well, it seems to me that there isn't much left of the Book after the lady that found the key gets through with it."

And that was the way I felt as I studied the textbook, but I was so determined to be healed that I tried to shut my eyes to its blasphemous heresies and to swallow it holus-bolus.

My practitioner was a lady with exquisitely beautiful hair, which was always so artistically puffed that it seemed there was not so much as a single hair out of place. She was placid as a summer sea and assured me, in the sweetest, calmest way possible, that my sin and sickness were only bad dreams from which I should shortly awaken to find everything all right, and at last I really began to half believe it. Like Jonah I was sinking down, down, down, and like Jonah I was saved by the direct intervention of God.

I made up my mind to go on with the thing and see what it could do for me: "But God" had far other plans for me, and He sent a whale; it was a big one, to swallow me.

One morning I awakened to find that complete paralysis of the right arm had come on during the night, and as I am not in the least ambidextrous, it would be hard to find anyone in a worse predicament than mine.

Of course, I rushed to my practitioner to find her wholly undisturbed by the catastrophe. How could she be disturbed when she knew that not only had I no paralysis of the arm but no arm to be paralyzed? She never turned so much as a silver hair, but assured me that, "There is no life, truth, intelligence, nor substance in the matter. All is infinite mind and its infinite manifestation, for God is all in all. Spirit is immortal truth; matter is mortal error. Spirit is real and eternal; matter is unreal and temporal. Spirit is God and man is His image and likeness. Therefore, man is not material; He is spiritual." Which clearly proved as you will no doubt perceive, that I had no arm, and therefore, could not have paralysis in it.

Whether or not I had an arm, there is one thing that I didn't have, and I was so sure of it that I didn't need to resort to Christian Science to tell me that I didn't have it. That was money to stay on in New York in my helpless condition, and pay, in addition to room rent in a very expensive house just off Central Park, and the large fee charged for treatments, to have my hair dressed, and my meat cut up, not to mention board at the rather high-class cafes in the exclusive neighborhood in which I was rooming. So I had no alternative but to return to my home which was then in Winnipeg, Manitoba, Canada.

Indeed, I thought it advisable to take my immediate departure before any of my other limbs went out of business. So I said farewell to my practitioner, who was still floating on a summer sea up to the last glimpse I had of her, and having fortified myself with Christian Science literature to enable me to continue my treatment after I reached home, I embarked.

And there, God provided just what I needed. An old friend, an aged minister of the gospel whom I deeply reverenced, was sent from a far land to minister to me. His heart went out in Christ-like sympathy when he beheld the havoc Satan had made in me, the utter destruction of everything that could make life worth living. He did not chide me when he saw me clinging to *Science and Health,* but he did say, and most solemnly: "Sister, that book is straight from hell, and the first step you must take to get deliverance is to put it in the kitchen range."

He did not argue but he prayed, prayed, I believe, without ceasing; I know of one whole night he spent in prayer for me. And, at last, one day I staggered down to the kitchen, I was almost too weak to stand upright, and deposited my copy of *Science and Health* on the glowing coals. It is the only proper place in the universe for it.

Not very long afterwards, the light of the glorious gospel of Christ, for soul and body, shone into my heart, and the drugs, with the resultant diseased conditions, vanished like snow wreaths, not because they have not been real, but because Jesus Christ, who died and rose again to deliver me from them, is real. They were real sin and sickness, but in Him I found a real Savior able to save to the uttermost.

To recapitulate: The Word of God, which "endureth forever," and *Science and Health,* produced by Mrs. Mary Baker-Eddy, during the last fifty years, are diametrically opposed to each other on all essential points, so we have to choose between them. Which shall it be then? The Bible or Christian Science?

BRIEF OUTLINE OF CHAPTER 11

The Bible and Christian Science are opposed to one another in all essential points. Christian Scientists carry a copy of the Bible along with Mrs. Eddy's *Science and Health with Key to the Scriptures,* but they do not believe the Bible to be the eternal, immutable Word of God. Where Mrs.

Eddy differs from the Bible, the Bible statements are discarded in favor of Mrs. Eddy's opinions. Mrs. Eddy does not hesitate to say that the account of the creation of man according to Genesis 2:7 "must be a lie" (*Key to the Scriptures* page 524). Plain scripture statements on the creation of man, virgin birth, vicarious death on the cross, resurrection and ascension of Jesus are all denied as actual material occurrences.

> *For many deceivers are entered into the world, who confess not that Jesus Christ is come in the flesh. This is a deceiver and an antichrist* (2 John 7).

The Bible teaches healing as coming to us through the atoning work of Christ on Calvary. Christian Science does away entirely with the necessity for the atonement by the teaching that there is no sin, and therefore, no need of redemption.

No doubt, healings have been effected through Christian Science, and we need not wonder at that for we may expect to see miracles wrought by satanic power in these last days before the coming of the Lord (see 2 Thess. 2:9).

> *And he doeth great wonders, so that he maketh fire come down from heaven on the earth in the sight of men, and deceiveth them that dwell on the earth by the means of those miracles which he had power to do in the sight of the beast; ... And he had power to give life unto the image of the beast, that the image of the beast should both speak, and cause that as many as would not worship the image of the beast should be killed* (Rev. 13:13-15).

Far better to be in physical torment for a lifetime than be healed by a lie.

Mrs. Eddy's colossal presumption is shown in the statement that God did not create man, as God and man are coexistent and are eternal (*Science and Health*, page 336, line 30).

Science and Health (page 29, line 14-18) teaches that the Virgin mother conceived the "idea" from God and gave to her ideal the name of Jesus. Compare this false statement with Luke 24:39.

Mrs. Eddy also taught that the Lord Jesus did not rise that "sin, sickness, and death" are a "dream" (*Science and Health*, page 347, line 28). (Cf. 1 John 1:10; 2 John 10-11; 1 Cor. 15:14- 17; Rom. 4:25.)

Mrs. Eddy also taught that the Lord Jesus did not rise in His material body from the grave but that to: "accommodate Himself to immature ideas Jesus called the body which by spiritual power He raised from the grave 'flesh and bone'" (*Science and Health,* page 313, lines 26-29). (See 1 John 4:3; 2 John 10:11; 1 Cor. 15:14-17; Rom. 4:25; Acts 1:21-22.)

The most dangerous of all the many heresies taught by Christian Science is the one that robs God of all personality and makes Him merely a Principle to whom one need not pray, thereby cutting off all communication with the only One who is able to lead the seeker into the light. Prayer is considered a positive hindrance.

Prayer is the very life of a Christian. "Pray without ceasing" (1 Thess. 5:17). (See Matt. 6:6; 9-14; Matt. 9:38; Matt. 26:36, 41; Mark 11:24; Luke 18:1; John 14:16; John 17:9; Col. 1:9; 1 Thess. 5:25; 1 Tim. 2:8; Jas. 5:13-16; 3 John 2; Phil. 4:6; 1 Cor. 7:5; Luke 1:13; 2 Chron. 7:14.)

QUESTIONS ON CHAPTER 11

1. Did Mrs. Eddy, in her book *Science and Health with Key to the Scriptures*, frankly refute the inspired declarations of the Word of God?

_____

_____

_____

_____

_____

_____

_____

_____

2.   What statement does she make in regard to the account of the creation of man as given in Genesis 2?

_____

_____

_____

_____

_____

_____

3.   Does Science and Health teach that Christ has come in the flesh?

_____

_____

_____

_____

_____

_____

4.   What does the Bible say of those who do not believe that Christ has come in the flesh?

_____

_____

_____

_____

_____

_____

_____

_____

5. How should Christians treat those who deny this most important Bible truth?

_____

_____

_____

_____

_____

_____

6. Is healing in the atonement?

_____

_____

_____

_____

7. Did Mrs. Eddy teach healing through the atonement?

_____

_____

_____

_____

_____

_____

_____

8.   Does Christian Science effect any real cures, and by what power are the healings accomplished?

_____

_____

_____

_____

_____

_____

9.   What presumptuous statement does Mrs. Eddy make in reference to the creation of man by the Lord?

_____

_____

_____

_____

_____

10.   What does Science and Health teach about the resurrection of the material body of Christ?

_____

11. Is the resurrection of Christ of importance to the one who hopes to attain unto eternal life?

12. Do Christian Scientists pray?

13. What does the Bible teach about prayer in the life of a Christian? Give references.

_____

_____

_____

_____

_____

_____

_____

_____

CHAPTER 12

FOREVER SETTLED

Forever, O Lord, thy word is settled in heaven.
(Psalm 119:89)

My word…that goeth forth out of my mouth…shall not return unto me void, but it shall accomplish.
(Isaiah 55:11)

R alph Waldo Emerson says, "No accent of the Holy Ghost this heedless world hath ever lost," which is true; not that the heedless world has safeguarded the priceless treasure, but that the Word of God can't be lost. "It abideth forever" (1 Pet. 1:23). It is incorruptible seed; frost will not kill it, the sun cannot scorch it. It liveth, and behold! It is alive forevermore. It is not only true; it is truth, "Thy Word is truth" (John 17:17).

"Where the word of a king is, there is power (Eccl. 8:4), and where the Word of the King of Kings is, there is omnipotence. In order to make that Almighty Word operative in us and for us, one thing only is necessary and that is to *believe it*.

So as the Word of God is with us today, for it cannot be lost, just as omnipotent as it has always been and always will be for it is incorruptible, i.e., cannot suffer change of any kind, we have but to make connection with the batteries of Heaven by pressing the button of faith, to have the exceeding greatness of God's power revealed in our lives.

Possibly we have all read the story of the blowing up of "Hell Gate" in New York Harbor, an engineering feat which was considered very wonderful at the time of its performance a number of years ago.

When it was decided to remove the dangerous rocks which had caused the loss of many ships and precious lives, large gangs of men were set to work to honeycomb them with drills. I do not now recall how many months, or years, they worked, but it was a colossal task. When the drilling was completed, powerful explosives were placed in position, and the whole was wired and connected with batteries located many miles away.

When the hour announced for the explosion arrived, the chief engineer was in his office in New York City with some officials and his staff of assistants. On his knee sat his tiny granddaughter and in front of him on his desk, was an insignificant looking key, or button, by means of which little Mary was to blow up Hell Gate.

How it was to be accomplished she had not the remotest idea, that was Grandpa's business, but that it would be done she could not doubt, for had not Grandpa, who had never told a lie, said so, and with perfect confidence that, as she did it, those gigantic rock masses were splintered into fragments and scattered to the four winds, just as Grandpa had told her, she pressed the button with all her might, and far away in the distance a dull booming sound was heard, and in a moment the message was flashed over the wire, "Hell Gate is no more."

The touch of a child's finger, in obedient faith in her grandfather's word, unlocked the forces which his wisdom had provided for the demolition of the frowning obstacles, but the touch, feeble as it was, was requisite. Though everything necessary to the clearing of the channel was finished, the child's finger must release the power.

Do you understand the allegory? God's Word of full salvation for spirit, soul and body, eternal and glorious deliverance for the entire man has been spoken; nay, is being spoken, for it liveth and back of it is Omnipotence; but we, children as we are, must press the button with our tiny fingers. When God's people do this, in its fullest sense, the message will be flashed to Heaven, "Hell Gate is no more," and the day is coming when this will happen for we are told that the gates of hell shall not prevail against the Church which does not mean that we are merely to defend ourselves against Satan's aggressions, but that we shall march against his gates and demolish them.

In Luther's time, the enemy had the harbor of peace with God so blocked with dangerous rocks that many were lost in their attempts to make it. With all their penances, fastings, pilgrimages, scourgings, and grovellings before popes and priests, perhaps comparatively few in his day knew what it was to be free from condemnation before God; the way was a veritable "Hell's Gate." But by believing the Word, "The just shall live by faith," "To him that believeth on Him that justifieth the ungodly his faith is counted for righteousness" (Rom. 1:7; 4:5), Luther pressed the button, Omnipotence was brought into action, the channel was cleared and countless myriads sailed safe into port and proved for themselves that "being justified by faith we have peace with God through our Lord Jesus Christ" (Rom. 5:1).

The Word regarding our bodies is just as express as that concerning our souls. Jesus healed the sick and said, "Thy faith hath made thee whole, go in peace" (Luke 8:48), and the way into healing, and wholeness is just the same today, for He is the same, and if someone will be small enough, and humble enough, and trustful enough, to obey Jesus as exactly and simply as little Mary obeyed her Grandfather, we shall have an explosive of divine power one of these days that will shatter the rocks, and clear the channel into the harbor of perfect soundness through faith in His name. Thank God for what He has done, but "there's more to follow," as the old hymn says.

God's Word regarding healing is "forever settled," and it has always been made living and real in exact proportion to the degree of faith exercised by His people. To show that this statement is amply borne out by recorded facts, let us briefly review the history of divine healing from the earliest ages to the present time, dwelling a little on the work of some of the more modern exponents of this truth.

It is a noteworthy fact that there is in every religion that has ever existed, some belief, either clearly expressed or tacitly implied, that the healing of the human body is part of the functions of the God of Gods, worshiped by the followers of that creed. One writer, the president of a university, says that the fact that the healing of the sick has been mixed up from time immemorial with religion has most seriously hindered the development of medical science.

I believe that the widespread existence of this belief is due to the common origin of mankind, and the retention, to some extent at least, by all peoples and races, of the original revelation of God to our first parents, including the fact that sickness is the result of sin, and that the Supreme Being, whose law has been violated, is the only one who can effectively deal with it. I further believe that the healing of disease is "mixed up with religion," as the writer I have quoted puts it, because God has joined them, and what God hath joined together man may not put asunder.

History shows us the ancient Babylonians, Chinese, Egyptians, East Indians, Greeks, and Romans, as well as other races, having recourse to religious observances, sacrificed to their demon deities prayers, and various other ceremonies in case of sickness, while of the Jews one historian states: "Disease was considered a punishment for sin, and hence, the cure was religious rather than medical."

From the foregoing, it is evident that it has been the general conviction of mankind in all ages that sickness has a spiritual origin and requires to be dealt with by divine power, and that even the heathen, in their benighted way, bear witness to this truth. So far from being a modern fad, as it has sometimes been called, divine healing is the ancient and original method of dealing with the ills that flesh is heir to, even among heathen peoples, while among God's chosen people, the Jews, nothing else seems to even have been thought of until after the reign of Solomon during which so much that was idolatrous was introduced.

It was prophesied of the Christ, some 700 years before His first advent, by the prophet Isaiah, that He would bear, not only the sins of the world, but their infirmities and sicknesses as well, on the cross, which word He fulfilled, healing all that were oppressed of the devil, and commissioning His followers to carry on the work after His ascension, promising to be with them until the end of the age.

In the book of the Acts of the Apostles we learn how literally they understood, and how faithfully they executed, this command, and for the first three centuries at least of the church's history their example was closely followed by believers on the Lord Jesus Christ.

Listen to the following quotation from one of the best-known fathers of the early church, Irenaeus, dated about A. D. 180; (he is drawing a comparison between heretics and true believers on the Lord Jesus Christ):

> *They (the heretics), can neither confer sight on the blind, nor hearing on the deaf, nor chase away all sorts of demons nor can they cure the weak, or the lame, or the paralytic; or those who are distressed in any other part of the body. Nor can they furnish effective remedies for those external accidents which may occur, and so far, are they from being able to raise the dead, as the Lord raised them, and the apostles, and as has frequently been done in the brotherhood, the entire church in that particular locality entreating with much fasting and prayer the spirit of the dead man has returned in answer to the prayers of the saints that they do not even believe that this could possibly be done.*
>
> *In another place he says:*
>
> *Others again heal the sick by laying their hands upon them, and they are made whole. Yea, moreover, as I have said, the dead even have been raised up, and remained among us for many years.*

The great Christian father, Origen, writing well on in the third century, says, speaking of the Christians of his day: "They expel evil spirits and perform many cures. Miracles are still found among Christians, and some of them more remarkable than have ever existed among the Jews; and these we have ourselves witnessed." These statements would have been challenged by Origen's opponents if they had admitted of being disputed.

It would appear that praying for the sick and anointing them with oil, never ceased to be practiced for the first seven centuries of the Christian era, though after that it began to decline as the result of the changed attitude of the Church due to the apostasy that had set in. But in spite of this, many notable healings took place after that date and the fact that as superstition became rife it was usual to connect these with the name of some saint or other, instead of giving all the glory to Him to whom it rightfully belongs—our blessed Jesus—does not invalidate the fact that the healings, which were prayed for in the name of Jesus, actually occurred.

Perhaps these old people did not grieve the Lord any more when they connected their healings with the prayers of Saint Solemundygundus, or some other saint or a relic of Saint Ann, or a piece from the Virgin's robe, than we do when we think that if this brother or sister, prays with us we shall be healed, instead of placing all our confidence in Jesus alone.

That the healings actually occurred, all historians are agreed, and as one of them, not a religious writer, says, if we refuse to believe it, we may as well decline to accept the whole historical record, for they are as well attested as any part of it.

In the beginning of the 12th century, we find Bernard of Clairvaux, author of the famous hymn "Jerusalem, the Golden," a leader of Christian thought in his day, and a man eminent for holiness of life, mightily used in healing the sick, thirty-six miraculous cures being reported as taking place under his ministry in a single day, the halt, the blind, the deaf, the dumb, being perfectly restored in answer to his prayer in the name of Jesus. On one occasion, a dying man was brought to him who was so emaciated that his legs were no larger than a child's arms. When Bernard prayed, "Behold, O Lord, they seek for a sign, and our words avail nothing unless they be confirmed with the signs following," and laid hands on the living skeleton in the name of Jesus, the sick man arose from his couch healed.

Toward the close of the 13th century, an Englishman, called Thomas of Hereford, was much used in healing, documentary evidence, which is still extant, showing that no fewer than 429 miracles of healing were performed by him through laying on of hands in the name of the Lord Jesus Christ. Though it occurred long after his death, his faith and teaching seem to have inspired the trust in the Word of God that brought the following miracle to pass at the beginning of the 14th century. I quote from the original account of the occurrence:

> *On the 6th day of September, 1303, Roger, aged two years and three months, the son of Gervase, one of the warders of Conway Castle, managed to crawl out of bed in the night and tumble off a bridge, a distance of 28 feet; he was not discovered until the next morning when his mother found him half naked, and quite dead upon a hard stone at the bottom of the ditch, where there was no water or earth, but simply the rock which had been quarried to build the castle. Simon Waterford, vicar who had christened the child, John de Bois, and John Guffe, all sworn witnesses, took their oaths on the gospel that they saw and handled the child dead. The King's Crowners (Coroners), Stephen Ganny and William Nottingham, were presently called and went down into the moat. They found the child's body cold and stiff, and white with hoar frost, stark dead. While the Crowners, as their office required, began to write what they had seen, one John Syward, a near neighbor, came down and gently handled the child's body all over and finding it as dead as ever*

any, prayed earnestly, when the child began to move his head and right arm a little, and forthwith life and vigor came back into every part of his body… That same day the child, feeling no pain at all, walked as he was wont to do up and down in the house, though a little scar continued in one cheek, which, after a few days, quite vanished away.

I used to be very much puzzled at the reports I read in the course of my studies in history of the healings of hopeless cases of tuberculosis, then called "scrofula" or "kings evil," some of them signed by eminent doctors of the age in which they were stated to have occurred, as the result of the king's touch. These patients were carefully examined by court physicians before being allowed to present themselves for the king's touch, as sometimes those who were not grievously afflicted were anxious to be touched, and to receive the small gold coin which it was the custom for the king to give to those to whom he ministered in this way, and which was worth far more than its intrinsic value, and in some instances these very doctors solemnly attested that the people had been perfectly cured.

When I came to look into the matter, I found to my great surprise that the ceremony was a solemn religious one based on the words in the last verses of Mark's Gospel. "In my name they shall lay hands on the sick and they shall recover," and that this scripture among others, was read aloud to each person who sought healing, also that the king prayed as he touched the sufferers, in which prayer his chaplains and all bystanders, were supposed to join. In view of these circumstances, it is no wonder that real healings took place, in some instances, through the power of the Word operating on souls and bodies.

Indeed, the reports of some of these healings are so convincing that I cannot doubt, for my part, that the boundless grace of God found out a way to honor the Word, and magnify the glorious name of Jesus, even though the instruments employed were not always all that might have been desired.

One case of a young woman who was prayed with by King Edward, the Confessor, who was a real Christian, is very striking. She was afflicted with large abscesses in the neck on which the king laid hands gently stroking the diseased tissues as he prayed for her recovery, when the abscesses opened, discharging tremendous quantities of putrid matter filled with maggots, and so completely emptying themselves that in one week no trace of them was to be found.

With the Protestant Reformation, there was a revival of faith for healing, and the tide has been gradually rising ever since that time. Martin Luther, George Fox, founder of the Quakers; John Wesley, Charles G. Finney, Dorethea Trudel, whose work became so extensive that it had to be investigated, and finally in some sense licensed by the Swiss Government; Dr. Charles Cullis of Boston; A. J. Gordon, Dr. A. B. Simpson of New York; Mrs. Carrie Judd Montgomery, formerly of Buffalo, New York, now of Oakland, California; Mrs. Elizabeth Mix of Connecticut, a woman through whom Mrs. Montgomery was healed; John Alexander Dowie of Zion City, Illinois; Dr. William Gentry of Chicago; Mrs. Aimee Semple McPherson, and many other names stand out in this connection as we pass the centuries in review.

Some of these men and women it has been my privilege to know personally, and in passing, I should like to dwell for a few moments on recollections of two of them who have passed to their reward, Dr. John Alexander Dowie and Dr. A. B. Simpson.

It is about 26 years since I met Dr. Dowie. He introduced himself to us and dwelt on the meaning of his name, *John,* "by the grace of God," *Alexander,* "a helper of men." As for the *doctor,* it has been bestowed upon him by grateful people who were healed in answer to his prayers. While I could never fully follow Dr. Dowie in his teachings, I could not doubt the truth of his statement that God had conferred upon him the gifts of healing. The Holy Spirit answered to it in my soul, and he was approved of God by miracles and wonders and signs which God did by him, which the very man in the street could neither gainsay nor resist.

For instance, I once asked one of the very best dentists in Chicago what he thought of Dr. Dowie. He did not know that I had any acquaintance with him. He replied, "Well, it is impossible to deny the genuineness of his healings; how he does them I cannot explain, but he does them without a shadow of a doubt. I myself know a young lady who had her leg lengthened three inches, and who now stands on even feet. You can see her any Sunday in Dr. Dowie's choir."

When Dr. Dowie began his work in Chicago, some time in 1893, I think it was he set up a wooden hut at the World's Fair and rang a dinner bell to get people to the meetings. This is history. He had some wonderful healings, among others that of Ethel Post, a little girl of 13 years of mouth was so full of a bloody, spongy cancer that she could not close it day or night. The surgeons would not touch it for age whose fear she would bleed to death, for the blood vessels in it were so infiltrated with cancer cells that they would not hold ligatures. As Dr. Dowie drove across Lincoln Park to pray with her, the Lord gave him the scripture that He is God to kill and make alive (2 Kings 5:7), and he prayed, "O Lord, kill the cancer and heal the child."

The malignant growth withered away and fell out of her mouth and throat, and she was completely and permanently healed. When I alluded to her case in a meeting quite recently, a lady rose and stated that Miss Post is alive and well, and actively engaged in some branch of commercial art. She used to sell her photographs, *Before and After the Lord's Healing Touch,* for the benefit of the Lord's work, and they in themselves constituted a wonderful testimony to the faithfulness of God toward those who trust Him.

I visited at Dr. Dowie's Divine Healing Home in 1898; it was then on Michigan Boulevard, Chicago, and was a most luxurious hotel fitted up in approved modern style. But it had something no other hotel I ever stayed at had, and that was a staff of helpers all of whom were filled with faith in the Word of God. Their faces shone, and any of them, from the furnace man to the elevator boy, was ready to preach you a sermon at a moment's notice if you dared to doubt that Jesus Christ is the same yesterday, today, and forever.

Dr. Dowie's devotion to the Word of God was beautiful; he would read it to his sick folk for hours on end sometimes, not even stopping for dinner, and they would visibly lift up their heads, like flowers after a gracious shower, as he did so. I have known him to put dinner back when it was served and the waitresses waiting to attend the tables, because he said we needed the Word so much more. He simply brought you right up against the Word, "I am the Lord that healeth thee," (Ex. 15:26) and expected you to believe it then and there without any regard to symptoms.

One of his favorite hymns, which we sang very frequently, was a sort of keynote to his character and work, and I will quote part of it here. If you are familiar with it, you will notice that he altered it to suit himself:

> *Have God's own faith and trust His might,*
> *That He will conquer as you fight,*
> *And give the triumph to the right,*
> *Have faith, have God's own faith.*
> *Have God's own faith,*
> *What can there be*
> *Too hard for Him to do for thee?*
> *He gave His Son, now all is free,*
> *Have faith, have God's own faith.*

Dr. Dowie had invincible, God-given faith in the Word of God as just the same today as it ever has been and ever will be, "forever settled" (Ps. 119:89), absolutely supreme and unconquerable, "whose faith follow" (Heb. 13:7). If there was anything in life or teaching that you do not see to be in accordance with God's Word, you are not called upon to follow it, but his faith in God's Word, you are exhorted to imitate.

> *It was hopeless, organic disease of the heart, which threatened to end his life in the very midst of his career of usefulness as a minister of the gospel, that brought Dr. A. B. Simpson to a knowledge of the truth of divine healing. When he was in such a condition that there was constant danger of his falling from the pulpit or into the open grave as he officiated at funerals, Dr. Simpson was ordered by his physician to stop work and take a prolonged rest. He was given but little hope that he would survive long, no matter what precautions he took, and was earnestly looking to God when the truth was revealed to him through the Word.*

Without the faintest improvement of any kind in his symptoms, he took God at His Word and believed himself healed, ever after acting on this through a long and most arduous life of service. God never failed to meet his physical need, and eternity alone will tell the story of the work accomplished in practically every country of the world by this faithful soldier of the cross, for the great burden of his soul was world evangelization in preparation for the coming of the King.

In a little verse by him, which I shall quote, is found the explanation of the great work which, by divine grace, he was able to perform:

> *I am crucified with Jesus, and He lives and dwells in me;*
> *I have ceased from all my strugglings, 'Tis no longer I but He.*
> *All my will is yielded to Him, and His Spirit reigns within;*
> *And His precious blood each moment,*
> *Keeps me cleansed and free from sin.*
> *I'm abiding in the Lord, and confiding in His Word,*
> *And I'm hiding, sweetly hiding, in the bosom of His love.*
> *All my sicknesses I bring Him, and He bears them all away,*

All my fears and griefs I tell Him, all my cares from day to day.
All my strength I draw from Jesus, by His breath I live and
move,
E'en His very mind He gives me, and His faith and life and
love.

Dr. Simpson had some wonderful healings in his ministry. Only a few days after he accepted Christ as his physician, his little daughter, their only child, was taken with malignant was diphtheria. Her throat filled with awful membrane, and her condition was most critical. He took her out of her mother's arms and into a room where he was alone with God, and there anointed her with trembling hand. She was only the second or third person he had ever anointed. He knew that unless God manifested His power quickly, there was going to be a crisis in the family for his wife was not at that time one with him on the subject of healing.

All night he knelt beside the child in prayer, and when with the first streak of dawn the mother entered the room with haggard face and eyes heavy with weeping, the little one opened her eyes and smiled at her the smile of health and happiness, and not one vestige of the dread disease remained.

All Hail the Power of Jesus Name!

BRIEF OUTLINE ON CHAPTER 12

The Word of the Lord abideth forever. The heedless world may reject it, but every word spoken by the Lord will accomplish the purpose of God. His Word is just as omnipotent as it has always been. His power is waiting for the prayer of faith.

During the dark ages, when the church usurped the prerogative of Christ to forgive sin and stood with her pride and power between the penitent and his Savior, six words, "the just shall live by faith" from the Word of God breathed by the Spirit of God into the ear of Martin Luther changed the whole course of the world. The obstacle imposed by the thirst for priestly power was set aside, and countless millions have swept unhindered into the presence of God.

The healing of the sick has been considered a part of all religions from earliest times. The idea that sickness is the result of sin, and therefore, a matter of religion must have been handed down from our earliest parents.

Isaiah prophesied seven hundred years before the birth of Jesus that He would bear our infirmities and sicknesses. This prophecy was perfectly fulfilled by the Lord during His earthly ministry, and just as He was leaving this earth, He commissioned His apostles to carry on the work of healing and promised His presence and power to the end of the world. The apostles carried out His command literally, as did the early Christian leaders for three centuries.

Irenaeus (about 180 A. D.) designated as heretics those who lacked the faith to pray for the sick and afflicted, cast out demons, and even raised the dead.

Anointing with oil and praying for the sick was continued with miraculous results for the first seven centuries of the Christian era, until with the coming of the apostasy, the healings were attributed to dead saints and relics.

In the beginning of the 12th century, Bernard of Clairvaux, author of the famous hymn "Jerusalem the Golden," was reported to have been mightily used through prayer in the name of Jesus, in the miraculous healing of as many as thirty-six cases in one day.

Toward the close of the 13th century, Thomas Hereford an Englishman, through prayer in the name of Jesus, was used of the Lord to effect 429 miracles of healing.

The "king's touch" was a solemn religious ceremony. Mark 16:17-18 was read to each of the afflicted ones who came for healing. The king's chaplains and the bystanders joined the king in prayer as he touched the sufferer, and many healings were affected by prayer according to the Scriptures.

The children of God are not called to follow the example and teaching of all the illustrious ministers of the gospel who have been blessed in their ministry of healing, but it is the duty of all believers of the Word of God to follow their faith in God.

QUESTIONS ON CHAPTER 12

1. Does the lack of faith in this age annul the power of the Word of God?

_____

_____

_____

_____

_____

_____

2. What six words spoken to Martin Luther by the Lord resulted in the Reformation?

_____

_____

_____

_____

_____

_____

3. Has healing always been considered a part of religion? Why?

_____

_____

_____

_____

_____

_____

4. Where do we find the prophecy that Messiah would heal the sick? When was the prophecy written? Who fulfilled it?

_____

_____

_____

_____

_____

_____

5. Why did the apostles continue to pray for the afflicted?

_____

_____

_____

_____

_____

_____

6. (a) Did the Christians who followed the apostles pray for the sick and cast out demons?

_____

_____

_____

_____

_____

_____

(b) How did they designate those who did not pray for the afflicted?

_____

_____

_____

_____

_____

7. Describe some miraculous healings in the 12th and 13th centuries.

_____

_____

_____

_____

_____

_____

8. How were healings effected by the "king's touch"? Describe the proceedings.

_____

_____

_____

_____

_____

_____

_____

9. Should Christians repudiate healing according to the Word of God because of the teachings and examples of some of the exponents of divine healing during the past generation?

_____

_____

_____

_____

_____

_____

_____

_____

CHAPTER 13

SIGNS FOLLOWING

Now when Jesus was risen early the first day of the week, he appeared first to Mary Magdalene, out of whom he had cast seven evils. And she went and told them that had been with him, as they mourned and wept...Afterward he appeared unto the eleven as they sat at meat, and upbraided them with their unbelief and hardness of heart, because they believed not them which had seen him after he was risen. And he said unto them, Go ye into all the world, and preach the gospel to every creature. He that believeth and is baptized shall be saved; but he that believeth not shall be damned. And these signs shall follow them that believe; In my name shall they cast out devils; they shall speak with new tongues; they shall take up serpents; and if they drink any deadly thing, it shall not hurt them; they shall lay hands on the sick, and they shall recover. So then after the Lord had spoken unto them, he was received up into heaven, and sat on the right hand of God. And they went forth, and preached every where, the Lord working with them, and confirming the word with signs following. Amen.
(Mark 16:9-10, 14-20)

Here we have, in the plainest possible words, God's program for the age in which we are living—a program in which every believer has his or her appointed part to play. It is not too much to say that we are here simply and solely for this purpose, for we are ambassadors for Christ, as though God did beseech by us "be reconciled to God." As faithful ambassadors, we have all the resources of Heaven to draw upon and Omnipotence to empower and protect us.

I have worked under the government and know what it is to receive instructions, often by telegram, directing that certain changes be made, new regulations promulgated and enforced, and as these were complied with the government invariably confirmed them by official letters bearing the great seal, and by such action as might be necessary to ensure the discharge of all governmental obligations in connection therewith. I do not remember that they ever failed to confirm their word, but if they did, the government of Heaven never fails to make the Word of God good in every respect, to fulfill every promise contained therein, and to inflict every penalty threatened for disobedience thereto, for the Lord Himself is working with us confirming the Word with signs following. So we can be absolutely certain that if we speak as the oracles of God, as we are directed to, He will not let any of our words fall to the ground, but will confirm them with signs following, setting the seal of Heaven on our utterances.

As we proclaim salvation from sin, and deliverances from its guilt and power, through the cross of Calvary, men and women will have their shackles struck off before our eyes, and as we preach a Savior who bore our pains and sickness, as well as our sins, the sick will be healed, the deaf will hear, blind eyes will be opened, the lame man will leap as a hart, and the tongue of the dumb sing.

If the puny governments of earth cannot afford to let their utterances go unconfirmed, is it likely that the King of kings will allow His eternal Word to be unfulfilled? It is unthinkable.

I am going to relate a few instances which have come under my personal observation of the confirmation of the Word of God by the signs following with the view, first, of glorifying Jesus, and second, of inspiring faith in the hearts of those who hear them or of increasing and strengthening it if it has already been inspired.

People sometimes speak as though the healing of the body through faith in the sacrifice of Calvary were something quite distinct from salvation, instead of part and parcel of it. Let us look for a moment at the case of the paralytic, who was brought to Jesus by four, in the 5th chapter of Luke. Jesus first speaks the word of pardon—first things first: "Man, thy sins be forgiven thee." After follows the man's physical healing, as a visible sign of his forgiveness and evidence before the eyes of all of the power on earth of the Son of man to forgive sins.

Jesus desires to convince the unbelieving world of the reality of His gospel by His healing miracles on the bodies of the sick who come to Him for deliverance. Often in this way, a door of utterance is opened for the heralds of the Cross which would otherwise remain closed, and the first incident which I shall relate is an illustration of this.

Just before leaving Canada for California, my sister and I received an urgent call to hold meetings in a rural part of Alberta. We had to drive a long way in a car to get there; it was a considerable distance from the railway, and the roads are not like the ones in California. We seemed to have to pray the car along almost every foot of the way, partly because the roads were bad, and partly because the car was none too good. However, we got there at last and were soon hard at work holding meetings in schoolhouses and homes, visiting the sick, tarrying with seekers for the Baptism of the Holy Ghost, and doing other work that came to hand, and we had the joy of seeing God move in a blessed way.

Finally, we felt that we were free to return to complete our arrangements for going south, so we bade them all a loving farewell and told them to have the famous car ready for an early departure the following day. Quite late the last evening, we expected to spend there, a man called to see us, bringing his wife and family. He was an unbeliever: and I noticed that one of his children, a little boy, had a marked squint in one eye. I told the parents that it was not God's will that the little thing should be so deformed and afflicted and that we would pray for him if they wished. As they replied in the affirmative, we laid hands on the child in the name of Jesus, and they went home.

I cannot remember that I noticed any change in the eye directly after we prayed, but as we were very busy seeing people who came to say good-bye, it may have escaped our notice. In any case, early the next morning before we had finished breakfast, the man returned and reported that the child was so improved that they were all amazed and recognized God's hand in the healing. He implored us to stay a while longer and promised to come and bring his family to the meetings if we would do so, which meant something as he lived a long distance from the place where we held them.

As he added that he and his family were ready to make an unconditional surrender to the Savior who had healed the child, we decided that the happening was a token from the Lord that He still had work for us to do there. We announced that we would continue the meetings, inviting all who were really seeking the Baptism in the Holy Spirit, but *no others,* to come to a tarry meeting in the upper story of our host's barn that very evening. It was a wonderful barn, the finest one in the whole district. And I certainly shall never forget that meeting: it was in some respects, the most wonderful one I ever attended.

As I was on my way to the meeting, I saw a man with a most unhappy expression on his face, skulking in the distance but casting longing glances all the same toward the huge, gray barn. I called to him and asked him if he wanted to come to the meeting.

"Yes," he said, "I want to come, but I am too bad a man. I am known all over this district as a bad man. My wife is at the meeting; she is a godly woman, and I have led her an awful life. I am a bad man."

"Well," I said, "You are the kind the meeting is for, for the worse you are the more you need Jesus; and we are going to seek Him there tonight as Savior, Healer, Baptizer, and all in all. Come along."

So, the "bad man" (we'll call him John) accompanied me to the meeting. Maybe the people were astonished to see him come in, but that was as nothing to the astonishment that was to fill them a little later.

The people knew almost nothing about the baptism; and as they were from various churches and societies, I explained the way of full salvation in the simplest manner possible, including the Baptism in the Holy Spirit as in Acts 2:4 and told them to look to the Lamb of God and praise Him for all He had procured for them. And they began. Everybody expected John's wife to receive the baptism first. I found that she was considered the best person in the district.

I can see those people now if I close my eyes. It was a beautiful loft, a real "upper room," the floor covered with new mown hay and the whole place lighted by lanterns hung around the walls. The faces of the seekers looked so earnest in the flickering lantern light. There was a spirit of love and harmony, for all who were not seeking the baptism were asked to stay at home. John knelt on the outside of the ring where the shadows were deep as the lantern light hardly penetrated to that distance. I wondered how he was getting along and intended going to pray with him; but before we had been on our knees many minutes, the power fell and a sister—not John's wife—received her baptism. As she was kneeling next to me, she fell over on me; and I could not get away.

When John's wife actually heard this sister praising in other tongues, she seemed to grow desperate in her longing and began with all her might to call upon God for the baptism.

I was encouraging her when suddenly, as a flash of lightening, the power of God struck John where he was kneeling, bolted him upright at the edge of the group and felled him to the floor with a crash so mighty that it seemed as though it must pull the building down. And he lay there under the power, which moved and manipulated every part of his body with such force and lightening-like rapidity that the people thought he was having an awful attack of convulsions. Indeed, it was with great difficulty that I calmed their fears. At last, the Spirit began to speak through him, first in English, describing the vision he was having of Calvary. Would to God that every sinner in the world could have heard him! It would have melted a heart of stone. After that, he spoke with awful power and majesty in a new tongue.

His wife was so dumbfounded when she heard him that she said to me: "He's got the baptism before me, and he was so bad. Perhaps I need to be saved from my goodness more than he needed to be saved from his badness."

I said, "Perhaps you do. Just repent of everything and cast yourself on Jesus."

Just then, to the amazement of all, the "bad man" raised himself to his knees and came along to us and placing himself in front of his wife, he preached the most wonderful sermon on Calvary I ever heard.

"Oh, look away from yourself, bad or good," he cried. "See, where He hangs bearing your sins away forever and making your peace with God—everlasting peace, sure as Jehovah's throne!"

It was thrilling. He seemed to see Jesus and to be able, through the power of the Spirit, to make us see Him, too.

As he kept pointing her to Calvary, the power caught another sister up as though on a whirlwind, and she danced all around the loft lighter than a feather she had never seen dancing in the Spirit—praising and singing meantime in Gaelic. Later the language changed to High German, which I had studied for years and understood a little, and she was unable to speak anything else for a couple of days. When spoken to in English, she replied in German. She had no knowledge of the language.

A sister who was taking charge of her baby—he had awakened by this time—asked for his bottle and she danced all-round the loft looking for it but was unable to stop dancing and singing.

In the meantime, the power was falling on others and there were days of Heaven on earth, and the salvations and baptisms came about through the healing of the child's eye. It is pretty hard to separate healing from salvation, isn't it? For my part I have given up trying to.

I am now going to relate another healing which we always called, "The man borne of four" because he came in the light of that scripture in Luke 5, which was referred to earlier in this chapter.

He was an old man between 70 and 80 years of age with a cancer on his face, on the temple near his eye. Sometimes people say that the disease of which we claim to be healed are imaginary but they could not say that about this case, for he had a face and he had a cancer on that face. He was not at all a good-looking man and with this hideous excrescence he presented a most repulsive appearance. As far as you could see him you would notice it and, unless you were careful, you were likely to exclaim: "Isn't that awful?"

The old man was genuinely saved and was quite willing to bear the affliction until he was called home if God so willed. But as he listened to the teaching from the Word, he became more and more certain that Jesus had purchased his full deliverance on the cross of Calvary and more and more determined to have that deliverance manifested in his mortal body.

As he considered himself weak in the faith, he asked God to give him some special help and was directed to request four sisters of whom I was going to say that they were seldom off their knees. That would be something of an exaggeration, but I can truthfully state that their prayer joints were kept well-oiled to carry him to the feet of Jesus as the bearers carried the paralytic. Nothing loath, they accepted the task and performed it so faithfully that the cancer simply dropped off and vanished forever.

It seemed to me that it went so quickly that it was there one day and gone the next, but I know there was an interval between the prayer and his manifested deliverance, though I cannot say exactly how long it was. God enabled them to fight the good fight of faith during it anyway, and the disappearance of the cancer was a grand testimony for Jesus in that town, for no one could deny that Grandpa had had a cancer, and no one could find a trace of it after his healing. I have heard him preach an eloquent sermon on the Lord's healing with the cancer for a text more than once, and I have never heard anyone attempt to dispute his statements.

The next case of which I shall speak was one of blood poisoning following childbirth, and the woman, who was healed was actually moribund when the miracle occurred, by which I mean that she was in the very article of death. Indeed, I could not find the faintest trace of a pulse when I laid my hand upon her as I entered the room. I had taken a long drive to reach her, and as it was raining and we were in an open vehicle, rivers of water were pouring from my slicker. But her husband insisted on my going in without a moment's delay, saying when he met us at the door, with a face as white as chalk, that she was just passing away.

As I felt the immediate presence of death, and the power of darkness rolling over the woman, who was perfectly unconscious, like a flood, the Spirit of the Lord within me raised up a standard against the enemy. I could not have done it. I was too scared, but through my lips came the words, "The prayer of faith shall save the sick, and the Lord shall raise him up, and up you come!" The same instant she opened her eyes and said to her husband, who was bending over her weeping—he never expected to hear her voice in this world again:

"Don't cry, sweetheart; Jesus is here! He has healed me." She had a vision of Jesus and was so occupied with Jesus, and His beauty and sweetness, that she did not even know that I had been there until after I left.

I met her some little time afterwards on the principal street of the town on a shopping expedition with a flock of curly headed little ones after her, and she was certainly very much alive.

The last case I call "The Story of Samuel," not the Samuel of the Bible, but another Samuel who was named after the Samuel of the Bible, because he was, like him, a child of faith.

Samuel's father and mother were godly people, who had a good, comfortable home with the benediction of God resting upon it but no children to brighten it and inherit the blessing promised to the seed of the righteous. This was a great grief to them, especially as Samuel's mother (she wasn't anybody's mother then) suffered a great deal at the hands of physicians, who endeavored unsuccessfully to remove, by means of painful operations, the trouble that prevented her from bearing a child.

But alas! Like the woman in the Gospels, she grew worse rather than better, and the only results attained were physical debility and suffering, and large doctors' bills. She was getting well on in years when she and her husband received the Baptism of the Holy Ghost, and a fresh illumination on the sacred page. With this came a conviction that barrenness and disease were not God's will for her, but part of the curse of the broken law which Jesus had borne in her stead, when He was made a curse for her, that the blessing of Abraham, which includes fruitfulness, might come upon her, and a determination to prove God and see if He would not open the windows of Heaven and pour out upon her the blessing of motherhood.

So, we gathered around her, a little praying band of earnest people, and with her took our stand on the unchanging Word. So real was our part in the matter that when the child arrived (he had to arrive for the scripture cannot be broken), we with one accord named him "Samuel," saying with Hannah, the mother of Samuel, I mean the Bible Samuel, "For this child I prayed" (1 Sam. 1:27) and all felt that he belonged to us quite as much as to his father and mother. We used to set him in our midst, and gloat over him, and when a year and a half later, the Lord graciously sent him a little sister, just for good measure, she was called "Ruth" (completeness), and our cup of rejoicing was full.

But what shall I more say? Time would fail me to tell of the sick I have seen healed of almost every disease that flesh is heir to, the goiters that have melted away, the blind that have been made to see, the deaf to hear, the lame to walk, the cases of tuberculosis, heart disease, kidney disease, indigestion, gall stones (one woman who had pulmonary consumption and gall stones was instantly healed on her death bed after receiving extreme unction—she was a Roman Catholic—the Holy Ghost falling upon her at the same time so that she praised God for her deliverance in a new tongue), tumors of various kinds, including cancer, which have been perfectly cured, sometimes instantly when hands were laid on and prayer made in the name of Jesus.

A woman who was healed of cancer of the breast in our home in answer to prayer, seemed to constitute herself a publicity agent for the Lord's healing, and every now and then our phone would ring and somebody would say, when we answered it, "Do you remember Mrs. Campbell, who was healed of cancer in your house? She told me that if I would ask for prayer in Jesus' name I would be healed too."

Yes, the signs follow. God always confirms His Word. Step out upon it this minute, whether for yourself or others, without a tremor. It has never failed and it never will fail, for they that trust in the Lord shall never be confounded.

BRIEF OUTLINE ON CHAPTER 13

God's program for the age in which we are living is given in plain words. We are the ambassadors of Christ, with a definite commission, which we are to bring to the people (2 Cor. 5:20):

> *Go ye into all the world and preach the gospel to every creature. He that believeth and is baptized shall be saved; but he that believeth not shall be damned. And these signs shall follow them that believe* (Mark 16:15-17).

Here we have an explicit command from the great King, which we have no more right to revise than we have to revise an order from our earthly government. The Lord's commands carried out faithfully will bring the promised results:

> *In my name shall they cast out devils; they shall speak with new tongues; they shall take up serpents; and if they drink any deadly thing, it shall not hurt them; they shall lay hands on the sick, and they shall recover* (Mark 16:17-18).

All human governments confirm orders and regulations by placing the great seal of state upon their documents. The great seal which God places upon the work of His faithful, believing ambassadors is the operation of the Holy Spirit in miracle-working power, both in the salvation of souls and in the healing of bodies.

The healing of the paralytic was a visible sign of the power of the Lord Jesus to forgive sins, and so it is today (Mark 2:7-11). Miracles of healing bring conviction to sinners, and many are saved through seeing the power of God thus manifested.

The Lord has not rescinded the great commission, neither has He deleted a single word of it. He stands waiting to add His manifested power wherever this commission is faithfully carried out, and He has promised to be with us until the end of this age. "Lo, I am with you always, even unto the end of the world" (Matt. 28:20).

QUESTIONS ON CHAPTER 13

1.   (a) What is God's program for the age in which we live?

_____

_____

_____

_____

_____

_____

_____

(b) What is the Great Commission?

_____

_____

_____

_____

_____

_____

2. What seal does God place upon teaching and work of His faithful
    messengers?

_____

_____

_____

_____

_____

_____

3. Have we any right to delete a single word from our Lord's command?

_____

_____

_____

_____

_____

4. What is the Lord's motive in showing signs and miracles of healing?

_____

_____

_____

_____

_____

_____

5. Did the apostles take the command of the Lord literally and carry it out? With what results?

_____

_____

_____

_____

_____

_____

6. Has the Lord ever rescinded this command?

_____

_____

_____

_____

_____

_____

7.   Does the same preaching of the Word by stretching of His hand to heal bring the same results today? (See Acts 4:29-31.)

_____

_____

_____

_____

_____

_____

8. How long is this command to be in effect? How do we know?

_____

_____

_____

_____

_____

_____

_____

CHAPTER 14

TEACHING, PREACHING, AND HEALING

MATTHEW 8

Among the last words uttered before the closing of the Old Testament canon, before the sad, silent centuries which intervened between Malachi, and the first coming of the Lord Jesus Christ, by whom God hath spoken to us in these last days, we find predicted the rising Sun of Righteousness with healing in His Wings (Mal. 4:2), which prediction was fulfilled when Jesus, the Dayspring from on high, visited us, and, as He was manifested to destroy the works of the devil, including sickness as well as sin, healed all that came unto Him, all that were oppressed of the devil.

And, thank God, He is still the Sun of Righteousness with healing in His Wings, and is beaming love, forgiveness, cleansing, and healing on all who will let the blessed Sunshine, the life which is the light, into our hearts and lives. "Clear the darkened windows, open wide the door, let the blessed sunshine in."

It is hard to keep sunshine out. Even when you have drawn every curtain close, pulled down the blinds, locked the shutters, and shut every avenue of approach, it has a way of stealing in and making a spot of glory in the midst of the gloom. And God is not willing that any should perish, and, even when the doors are barred against Him, He loves us so much that He is always sending some ray of divine light through the prayers of His people, or their testimonies, or their loving smiles, or some Word of God dropped into our minds by the Holy Spirit, to lighten our darkness, and to invite us to throw our whole beings wide open to the illuminating, warming, electrifying, healing, energizing, vitalizing, magnetizing rays of the Sun of Righteousness.

I saw some little children once who were the very incarnation of health. They were nut-brown from head to foot, and they radiated physical vigor and well-being from every pore. I said to their mother, "What have you been doing to them?" She replied like this: "I had them at the seaside, and it was beautiful weather; just sunshine all the time. I stripped off their clothes and put tiny bathing trunks on them so there wasn't a thing between them and the sunshine, and the sun did all the rest. Dr. Sun is my doctor from henceforth."

Yes, the sun is a wonderful doctor but even he sometimes fails, but the Sun of Righteousness never fails to illuminate the darkest heart that is opened wide to receive Him, and to heal the most helpless case that comes to Him. Only we must be like the tiny children; we must have nothing between us and the Sun; not so much as a cloud to arise and darken our skies or hide for a moment our Lord from our eyes, nothing of sin or self that could separate us from Jesus.

Shall we open wide the doors and windows? If they are already open, throw them wider, or better still, step right out of ourselves into Christ. As a song in the Spirit which the Lord gave to my sister, says:

> *Step out into the light, and stay there,*
> *Walk there, sit down there;*
> *Step out into the light, and grow there,*
> *Praising the Living Word;*
> *In Jesus all is bright, so live there,*
> *Rest there, abide there;*

Step out into the light,
Pass on through faith, to sight,
The light of God.

Now, let us study for a short time the work of Jesus, the Savior and Healer, as described in the New Testament, noting, first of all, that He followed a definite method and order in its performance, viz: (1) "teaching," (2) "preaching" and (3) "healing" (Matt. 4:23).

1.   Teaching – Jesus first teaches, i.e., reveals to man God's will for him, and shows how far he has wandered from it.

2.   Preaches – proclaims to man the salvation provided for him through Christ Jesus, which, accepted by faith, brings him into perfect harmony with the divine will.

3.   Heals – Jesus removes from human bodies the results of sin. This is God's order, and it is well to remember that it is unchanging.

Sometimes people who come to be healed of some distressing complaint are likely to feel rather impatient when, instead of at once praying for their immediate deliverance, we deliberately, prayerfully, and reverently, read to them from the Word, even for hours, if the Spirit so leads. They forget that the words themselves are "Spirit and life," and that "He sent His word and healed them."

I have seen patients who were so completely drained of vitality that, from a medical standpoint, I should have thought it necessary to administer powerful heart stimulants at frequent intervals, to prevent collapse, listen to the Word of God for hours continuously, and lift up their heads, under the distillation of its heavenly dews, like a parched garden after a gracious shower.

The Word teaches, reveals God to man, so that man abhors himself in dust and ashes. As Job says, "Now mine eye seeth thee. Wherefore I abhor myself and repent in dust and ashes" (Job 42:5-6). Preaches, shows him the way out of defilement into holiness, by the blood of Jesus— "Having therefore, brethren, boldness to enter in the holiest by the blood of Jesus" (Heb. 10:19), and heals all who will through the boundless grace that flows from Calvary, accept God's perfect will for spirit, soul, and body, "that they may be preserved blameless unto the coming of our Lord Jesus Christ" (1 Thess. 5:23).

When Jesus said to the impotent man in the 5th chapter of John's gospel, "Wilt thou be made whole?" He meant nothing short of this. Not only that his poor atrophied body should arise from its supineness but that the whole man should rise to walk in Heaven's own light, above the world and sin, for in the 14th verse of the same chapter we find Him telling the man to sin no more. It is God's revealed will toward us, not only to remove all sin and disease, but to lift us far above the realm in which sin and disease operate, even into the resurrection life of Christ: "The law of spirit of life in Christ Jesus hath made me free from the law of sin and death" (Rom. 8:2); and He is saying to each one, "Wilt thou be made whole?" Not half, not 60 percent or even 90 percent, but 100 percent, whole!

So much for a general consideration of the teaching of the New Testament regarding healing, and now we will study more especially some particular cases found in Matthew 8.

The first thing that strikes us as we enter upon this, is the fact that each case in the New Testament has certain features peculiar to itself, not to be found in connection with others. I believe that this is to show us how inexhaustible are God's resources and how perfectly able He is to meet the need in each case that is unreservedly placed in his hands.

The first patient in the 8th chapter of Matthew is the leper who believed implicitly in the power of the Lord to heal him, but doubted His willingness. "Lord, if thou wilt, thou canst make me clean" (Matt. 8:2). Jesus, the author and finisher of our faith, completes the supplicant's faith by His "I will," and the result is his immediate healing.

The Bible, from Genesis to Revelation, is God's "I will" to every seeker for full salvation for soul and body. Jesus, the only begotten Son of God, hanging on the cross in agony and blood, is God's "I have delivered you, and this is what it cost me. Can you doubt My willingness?"

Jesus speaks of healing as "the children's bread" in the 15th chapter of Matthew, and no earthly father, worthy of the name will withhold bread from his children, much less our heavenly Father.

We are taught to pray, "Thy will be done on earth as it is in Heaven," and there is no sin or sickness in Heaven, for nothing that defileth can enter there.

God desires our bodily healing just as He desires our spiritual well-being for the apostle John prays for the well-beloved Gaius, "Beloved, I wish above all things that thou mayest prosper and be in health, even as thy soul prospereth" (3 John 2).

Some say that this leper was told not to testify, but that is a mistake. Rather he was directed just how, when, where and to whom, he was to testify. He was to testify to the priest, the official appointed to examine lepers and pronounce them clean in the event of their healing, and he was to bring the required offering. One reason for this was that leprosy is a type, as well as a result of sin, and the righteousness which is by faith of Jesus Christ is to be witnessed to by both the law and the prophets (Rom. 3:21). After I was healed of the morphine habit some of my Christian friends begged me never to mention the fact that I had been a drug addict. But the Lord told me to show what great things He had done for me, even if it humiliated me to do so, and He told me just when, where, and how, I should testify. Shortly after I was delivered, I went to a church in Chicago, a Methodist church, and as soon as opportunity was afforded for testimony, I rose and told what a marvelous deliverance God had wrought in me.

After I sat down, a young man stood up in back of the church and said that he praised God for my testimony for it gave him courage to tell what God had done for him. He had been a hopeless drunkard and had been completely delivered and gloriously saved. His friends had begged him to keep quiet about it, he belonged to a wealthy family, but my example so inspired him that he declared he was going to testify for Jesus every chance he got, and preach Him too, for he felt called to preach, and I heard him give a splendid sermon that very evening at the hall of the Volunteers of America.

After the service in the Methodist church, a gentleman walked up to me and introduced himself as Dr. William Gentry. He was in medical practice in Chicago then, and told me how impressed he was with what I had said, the truth of which he could not doubt. Later he gave up the practice of medicine and devoted himself to the Lord's work from that time.

The next case in this chapter in Matthew is that of the Roman centurion who sought healing for his servant, who was delivered in answer to his master's great faith. Note that the centurion asked for nothing but the word, "Speak the word only," and also observe that he did not base his request on any merit in himself. "Lord, I am NOT worthy; speak the word." I believe that if we could and would, divest ourselves of every vestige of self-righteousness and settle it once and for all that we, in ourselves, are worthy of nothing but eternal doom, but that the Lamb of God that was slain for us, Christ Jesus, in whose name we come, is worthy to receive "power, and riches, and wisdom, and strength, and honour and glory, and blessing," we should witness signs and wonders such as have not yet gladdened the eyes of men.

One of the most prompt deliverances I ever witnessed was that of a young ballet dancer, who had an awful attack of appendicitis and had been ordered to the hospital for operation, and I believe that one secret of her instantaneous healing was the fact that she knew as everybody else knew, that she had nothing in herself to recommend her to God. It had to be "all Jesus."

She was just a little, wicked, flirting, swearing, smoking sinner, who had cast herself in self-despair at the feet of Jesus, and He taught her that way, and brought that way, "Lord, I am NOT worthy ... speak the healing word," and He spoke it, and in one minute after that she had no more need of an operation for appendicitis than I have this moment. She was a perfect little heathen when I first met her and she was transformed into the most earnest advocate of the Lord Jesus as the healer of His people that I have ever known.

The next case in this chapter is the healing of Peter's wife's mother (Matt. 8:14-15), in which I call Jesus the Family Physician.

Here there does not seem to have been any special question to settle prior to the healing, as in some other healings recorded in the Word. Peter, the head of the family, had accorded to Jesus the rightful place of preeminence, and He enters the home and banishes the works of Satan from the premises. Luke tells us (he was a physician, remember) in correct medical phraseology that she was suffering from a "great fever," following the teaching of the famous ancient Greek physician, Galen, who divided fevers into lesser and greater. But, as the sufferer tossed uneasily on her bed of pain, with flushed face and aching head, Jesus drew near and touched her hand and the fever left her, for vital contact with Christ banishes disease." Someone hath touched me," and by vital continuity with Him we are delivered from the power of sin and sickness, and quickened by resurrection life (Rom. 8:2, 11). As the result of her healing, Peter's wife's mother arose, took higher ground—everyone who is healed by faith in Jesus does that—and ministered unto Him (Matt. 8:15, margin). We are saved and healed, to serve Him.

It is a glorious thing to have Jesus as our Family Physician, and no one is too poor to secure His services, for they are "without money, and without price." Let me tell you a true story of what He did for a little girl whose father and mother placed their home under His almighty care and keeping.

At a tent meeting in western Canada at which I was one of the workers, a sweet little girl, five years of age, whose ears had been destroyed by the ravages of scarlet fever, was brought to the altar by her mother to be healed of deafness.

The child was so deaf that it was impossible to make her hear any sound, no matter how loud, and there was no prospect, humanly speaking, of any improvement in her condition. I asked the mother, who led the child to the altar, if the father was saved, and on receiving a reply in the affirmative, asked him to come with his wife and child, and definitely receive Jesus as the Family Physician, claiming perfect spiritual and physical deliverance for all under the roof-tree through the power of the blood upon the door.

> I'll sing it, yes, and I'll shout it!
> The blood! the blood!
> There was never a soul saved without it,
> The blood of Calvary!

After they had unitedly and publicly taken this stand the child was anointed and prayed for in accordance with James 5:14-15, and left in the hands of the Family Physician. The meeting was a very large one and I never happened to see her again, but some months after our return to our home, we received a beautiful feather pillow. I really think it is the finest one I ever saw in my life, as a thank offering from the mother for the child's complete recovery, with the statement that she could hear a pin fall. We handed the pillow over to my own little adopted daughter and as she laid her head on it every night for years, the fact that it was an offering from a little girl who had been healed of deafness was a constant inspiration to her faith in Jesus as the Family Physician.

Well, perhaps you say, "But my case is quite different from any of those you have cited. It is not like the leper's, nor than of the centurion's servant, nor Peter's wife's mother. How can I be sure from this scripture that there is healing for me?"

If that is your feeling, just come with me to the 16th verse of this same chapter where we read: "…They brought unto him many…and he cast out the spirits with his word and healed all that were sick." "All that were sick"—He healed *all* that were sick. How many did He heal? All. No matter what kind of people they were, or what the nature of the diseases from which they were suffering, whether acute, subacute, chronic, functional or organic. He healed all that were sick. "ALL." You cannot get outside of that, can you? So bring your case to Him, now, singing:

> *Just as I am without one plea,*
> *But that Thy blood was shed for me,*
> *And that Thou bidst me come to Thee,*
> *O Lamb of God, I come.*

And you will go away not only healed in body, but in soul also; for Jesus removed not only symptoms, but the deep-seated cause of symptoms, sin in the heart, which no remedy but the blood can reach.

BRIEF OUTLINE ON CHAPTER 14

In the last chapter of the last book of the Old Testament in prophecy the healing power of the Lord Jesus is clearly shown: "But unto you that fear my name shall the Sun of Righteousness arise with healing in his wings" (Mal. 4:2). (See also Ps. 36:7; 61:4-6; 91:3-6; Matt. 23:37.)

The sad silent centuries passed between the closing of the Old Testament and the opening of the New Testament with the account of the coming of this very Sun of Righteousness, the Lord Jesus, who continues "with healing in His wings," ready to bring this same blessing of healing to the ends of the earth through the prayers and testimonies of His believing people.

The sun is a wonderful doctor, though he sometimes fails, but the Sun of Righteousness never fails to illuminate the darkest heart that is open to receive Him and to heal the most hopeless case that comes to Him. We must have nothing between us and this Sun of Righteousness, not a cloud must arise.

Jesus followed a definite method (Matt. 4:23):

(a) Teaching: reveal to man God's will for him and show him how far he has wandered from it.

(b) Preaching: proclaim to man the salvation provided for him through Christ Jesus, which if accepted by faith will bring him into perfect harmony with the divine will.

(c) Healing: removes from human bodies the results of sin. This is God's order, and it is well to remember that it is unchanging.

Sometimes people who come to be healed of some distressing complaint are impatient when time is spent in reading the scriptures to them, forgetting that the Words of God are "Spirit and life" and that "He sent His word and healed them" (Ps. 107:20). Sufferers on the verge of collapse are enabled to listen to the reading of the Word for hours continuously, and will revive like a parched garden after a gracious shower.

When Jesus asked the impotent man "Wilt thou be made whole," He meant nothing short of perfect soundness for soul and body. It is God's revealed will toward us to remove all sin and disease and to lift us into a spiritual realm where sin and sickness does not operate (Rom. 8:2).

The Bible, from Genesis to Revelation, proclaims God's "I will" to every seeker for full salvation for soul and body (Rom. 8:32). He desires our bodily healing as He desires our spiritual well-being: "I wish above all things that thou mayest prosper and be in health, even as thy soul prospereth" (3 John 2).

Jesus directed the leper just how, when, where, and to whom he was to testify. He will do the same for those who are healed today, and their testimony will bring results according to the will of God (Matt. 8:4).

The centurion furnishes another example to be followed. He did not base his request on merit, but said humbly: "Lord, I am not worthy speak the word" (Matt. 8:8). If we would divest ourselves of every vestige of self-righteousness and ask the blessing of healing for the honor and glory of the Lord Jesus, we should witness such signs and wonders as have never yet been seen.

Jesus as the Family Physician is shown in the healing of Peter's wife's mother who had a great fever. Jesus touched her and as a result of this touch she arose to a higher plane and entered into His services (Matt. 8:14-15).

Our particular ailment may not be mentioned among the special cases in the Bible, but the inclusive "all" covers every disease: "When the even was come, they brought unto him many that were possessed with devils: and he cast out the spirits with his word, and healed all that were sick" (Matt. 8:16).

QUESTIONS ON CHAPTER 14

1.   (a) By what title does the prophet Malachi speak of the Lord Jesus?

_____

_____

_____

_____

_____

_____

(b) With what particular ministry is this wonderful title associated?

_____

_____

_____

_____

_____

_____

2.   What meaning is conveyed by the words "His wings"?

_____

_____

_____

_____

_____

3.   What definite method did Jesus follow in His ministry, and are we privileged to change this order?

_____

_____

_____

_____

_____

_____

_____

4.   What results may we expect from the reading of the Word of God
     to sufferers?

_____

_____

_____

_____

_____

_____

5.   How much was included in the question which the Lord Jesus asked
     the impotent man? (Matt. 8:2)

_____

_____

_____

_____

_____

_____

6.   Does the Lord desire our bodily healing as well as the healing of our
     souls? Give references.

_____

_____

_____

_____

_____

_____

_____

7.   How may our testimony of healing best be used for the Lord?

_____

_____

_____

_____

_____

_____

8.   What is the essential attitude of heart if we would see the mighty working of the power of God in miracles of healing?

_____

_____

_____

_____

_____

_____

9.   How inclusive is the word "all" in Matthew 8:16?

_____

_____

_____

_____

_____

_____

_____

10. Give scripture references to show that the Lord did miracles of heal-
    ing during the ministry of the apostles and that He is just the same
    today.

_____

_____

_____

_____

_____

_____

_____

Lilian B. Yeomans, M.D.

PART 2

RESURRECTION RAYS

A BOOK BY LILIAN B. YEOMANS
UNPUBLISHED SINCE THE 1930S

Resurrection Rays! Can you see them?
Streaming straight from Heaven above!
Resurrection Rays! Do you feel them?
Tokens of a Savior's love.
Resurrection Rays! Hallelujah!
Lo, He maketh all things new!
Resurrection Rays through eternal days,
Resurrection Rays for you!

Chapter 1

Our Letter of Introduction

Aman is given courage to go among strangers, breast opposition, and overcome indifference to the cause which he represents, if he has with him proper credentials, a letter of introduction from someone in a position of undoubted preeminence. He presents his testimonials, holds up his head, and looks everybody square in the eye.

More and more we, as workers together with God, are beginning to realize that the ministry of healing, exercised in the power of the Holy Spirit, is a God- appointed letter of introduction to a gainsaying generation. It is an "Open Sesame" before which barriers melt away, bolts shoot back, and doors long barred fly open.

When God bears witness with signs and wonders you are not asked for references.

The only question is, "How long can you stay?" or, if you are compelled to leave, "How soon will you return?"

Not long ago an evangelist stopped over between trains in a strange city, and upon being asked to preach, spoke on "Jesus Christ the same yesterday, today and forever," and prayed for the sick. A man, well known locally as a hopeless cripple, was healed, and hearts and homes flew open immediately. That evangelist needed no further introduction in that city.

Sometime ago Dr. Finis E. Yoakum, who used to live in Los Angeles but changed his address to Heaven a few years since, came to hold a campaign in a town where he was a stranger to everybody. Some of the best people there were inclined to be exceedingly conservative about countenancing or supporting him.

But he had not left his credentials behind him, and before long a man who had been deaf from childhood, or early youth—following scarlet fever—received his hearing so he said he believed he could almost hear the grass grow. I was there and can personally testify as to the genuineness of the case, and also as to the permanence of the cure.

Then a messenger boy who was suffering from inguinal hernia was healed, and a young lady who was brought a distance to the meeting, looking like a lily with a broken stem, suddenly bloomed out like a rose and plunged at once into the thick of work for the Master.

A brother who had stood aloof from the campaign was meditating on these, and other similar happenings, when the Holy Spirit called his attention to these words in Acts 2:22: "A man approved of God among you by miracles, and wonders and signs, which God did by him in the midst of you, as ye yourselves also know."

As a result of this, he called upon Dr. Yoakum and expressed his regret at the attitude which he had assumed toward him and his work, and turned right about face. He recognized his credentials. As ambassadors for Christ, we are accredited but only as we faithfully deliver the definite message committed to us. To this end we must be filled with the knowledge of God's will concerning our bodies, filled so full that there is no room for human opinions and reasonings.

There must be absolute certainty in our note as we sound forth the trumpet of jubilee and proclaim liberty to the captives of sin and sickness throughout the land.

As a child I used to watch the cavalry drill, where orders were all given by the bugle. (My father was a surgeon in the United States Army.) Both men and horses—the latter seemed to know the drill as well, if not better, than their owners—responded with accuracy and promptitude as long as the orders were given with accuracy and precision; but when the bugler failed to "do his stuff" right, absolute demoralization resulted.

"If the trumpet give an uncertain sound, who shall prepare himself to battle?" (1 Cor. 14:8). And it is a real battle, a "good fight of faith" in which we are engaged.

It is always God's will to save and heal, "Who healeth all thy diseases" (Ps. 103:3). "He is not willing that any should perish" (2 Pet. 3:9). "By His stripes we were healed" (1 Pet. 2:24). There can be no uncertainty about our message if we speak as we are commanded, "as the oracles of God" (1 Pet. 4:11).

Do not, I implore you, go to pray with a sick one for healing, pressing them out on the promises of God, which cannot fail if we will only release Omnipotence by believing them, and after prayer join in a discussion as to whether they had better wear a black or a white dress to be buried in! To such a pass have things come in some quarters.

Listen to the clarion call of the Scriptures summoning all who thirst, all who are burdened: "Ho every one that thirsteth, come ye…" (Isa. 55:1). "Come unto me all ye that…are heavy laden, and I will give you rest" (Matt. 11:28). Echo the message clearly and sweetly, and you will see them coming.

Make the message so plain that no one, no matter how sick and sinful, may have any excuse for delay or doubt. Never forget how all important it is that you should blow the right command, the "Thus saith the Lord" through your bugle.

In the year 1896 a terrible collision occurred, just outside of New York City, between two express trains traveling at a terrific rate of speed. There was tremendous loss of life and the whole metropolis was plunged into gloom by the tragedy.

The engineer of one of the colliding trains lay dying, pinned under his engine. He was in awful agony, blood spouting from his head, tears raining down his face, but he seemed almost unconscious of his condition, desperate as it was. He spent all his ebbing strength trying to draw the attention of pitying by-standers to a scrap of yellow paper which he held tightly clutched in his hand. "This shows that someone gave me the wrong orders," he gasped as his life passed away.

Don't let anyone be able to say that you failed to give them the right orders, to declare unto them the whole counsel of God. For ages men have grappled with the problem of disease; for centuries they have sought a panacea or cure-all for all the ills that flesh is heir to. They have hunted it in earth, air, fire, and water. They have delved into the mineral kingdom in search of it, have extracted the juices of plants, the sap of trees, have dissected animals, studied gases, investigated the operation of various forces, such as light, electricity, etc., but all in vain.

You may ask, "Is it reasonable to expect one remedy to cure everything?"

I think it perfectly logical, for a real remedy would do nothing less than this. A medicine that would effect a perfect cure of disease of the liver, for instance, would necessarily put every organ of your body into perfect working order, for the different organs, and systems of organs, which make up the human organism, are so intimately associated, so interdependent, that no one organ can be perfectly normal unless all are. So, this dream of a panacea is not all a dream. The only trouble is that men have failed to look in the right place for it.

Do not think I am disrespectful to men of scientific attainments; far from it! But Thomas Edison, one of the greatest of them, who was greeted the other day on the occasion of the 15th anniversary of his discovery of the electric lamp by earth's intellectual, political, and financial giants, said recently, "We do not know a millionth part of one percent about anything!"

So, I may venture to say that they do not know where to look for a panacea for sickness. It is to be found in God's Word, which teaches us that Jesus Christ healed, and heals, everything and all.

"And Jesus went about all Galilee, teaching in their synagogues, and preaching the gospel of the kingdom, and healing all manner of sickness and all manner of disease among the people. And His fame went throughout all Syria: and they brought unto Him all sick people that were taken with divers diseases and torments, and those which were possessed with devils, and those which were lunatic, and those that had the palsy; and He healed them." (MOF) adds "all" to the end of the verse.) (Matt. 4:23-24). There is the panacea—the dream come true.

"But is this power still available, operative on the earth today?" you may ask.

Yes, because the Lord Jesus Christ is operating on the earth today through those who believe.

"All power is given unto Me … in heaven and in earth. Go ye therefore, and teach all nations … and, lo, I am with you always, even unto the end of the world" (Matt. 28:19-20). "He that believeth on Me the works that I do shall he do also; and greater works than these shall he do" (John 14:12).

This includes the healing of everything and all who come in simple faith. How is it to be accomplished? John 14:13-15, answers this inquiry. By asking Him to do it and believing He answers your prayer.

The book of Acts is the only unfinished one in the New Testament. It begins, "Jesus began" (Acts 1:1), and we are to carry on. The very last chapter says. "All the other sick people in the island came, and were cured" (Acts 28:9 WNT). Not long ago I stood in the vestibule of Johns Hopkins Hospital, Baltimore, gazing at the colossal copy of Thorvaldsen's Christus." As I looked into that noble face beaming with love for fallen humanity, I said to myself:

> *If the poor patients could see Him as He is, Savior and Healer,*
> *they would need to go no further and the magnificent wards and*
> *glittering operating rooms would be vacated.*

As I mused thus, someone said to me: "Let me tell you a pretty little true story about this statue. It happened one day that a great tall man and a tiny girl were standing side by side looking at the work of art. The tall man found much fault with it, while the tiny child was entranced at its beauty and benevolence. After listening to his criticisms for several minutes, the little thing plucked up courage and said: 'O Mister, I know what is the matter, you're too big to see it right. If you would just kneel down you would see how lovely He is!'"

That's the solution of the problem. Give Him His place of undisputed supremacy and almighty power, and take yours in humble submission and unfaltering trust at His feet, and you will find in Him all you need for spirit, soul, and body, for time and eternity.

CHAPTER 2

HEALING BY THE POWER OF HIS RESURRECTION

That I may know him,, and the power of his resurrection....
(Philippians 3:10)
If ye then be risen with Christ....
(Colossians 3:1)
... The exceeding greatness of His power to usward who believe,
according to the working of His mighty power, which He wrought in
Christ, when He raised Him from the dead....
(Ephesians 1:19-20)

ealing through the sacrificial death of our Lord Jesus Christ on the cross of Calvary constitutes the negative side of the great work. There, on the cross, sin, the cause of sickness, was destroyed, root and branch. Jesus put away sin by the sacrifice of Himself, and by His stripes we were healed. In other words, sin, the cause of disease, and sickness, the effect, were taken away by the sacrifice of Calvary.

But something must be supplied to our redeemed bodies, and that something is life, which comes to us through the resurrection of our Lord Jesus Christ. This the positive side of divine healing and health.

We are baptized in water to show forth to the world that we died in Christ on the cross. "I have been crucified with Christ" (Gal. 2:20 WNT).

"How shall we that are dead to sin, live any longer therein? … Now if we be dead with Christ, we believe that we shall also live with Him" (Rom. 6:2, 8). We truly died, but we did not stay dead. We were lifted out of the water to, proclaim to all that God has raised us up together with Christ (Eph. 2:5-6). So we sing not only, "I was nailed to the cross in Thee," but also, "I was raised from the grave in Thee; on the cross crucified in Thee I died, and was raised from the grave in Thee."

And what life is to be manifested in us, according to God's plan and purpose? Our natural life paid the death penalty on the cross.

We are commanded to reckon ourselves dead unto sin, but alive unto God through Jesus Christ (Rom. 6:11), and it is the life of Christ which is to be manifested in our mortal flesh (2 Cor. 4:11).

The life of *whom?* Jesus Christ.

Manifested *where?* In our mortal flesh. That comprises every cell and fiber of the human body.

So we can add another verse to the beautiful song given through that sweet singer in Israel, Rev. F. A. Graves, who now beholds the King in His beauty and the land that is very far off, and sing:

> *And now I live in Thee,*
> *And now I live in Thee,*
> *On the cross crucified*
> *In Thee I died,*
> *And now I live in Thee.*
> *And Thou dost live in me,*
> *And Thou dost live in me,*
> *On the cross crucified*
> *In Thee I died,*
> *And Thou dost live in me.*

In Hebrews 1:3, we find the negative and positive sides of Christ's work beautifully and clearly set forth: "Who … when He had by Himself purged our sins" [taken them away—the negative side] "sat down on the right hand of the Majesty on high." What is He doing there? Exercising His high-priestly office as a priest after the order of Melchisedec, "made after the power of an endless [indissoluble] life" (Heb. 7:16). And He is interceding for us, living to make intercession for us, and ministering to us in this power of an endless life.

Get under the *Resurrection Rays* which our risen Lord is continually shedding forth! They are streaming from Him, for He is the Sun of Righteousness with healing in His wings, the Light of the world, and the light is the life of men.

> *Get out into the Light and stay there. Walk there, sit down there.*
> *Get out into the Light and live there, the Light of God.*

We hear much of "rays" these days: "death rays," spreading destruction and devastation over large areas, leaving nothing alive, and even sucking nutriment, which makes animal and vegetable life possible, from the very soil itself; "X rays," revealing the hidden secrets of the most deep-seated internal organs; "life-giving rays," imparting vitality to drooping, sickly organisms.

Let us learn to open our beings, to bare our bosoms, by faith, to the *Resurrection Rays* flowing to us from the risen, glorified Christ, that they may pierce to the deepest depths of our spirit, soul, and body, bringing us life, *life,* life—more abundant eternal life. In the Aaronic and Melchizedekian priesthoods we see law and life in contrast, the law of a carnal commandment and the power of an endless life.

We cannot abide in spiritual and physical soundness through the law, by reason of the weakness of the flesh, but by the power of an endless life! Not a weak link in the chain!

You do not have to make a law to force a fish to swim in the clear stream, or to prevent him from walking on the dusty highway. Something stronger than any law—life the fish life—is there, and he swims in the crystal water. You do not have to legislate to make an eagle spurn the earth and soar heavenward. The eagle life is there. And you do not have to try and try to be holy and whole, sound spiritually and physically. It does not come that way. Trying gets you back under the law of a fleshly commandment. It is the power of an endless life, the all-conquering life of the risen Christ you need. It is yours. Receive Him who is the Resurrection and the Life, by faith, and sing in your spirit:

> *Oh, the resurrection power in this hour*
> *Lives in me:*
> *Things that are not, lo, I call,*
> *They must come, for Christ is all,*
> *We shall see.*
> *It was God's eternal Word chaos heard,*
> *"Let there be!"*
> *He commands and it was done.*
> *Now this great unchanging One*
> *Speaks through me.*
> *Do not doubt Him in your heart,*
> *Nor depart*
> *From the Word;*
> *For it is not you but He,*
> *Moves the mountain to the sea,*
> *Christ, the Lord.*

Do you ask for the practical application of this lesson? It lies in the fact that our life flows not from our natural constitution but from our risen Lord.

How often people say to me, "But, Dr. Yeomans, I was always disposed to take cold."

To this I reply, "What does that matter? You died. It is no longer you but Christ, the risen Christ, who lives in you. He has conquered every form of death, and every death process, of which colds, so called, are one."

The fish swims because it has the swimming fish life in it; the eagle soars because it has the soaring eagle life. We are more than conquerors in all these things, if we shall have it so, because we have within us Christ life, which is conquering life.

CHAPTER 3

RESURRECTION FAITH

By faith…women received their dead raised to life again.
(Hebrews 11:35)

Long, long, long drink we milk,
Although strong meat awaiteth;
Long we wear swaddling bands,
Although all might is ours.
Just a little of God, our feeble longing sateth.
As you desire your God, your God is yours.
Look for vigor in Him,
'Tis yours just for the looking.
Look for daily supply
And that supply is yours;
Look for all that you need
And from His hand still taking.
Lo, He is yours with all things,
While time endures.

God is dealing with every one of us in relation to faith. This must be, for we are justified by faith, saved through faith, made physically whole by faith; and in direct proportion to it, is the work wrought in us by the power of God, for Jesus said, "According to your faith be it unto you" (Matt. 9:29). The Holy Ghost comes upon the soul in answer to faith: "The Holy Ghost fell on all them which heard the word"(Acts 10:44). We walk by faith, there is no other way of moving on in God. Our work is faith. "This is the work of God, that ye believe" (John 6:29). Without faith it is impossible to please Him, indeed whatsoever is not of faith is sin (Rom. 14:23). The Scriptures were "written that ye might believe" (John 20:31).

So it is all faith, faith, faith, and God is endeavoring to create it in your heart, or to bestow it upon you in larger measure, for faith "is the gift of God" (Eph. 2:8). To make a gift effective, a recipient is necessary. Will you receive?

A young girl earnestly desired to be saved but she could not see her way into the blessed consciousness of acceptance with God through the atoning merits of Jesus Christ. She turned from the world, as best she knew how, and with tear-stained face came to the evangelist after the altar meeting, to tell her that she could not be sure that she was saved. She happened to wear on her breast an exquisite rose, and the evangelist, taking her by guile, expressed great admiration for the lovely blossom.

"Will you accept it?"

"Certainly, with joy. Thank you so much." The evangelist pinned it on her own breast. "Now, whose rose is it?" she asked.

"Why yours," the astonished girl replied. "I gave it to you."

"God says He bestows upon you the unspeakable gift, Christ Jesus, as your personal Savior; is He yours? Fasten the Rose of Sharon over your heart as I did that rose you gave me."

"Is it that simple?"

"Yes, just that simple."

But the acceptance is only the initial stage of faith. Some people seem to think that when they have believed for soul and body, received the Baptism of the Holy Ghost, and confessed Christ by word and deed before earth and Heaven, they have graduated; whereas they have only been admitted to the kindergarten, and have all their work before them. For faith is not only a flashing diamond, a gleaming pearl, a wedge of fine gold—Peter calls it "precious" (2 Peter 1:1), but it is a living, incorruptible seed, compared to a grain of mustard seed (Matt. 17:20), and living things have within them the mysterious power of growth and development. God is concerned that the heavenly seed, which is planted in your heart, should have every opportunity of unfolding its divine potentialities, and He will spare no cost or pains to that end.

I have a friend who is a most successful horticulturist. Oh, what pains he takes with his choice plants! He secures the best seeds; and, when the seedlings show their tender emerald blades above the earth, he separates the strongest and most promising one of them from the others and plants the poor little forlorn thing all alone, very often turning a flower pot or box over it to protect it from the rays of the sun. Did the divine Husbandman ever tear you away from your companions and shut out the sunlight?

Again, when the plant has rotted and thriven, and perhaps budded prematurely, my friend often nips off the buds. It isn't a pleasant experience to have the plants all around you covered with blossoms while you display "nothing but leaves."

But even that isn't the worst. The other day I said to my sister, "Where are the geraniums?" We used to have a few bright scarlet blossoms in our grounds that delighted my eyes. "Oh," she replied, "I cut them all back." Did you ever have that happen to you?

Cut back—only a few withered-looking stalks left. Did you ever sing, "Oh, to be nothing, nothing!" Did you mean it? God has a way of doing that very thing in order to develop the infinite possibilities of the divine seed which He has planted in your heart. Do not be discouraged; these operations are beneficent, and designed to make you bring forth much fruit to His glory. Now for instance of this from the Word, a concrete case.

"Women received their dead raised to life again." The Shunammite woman of 2 Kings 4:8-37 is undoubtedly one of the women referred to. We may divide God's dealings with her, on the line of faith, into four stages.

PREPARATION

God inspired a faith in Him, as revealed through His messenger, that made her constrain Elisha to accept her hospitality. "She constrained him to eat bread" (2 Kings 4:8-9). God loves to have us constrain Him. "I will not let Thee go except Thou bless me" (Gen. 32:26). She "perceived" that he was a holy man of God as he passed by continually. What do people who see us, day after day going about our tasks, perceive us to be? Does our presence make them hungry for God?

PERMANENCE

This is the second stage. She believed so firmly that she made room in her life for the abiding presence of God in His messenger. We come to … a place, if we will let God move us on in faith, where He can rest in our hearts—because we wholly trust Him—feast with us, commune with us, and let His light shine through us; in other words when the chamber is furnished with bed, table, stool, and candlestick.

PROBATION

"What then is to be done for her?" (2 Kings 4:14). God wanted to do something for her; she didn't have to coax, cajole, and implore Him. He longed to do something for her. "For the eyes of the Lord run to and fro throughout the whole earth to show himself strong in the behalf of them whose heart is perfect toward Him" (2 Chron. 16:9). Or, in other words, He shows Himself strong for those who fully trust Him and depend upon Him. God's very choicest gifts are lying on the shelves in Heaven because we fail to accept them.

As Dr. Simpson says, "God has His best things for the few who dare to stand the test. He has His second best for those who will not have His best." Alas, how often is the better foe of the best!

Now this woman was a "great woman," and her choice was worthy of her. You say, "She didn't make any choice." But if you will read between the lines, I think you will agree that she did. She chose God and God alone. She said, in effect, "I did not go to this effort and expense for any reward that might come to me. I am satisfied; I dwell among my own people. I long for one thing only, the abiding presence of God in my home through His messenger, hence the chamber on the wall." She seemed almost hurt at the suggestion that any reward should be bestowed upon her.

Her words recall a hymn, centuries old, sung by one who laid down his life for Christ:

> *My God I love Thee,*
> *Not because I hope for heaven thereby,*
> *Nor yet because if I love not I must forever die.*
> *Thou, me, O Jesus, on the cross*
> *Didst tenderly embrace,*
> *For me didst bear the thorn and spear,*
> *And manifold disgrace.*
> *Then why, O loving Savior Christ,*
> *Should I not love Thee well,*
> *Not for the hope of gaining heaven,*
> *Nor of escaping hell,*
> *Not for the hope of gaining aught,*
> *Nor seeking a reward,*
> *But as thyself hast loved me,*
> *O ever loving Lord.*

She wanted God, and when God gets souls there, He can bestow anything upon them. "Delight thyself... in the Lord: and He shall give thee the desires of thine heart" (Ps. 37:4).

PROMOTION

And straightway she was promoted to the Abraham class. Why not? She was his daughter (Gal. 3:26, 29). Why shouldn't you be promoted to that class too? There are hard lessons there, to be sure, but there is a magnificent Teacher. She was promised a son. He came, but before many years he lay in her lap and died. But in this awful crisis her divine Teacher showed her the path to victory. He will show you how to meet the crisis in your life too, if you are *determined* to go through with God.

She didn't look at her son, now dead, any more than Abraham looked at his boy in the same predicament. She shut the door on that, put her will between herself and that sight and then (Oh, please note this), she shut her mouth about it.

If we would only shut our eyes to the works of Satan in our bodies, shut our mouths about them, and fly straight to God's Word for relief, as this Shunammite did, we would see signs and wonders. You say you wouldn't call a doctor, or listen to his diagnosis of your case, but you will listen to Satan instilling doubts and fears and even quote his lying words to others.

This woman flew to the feet of the man of God and there stayed till he followed her. "You promised me a son. Nothing can undo that. A son is what you promised and all hell cannot prevent the fulfillment of that word. It shall be well. It is well. I know whom I have believed."

> Faith, mighty faith, the promise sees,
> And looks at that alone,
> Laughs at impossibilities,
> And cries, "The work is done."

And Elisha rose and followed her! Followed her! Yes, it is there. Look for yourself. The prophet whose miracles most closely resemble those of the Lord Jesus Christ Himself, stirred into motion and directed in his action, by a woman. "He ... followed her," she resolutely leading the way to the bedside of the dead child, he, like a lamb, meekly following. Truly, "all things are possible to him that believeth" (Mark 9:23).

238

Arrived at the death chamber, Elisha went in and shut the door upon them twain. The Shunammite could see nothing, hear nothing, feel nothing. What was she doing outside that shut door? Following in the footsteps of her father Abraham; "accounting that God was able to raise him up, even from the dead" (Heb. 11:19) and that He could not break His promise. Sublime situation! Praising God outside fast-closed doors for His faithfulness, while He accomplishes resurrection within. Stand there, God is able to make you stand, and that promise of God on which you have gone down to death will yet be fulfilled. The door will open, your call will come, and bowing yourself to the ground in adoration, you will take up your son—that thing that God promised you that seemed as dead as the Shunammite's son, now quickened by resurrection faith.

> *Resurrection faith! The gift of God.*
> *Now, behold, through you 'tis shed abroad,*
> *As you will believe Him and count Him true,*
> *Resurrection faith for you!*

CHAPTER 4

PILLS OR PROMISES—WHICH?

2 CHRONICLES 16:1-13

To a tower tall, a high tower I flee;
That tower is God's Word to me.
'Tis there I take my stand, 'tis this,
What God's Word says is, IS.

The history of Asa, the king of Judah, great-grandson of Solomon, and great-great-grandson of King David, is a sad one, beginning as it does, so auspiciously, and ending so ingloriously. You cannot read it carefully and prayerfully without being convinced that God's gracious plan and purpose in his life was thwarted to a large extent; that he missed God's best. His sun rose to the zenith in a cloudless sky, and then sank out of sight amid lowering clouds and gloomy shadows.

I remember as a child sitting beside my mother on the broad veranda of a house that faced west at the sunset hour. It had been a dark and stormy day. The wind shrieked and howled among the branches of the trees that shaded our home. The rain fell in sheets, and the sleet was so cutting that, if you ventured to face it, it made your skin burn like fire.

But, as the day advanced toward its decline, the rain ceased to fall, the clouds scattered, leaving the clear blue of Heaven revealed, the wind sank to gentle breezes that sighed a lullaby amidst the pine tops, and, as a parting salute, the sun, so long obscured, broke out into a blaze of glory that immersed everything in a sea of rosy light. As we looked at each other's faces transfigured by the heavenly radiance, Mother said: "Isn't this beautiful? It reminds me of a Christian's farewell to earth. It seems to me that whatever the conflicts may have been God intends that 'at even-tide it shall be light.'" I thank God that it was even so with her. A hymn of which she was very fond beautifully describes her home-going:

> Sunset and evening star,
> And one clear call for me,
> And may there be no moaning of the bar,
> When I put out to sea,
> But such a tide as moving seems asleep,
> Too full for sound or foam,
> When that which drew from out the boundless deep
> Turns again home.
> Twilight and evening bell,
> And after that the dark,
> And may there be no sadness of farewell,
> When I embark;
> For though from out this bourne of time and place
> The floods may bear me far,
> I hope to see my Pilot face to face
> When I have crossed the bar.

"But," someone may say, "we have to have something, some disease or other—cancer, tuberculosis, diabetes, locomotor ataxia, or arterial embolism, or appendicitis, or bronchitis, or colitis, or duodenitis, or endocarditis, or gastritis, or meningitis, or nephritis, or pharyngitis, or peritonitis or proctitis, or some other 'itis or phritis' mostly fright-us,' to move us out, don't we?"

Why and where in the Bible do you find that? Please give me the chapter and verse. You can't, because it isn't there. Is God so short of bright angels to carry His loved ones home that He has to borrow some of the devil's black ones? Methinks not. Jesus said His Father would send twelve legions—72,000 angels—to His aid, and I believe that every believer can have all the shining servitors he needs, by asking for them in Jesus' name.

I certainly do not intend to let any of those black angels escort me. I shall not be at home when they call.

About three years ago a black angel, Mr. Pneumonia, by name, called and announced that he had come to take me home, but I didn't go. I wakened one morning to find myself with all the symptoms of pneumonia, one lung consolidated, the other affected; my face as blue-black as a stovepipe. I don't know what my temperature was. I took good care not to know. As to how I felt if any of you have ever had a really serious case of pneumonia, you know. If you don't know, thank God you don't.

I didn't waste a moment but got to prayer. I knew I must have been failing God some way, and He showed me just how. Then I yielded utterly, and told Him how sorry I was that I had inadvertently got into my own way instead of His and claimed immediate healing of the pneumonia.

Then He showed me a great, high, strong tower. It stood upon a massive rock in mid ocean, and oh, how the waves crashed, and dashed, and lashed, and smashed against it in their fury! Some of them had wolves' heads. Around the very top of the tower, in great white letters, were the words, "I Will Put None of These Diseases Upon Thee," and I knew I was to take my place on the very top of this tower. The waves with the wolves' heads could not reach me there, try as they might.

But you say, "I don't understand. Didn't you say you had pneumonia?" I didn't understand either, and I didn't waste time trying to. I was too near death for that. I just flew by faith to the tower top and said, "He will put none of these diseases upon me. He is the Lord that healeth me"

(Ex. 15:26). And the pneumonia took its flight. The altitude seemed too high for it. I believe in high altitudes.

To return to Asa; we cannot but feel deep regret that a life that shone for God, and His faithfulness to His Word, for so many years, as did Asa's should go out amidst obscurity and shadow, leaving no testimony of perfect victory, through the all-conquering Christ, in the last weariness, the final strife. Yet Asa was a man who proved God in hard places many and many a time. He stood, with his army of 300,000 men, on the battle field of Mareshah against Zerah, the Ethiopian, and with a thousand thousand, and 300 chariots, and cried to the Lord, his God, (see 2 Chron. 14:9) and said:

> *Lord, it is nothing with thee to help, whether with many, or with them that have no power: help us, O Lord our God; for we rest on thee, and in thy name we go against this multitude. O Lord, thou art our God; let not man prevail against thee. So the Lord smote the Ethiopians before Asa... and the Ethiopians fled* (2 Chron. 14:11-12).

They always flee before a prayer of faith like that.

What a pity Asa didn't remember that prayer, and its results, when he came to the final struggle with the powers of darkness!

After this notable victory God sent a prophet, Azariah, to tell him that, just as long as he would stay with God, God would stay with him, but that if he forsook God he would be forsaken by the Lord. And Asa took courage at these words and put away the abominable idols, and led his people in a regular revival of true religion, making offerings to the God of Israel, and entering into a covenant to seek the Lord, their God, with all their heart, and all their soul. And Asa brought into the house of God the things that he had dedicated, as well as the precious things that his father had dedicated.

In short, he appears to have tried to straighten things up in every possible way, and as the result of his submission to God, there was no more war unto the five and thirtieth year of his reign. Then a very sad thing happened. Asa handed over to Benhadad, king of Syria, things that belonged to God, and sought Benhadad's protection against Baasha, king of Israel. He had forgotten the God who had delivered him from Zerah, the Ethiopian, when the odds were so overwhelmingly against him. Then God, in His mercy, sent a messenger to Asa to warn him, and to remind him that the Lord was just the same as He had been in the battle with the Ethiopians, and that He needed no outside help. But Asa would not listen, but was wroth with the messenger, and put him in prison, and oppressed some of the people at the same time.

And when Asa would not listen, God sent sickness just as He says He does, when He speaks twice and man perceiveth it not, in Job 33. And in the thirty and ninth year of his reign Asa was diseased in his feet, and the disease was exceeding great, probably gangrene of the feet, a disease which is sometimes attended with fatal results (1 Kings 15:23).

And now we come to our subject proper, "Pills or Promises—Which?" For Asa had just the two alternatives before him. (I may say that I am using the word "pills" in a general sense as representing all that medical and surgical science had, or have, to offer.)

Does someone say, "I didn't know that those old fellows had pills. Didn't suppose they were up to date enough for that"?

Yes, they had an elaborate pharmacopeia. Perhaps, like us, they had pale pills for pink people, or is it pink pills for pale people? And blue pills for green people; sugar-coated pills, and gilt-edged pills. In other words, they had a fully developed system of medical and surgical science, imported from Egypt, and no doubt patronized by Solomon's wife, who was an Egyptian princess, and her admirers.

Yes; Asa had pills, powders, potions, fumigations, snuffs, injections, skilled surgeons who could handle the knife dexterously, and all the rest of the paraphernalia pertaining to medical and surgical science, as I tell about "Moses' Medical Chest."

Professor Breasted, of Chicago University, one of the most distinguished Egyptologists in the world, who deciphered the inscriptions in the tomb of King Tutankhamen, being sent for by the Lord Carnarvon for the purpose, states, as a result of the translation of an ancient Egyptian papyrus, recently made by him, that the old Egyptian physicians were true scientists, acquainted with the phenomenon of the circulation of the blood centuries before it was discovered in Europe by Harvey, and with many other things, and possessed a system of treating diseases in some respects closely resembling that of our own day.

Yes, Asa had pills, much the same as we have, and the same precious promises, though he didn't have as many of the latter as we have. To whom much is given of him shall much be required.

He had wonderful pills but much more wonderful promises. He had the covenant of healing (Ex. 15:26), "Deliver him from going down to the pit: I have found a ransom" (Job 33:24), clearly teaching healing in the atonement. "He sent His Word and healed them" (Ps. 107:20), "Who healeth all thy diseases" (Ps. 103:3).

His own great-grandfather, Solomon, had claimed, at the dedication of the Temple, the healing of every disease as part of God's covenant with His people (1 Kings 8:37, 39; 2 Chron. 6:28-30). *Pills or promises— which shall it be?*

If we arranged the subject in tabulated form we should have to place under "Pills," in order to be true to the facts of medical science, "Uncertain in their results." There is no note more strongly stressed in medical teaching, by the foremost men in the profession, than this one. They are only quacks and fakirs who promise certain results from their treatments. Thoroughly conscientious, capable, medical men promise one thing only their best efforts directed by the results of the latest medical research and experiment.

What do we place below "Promises" under this head? Is there any dubiety as to the result? Not the faintest. "He sent His Word and healed them." "Who healeth all."

Secondly, we shall have to place "superficial in their results" under "Pills," for as Dr. Weir Mitchell has said, "Back of each disease lies a cause which no remedy can reach," while under "Promises" we may write, "radical cure," for the blood of Jesus Christ removes the cause of sickness, which is sin.

Thirdly, under "Pills," or human remedies, we shall have to put the words, "not God's way for His people." When God announces Himself as your Physician, He forever puts all other physicians out of court, so far as you are concerned. When Moses undertook the leadership of the Israelitish people, two or three million in all, in the exodus, he, though familiar with all the resources of Egyptian medical science, which, as we have learned, was truly scientific in the modern sense of the word, took but one remedy in his medicine chest, the Word of God, the covenant of healing, "I am the Lord that healeth thee." And the remedy worked every time.

The other day a student in the class on Christian doctrine gave as a proof of the divine origin of the Bible, "It works." I thought that was a splendid answer. I gave her "A plus" for that. And Moses' remedy worked. He had the finest set of people physically that ever trod this globe, not one feeble person among all their tribes.

In saying that pills are not God's plan for His people we are far from belittling the wonderful results achieved, and the self-denying devotion displayed by students of medical science in all ages. We do not read that Moses berated his colleagues, or underestimated their work. The worst thing I would say about physicians, and the entire medical fraternity would perforce agree with me, is that they are men, and not God, and their activities flesh, and not spirit. God has deigned to assume charge of the bodies of His people, healing them through the atonement made on Calvary, and keeping them immune from disease as they trust and obey Him. That being the case no one else is good enough for our Physician.

But someone asks, "Doctor, why does it have to be 'Pills or Promises'? Why not 'Promises and Pills'? Because the two are incompatible. We were carefully taught that certain remedies were incompatible, and could not be taken together. There is chemical incompatibility and physiological incompatibility. And there is also spiritual incompatibility. The moment you really take a promise of present, perfect healing for what it is, the all-powerful, living, energetic, Word of God, you are healed, for "He sent His Word and healed them" (Ps. 107:20).

I used to take 56 morphine pills every 24 hours. One day I took a Word of God, a promise, and I have never had any use for the pills since.

Asa chose, and chose wrong. I sometimes wonder if he was not willing to repent of his wrongdoing in the matter of giving what belonged to God to Benhadad, trusting in the arm of flesh, persecuting God's messenger, and oppressing God's people. I once met a woman who said she was seeking healing, but upon having it pointed out to her that she would have to obey the commands of the Great Physician, and in His strength, and by His grace, sin no more, she said, "It's cheaper to die." And I fear that, like Asa, she died. How awful to have one's life go out in rebellion against God!

Yes, Asa chose, and chose wrong, but praise God, we are still in the valley of decision, and have an opportunity to choose right. Shall we accept God unreservedly as our Physician, and have every ill, spiritual, mental, and physical, healed by power divine?

Which shall it be? "Pills or Promises"?

If you really want a pill,
You may take one every hour—
Pill of promise, pill of faith,
Pill of resurrection power.
Search your Bible as you will,

You will always find a pill.
Praise and take one every hour,
Pill of resurrection power.

CHAPTER 5

THE LEAPING LAME MAN

Banished my sickness, those stripes did heal,
Because the work on Calvary is finished;
Now in my body His life I feel,
Because the work on Calvary is finished.

In Acts 14, we have the story of the lame man of Lystra, one of the most instructive cases of healing to be found in the entire Bible.

To begin at the beginning, generally a good thing to do, we find that Paul and Barnabas started out on what is known as the first missionary journey (Acts 13), from Antioch in Syria, being helped forward by the prayers and faith of that splendid body of believers, the church at Antioch. It was at Antioch that believers were first called by the beautiful name "Christians," which they have borne ever since (Acts 11:26).

And a son of Antioch, John Chrysostom, or Golden Mouth, so called because the exquisite melody of his voice would melt sinners to tears, speaking about 300 years after this occurrence, said that that fact, together with the readiness of the saints at Antioch to succor the poor saints in Jerusalem when grievous famine was approaching (Acts 11:28-29), and their zeal for the maintenance of the gospel of the grace of God from all Judaizing admixture as evidenced in their sending Paul and Barnabas to the Council at Jerusalem (Acts 15), constituted the city's chief glory, though in art and architecture, palaces, statues, and miles of marble-colonnaded streets, it vied with Rome itself.

So I think we may safely conclude that the church at Antioch followed their missionaries with unceasing prayers, and that the healing of the lame man at Lystra, as well as many other blessed fruits of this missionary expedition, were largely due to this fact.

In Antioch, of Pisidia, Paul preaches the gospel with such power that the whole city is stirred; and when the Jews reject the truth, he turns to the Gentiles. Relentlessly pursued by the infuriated Jews, he and Barnabas pass to Iconium, and again have a great revival, followed by fiery persecution and assaults by both Jews and Gentiles. Threatened with stoning they fly to Lystra and Derbe, and the lame man at Lystra has his chance at the gospel of the grace of God.

It cost something to get it to him. It is a costly affair all around, this gospel. It cost God His only begotten son, for the Father broke His alabaster box when the Lord Jesus died on the cross. It cost the Lord Jesus everything to redeem us; He became poor that we, through His poverty, might become rich. It costs something to carry it to the lame men about us, in all its pristine power and purity, in the 20th century as well as in the first, and if we are afraid of pebbles of criticism that may damage our reputation for sanity or integrity, or even hurt us in our pocket-books, the lame men are apt to remain cripples so far as we are concerned. It was not pebbles but jagged stones and ragged rocks that threatened Paul and Barnabas, but these had no power to make them swerve one hair-breadth from their appointed path as heralds of the cross.

Now we are at Lystra. The intervening centuries fade away like a dissolving view, and we find ourselves. in the midst of the great crowd that has gathered from town and country to listen to the message of these strangers, regarding whom fantastic stories and wild rumors have doubtless reached them from Iconium and other places.

In the forefront, perhaps accorded this point of vantage under the speaker's eye because of this sad affliction of so many years' standing, for he has been a cripple from his mother's womb, sits the hero of our story, the lame man of Lystra. His whole life he has been thus, "impotent in his feet."

He was born for motion, progress, and he knows it. It is written all over him. But how to attain to it? How to fulfill the purpose for which he was created? It is a heathen audience, and he is a heathen amongst heathen. His physical condition is typical of his spiritual state, and that of all by whom he is surrounded.

They were created for movement Godward, and "the law written in their hearts, their consciences their thoughts the meanwhile accusing or else excusing" (Rom. 2:15); something deep in their souls is telling them that they are missing the very purpose for which they were brought into being. "We were created for Thee, and can find no rest until we find it in Thee, God, Thou Ancient Beauty!" says Augustine of Hippo.

Alas, they are as impotent spiritually as the lame man is physically. Some force outside themselves, a divine power, is needed to set them in motion. How to link on to it? That is the question.

But listen; the little man with the shining eyes and gracious mien, Paul, the chief speaker, who is so eloquent that they nicknamed him "Mercurius," after the heathen god of eloquence, is about to address them. What will he say? Will there be any modification of his message because of his recent painful experiences? No, for we read in the 7th verse, "And there they preached the gospel."

Paul didn't have one message for Antioch and another for Lystra. He says he was ready to preach the gospel at Rome also. Not two-thirds of it but the gospel in its entirety.

No doubt he told them as he did in Antioch of Pisidia, that through the man Christ Jesus, he preached unto them the forgiveness of sins, "and by Him all that believe are justified from all things." He preached a crucified, risen Savior, who, when He was on earth in bodily presence, healed all that were oppressed of the devil, and who was still spiritually present in His representatives, performing through them the same and greater works, because of His ceaseless intercession at the right hand of the Father, and because of the outpoured Holy Ghost.

And this lame man had "no more sense" than to believe it all. If you are disposed to think him overcredulous, remember that he was only a poor heathen. His heart was virgin soil for the gospel. He had no one to tell him that "only part was then available" for him. He was just "foolish" enough to appropriate every word of it to himself personally then and there, and to believe that Jesus Christ was "just the same" in Lystra in 48 A. D. as in Judea in 31 A. D.

And Paul, "steadfastly beholding him." Paul wasn't preaching for fame or filthy lucre. It was a serious business to him. A life-or-death, a Heaven-or-hell matter. He knew it was God's will by the foolishness of preaching to save them that believed. He knew that those to whom the gospel was hid were lost, "perishing." And he steadfastly beheld his hearers, watching for the dawn of Eternal Day on their faces.

As he was searching their countenances with Spirit-anointed eyes, he beheld the light, that never was on sea or land, break on the face of the lame man. "And perceived that he had faith to be healed." Why? Because he believed the gospel. That was what he had just heard, and heard for the first time. Believing it, he had faith to be healed. Perceiving this, Paul addressed him directly. He would not have done this if he had not perceived that he had faith. You can't coerce men into believing, but when they are ready to accept God's Word you can have the blessed privilege of being a helper of their faith. "Lord, I believe, help thou…" (Mark 9:24).

Paul said, "Stand upright on thy feet," and he leaped up. There is an exuberance about our first faith for healing. I felt when, more than 28 years ago in the city of Chicago, I was healed of a hopeless condition resulting from advanced morphine addiction, that if the Lord told me to put one of my shoulders under a skyscraper and lift it, the building would go up. The power of God just surged and thrilled through my entire being. It was much easier to leap than to walk. Later a steady sustaining power is more in evidence and, thank God, it is unfailing. You mount up on wings like eagles, run and are not weary at first, and later you walk and jog trot day after day, week after week, month after month, year after year—that is the pace that kills if you like—and you do not faint. Ready each morning for your appointed task! That is what divine health means, "His saving health."

Not only are you ready each day for the appointed task, but if God so will, you can work all night too, and yet not faint. You say, "Oh, I can't believe that." Well, it's so any way, and many are proving it in these days. "Many" are coming "from the east and west" to "sit down with Abraham," because, like him, they believe God implicitly and unreservedly. Perhaps others will wait for the second table, or stand behind Abraham's chair.

So the man leaped and walked, and by works his faith was made perfect, and yours will be perfected the same way.

Did the multitude glorify Jesus Christ? Never. They had their own idols to whom they hastened to ascribe the praise for what had been accomplished. They called them Jupiter and Mercurius. Today they have different names—suggestion, mass psychology, the subconscious self (what wonders has that marvelous being not accomplished?), "every day in every way I am growing better and better," etc.

They came with their oxen and garlands to worship these new deities. There is plenty of solid sustenance and luxurious adornment for us if we will fall in with popular notions.

But Paul and Barnabas rent their clothes—their voices wouldn't carry far enough to express to all the crowd their horror—at the very thought of these vanities, and told the people they had come expressly to turn them from these things to the living God.

Then the stones came, and Paul had a glorious opportunity of practicing as well as preaching, divine healing. Both are essential in carrying on this blessed ministry.

A man who got saved in a town where none of the churches expected people to get saved was asked: "Under whose preaching were you saved, anyway?"

"Under no one's preaching," was the reply, "but under my Aunt Hannah's practicing."

When Paul was stoned, and his presumably lifeless body was dragged out of the city, as the disciples stood around him (Please don't forget that point but stand by your leaders in prayer under the most desperate circumstances; I can see that lame man who was healed standing like a rock) Paul rose and went on a much-needed furlough? No; he departed to Derbe and preached the gospel in that city also. Derbe, as well as Lystra, must have her chance at the gospel. Today we are getting our chance. What are we making of it?

> *Reveal Thy truth from Calvary,*
> *That Jesus, living now in me,*
> *From sin and sickness sets me free.*
> *Shine forth!*

CHAPTER 6

SPIRITUAL SANITATION

The just shall live by faith,
Faith in the Son of God,
Who bore our grievous sins away,
And cast them in the flood.
The just shall live by faith,
For in that awful load
Our sickness too was borne away,
Praise to the lamb of God!

The other day I came across a statement in an article emanating from presumably reliable sources, that many medical authorities greatly dread a recurrence of Spanish influenza, that awful epidemic which killed more people than the great World War, although that war was attended with greater fatalities than any war that preceded it. The article went on to say that as the cause of the disease in question had never been ascertained, nothing could be done to avert it, and as no effective treatment had been discovered for it, there was nothing to look forward to but another fearful death list, in the event of its reappearance.

This set me to thinking about the whole question of epidemic disease in the light of God's Word. Nowadays if we are visited by some general calamity, such as a famine, a huge conflagration, or a fatal epidemic, and any one ventures to suggest that it never could have occurred without God's knowledge and permission, and that He may have some lesson to impart by means of it, the newspapers come out with articles contending that the only lessons God is trying to teach us by these visitations are that we should improve our agricultural methods, use fertilizers more freely, practice intensive farming, increase our appropriations for experimentation in laboratories, and government-controlled farms, improve our fire departments, or be more stringent in our building regulations, or be more scientific in our drainage and sewage disposal, or be more rigid in food inspection, and other ordinances having to do with public health.

But what does the Bible say or has it anything to say on the subject?

In consulting the Bible, let us never forget that it is the only book on the contents of which we can absolutely rely. All other writings which attempt to state the real causes of things are confessedly made up largely of guesses. All the medical books and scientific works are full of them, but you will not find one in the Bible, not one. There is no guesswork there, for the Word of God is forever settled in Heaven.

And I believe that if medical men and scientists would take the trouble to find out what it has to say about epidemics, they would learn of something to their advantage and that of the human race at large.

First let us note that, while the Bible, both in the Old and New Testaments, exhorts us to physical cleanliness, it also demands a deeper and more radical form of cleanliness; namely, clean hearts (Ps. 51:10), and a cleansing from all filthiness, not only of the flesh, but of the spirit (2 Cor. 7:1). It also reveals that spiritual uncleanliness may lead to judgment in the form of epidemic disease, as well as to other punishments (Num. 16:46-50; 1 Chron. 21). Let us look then to our spiritual sanitation.

The time when the epidemic referred to in 1 Chronicles 21 occurred was one of great prosperity in Israel. Before this a census had been taken at God's command (Num. 1:2), but the one referred to here was apparently undertaken so that they might exult in numbers, and depend on them rather than on the Lord their God. Evidently, the whole nation was at fault, and all shared the terrible punishment.

We are not to count on our resources, gloat over our fancied strength, or mourn over our feebleness. Our help cometh from the Lord which made Heaven and earth. We are to look away from ourselves altogether, fix our gaze upon the Lamb of God, and if we do this no plague shall come nigh our dwelling.

> *Though influenza rage from sea to sea,*
> *The home that trusts Him shall be free.*

I know a man who was standing on Psalm 91:9-10, "Because Thou hast made the Lord which is my refuge, even the Most High, thy habitation; there shall no evil befall thee, neither shall any plague come nigh thy dwelling," and when a doctor declared that one of this man's children was suffering with diphtheria, he denied it, and absolutely refused to accept the doctor's diagnosis. When the doctor persisted and wanted to enforce the measures usual in cases of this kind, he said, "It is impossible that diphtheria, which is a plague, should come nigh my dwelling. God's Word says that it cannot happen to me. Have you had a specimen from the case examined at the government laboratory?"

The doctor said he had not done so as he did not deem it necessary.

"Well, I refuse to accept your diagnosis of the case," replied my friend. "And I am certain that if a specimen were forwarded to the laboratory the report would be negative."

He said this on the strength of Psalm 91:9-10, and God made His Word good, for the doctor accepted the challenge, forwarded the specimen, and received a report that no diphtheria germs were present.

When Spanish influenza was raging all around us, and nearly every house in sight bore a placard, my sister said boldly to everyone, on the strength of God's Word, "You will never see an influenza card on this house," and God made her boast in the Lord good, though we exposed ourselves freely to infection in ministering to the sick.

Thank God, there is not only immunity from epidemic disease promised in the Word, but an effective treatment for those who fall victims to it. In this same 1 Chronicles 21, we find the plague stayed by sacrifice.

Under divine guidance, David sets up an altar to the Lord in the threshing floor of Ornan, the Jebusite—type of Calvary's cross—and offers there sacrifices—types of the spotless Lamb of God, who bore our sins and sicknesses; and God answered him from Heaven, by fire upon the altar of burnt offering, and commanded the angel to "put his sword again into the sheath thereof," and the plague was stayed from the people (1 Chron. 1:21).

It was because of perfect spiritual sanitation, secured through the blood of the Passover Lamb, that the children of Israel were rendered immune to the plague that smote the first-born in Egypt, both of man and beast; "When I see the blood, I will pass over you, and the plague shall not be upon you" (Ex. 12:13). No expedients of hygiene or sanitary science could have averted the epidemic from their homes.

Is it not advisable for us living in these perilous times, to go deep enough in our sanitary precautions, and while strictly obeying scriptural injunctions as to physical cleanliness, and gladly availing ourselves of improved facilities, therefore, to see that we also meet God's demands for truth in the inward parts, purity of heart? This, by the manifold grace of God, we can do, through the power of Christ's death and resurrection, and by so doing can manifest to the world a deliverance from epidemic disease as undeniable as that vouchsafed the Israelites when Egypt, with all its advanced medical science, was ravaged by a destructive plague.

The Lord put a difference between the Egyptians and Israel, and He puts a difference between His people and the world today, for He says, "I will put none of these diseases upon thee, which I have brought upon the Egyptians: for I am the Lord that healeth thee" (Ex. 15:26).

CHAPTER 7

'PUT OUT YOUR TONGUE!'

Letters are we, all men must see
That as they read, they may glorify Thee.
So let me shine with likeness divine
That men may take knowledge,
That Jesus is mine.

When I was a child, I always had great misgivings when the doctor said, "Put out your tongue," invariably the first words addressed to me when my mother lined me up in front of him. For I had made the discovery that, in some mysterious way that I could not fathom, try as I might, my tongue told tales on me, for the doctor would take just one, keen, searching glance at the trembling little tongue that was obediently thrust out for his inspection and say: "This child has been eating trash. Let her have no supper; give her a dose, a full dose, of castor oil, and put her early to bed."

Oh, how wise he was, I thought, *to be able to tell about those big candy bull's eyes I had eaten, and the extra piece of lemon pie I had cajoled the cook into giving me, just by looking at my tongue!* How wonderful it must be to be a doctor! How could one possibly tell that a person had been naughty, had eaten things they should not have eaten, and needed to go without supper, take horrid medicine, and go early to bed just by looking at one's tongue? Perhaps he could see all the way down my throat into my tummy, where the contraband candy and surreptitious pie still lay heavy, both on my conscience and on my digestive apparatus. But I could reach no conclusion about the matter. These questions were "too high" for me. My childish mind could not cope with the problems which underlay them.

But there came a day when I, too, was a doctor able to say, in a commanding voice to the submissive patient trembling before me, with possible castor oil, calomel, rigid dieting, perhaps even fasting, looming darkly in their horizon, with all proper professional dignity, "Put out your tongue," and when that day came I knew that a perfectly clean tongue was a sure sign of physical well-being, while a dirty, furry, flabby tongue was as surely an evidence of ill health.

And how wonderful it seemed to me, after I had taken Jesus as my Great Physician, to find out that He lays such great stress on the condition of our tongues.

Let us look in our Bibles and carefully note some of the things He tells us about our tongues. In Proverbs 12:18, we find that "the tongue of the wise is health"—health to the owner of the organ, and to those to whom he may speak, because a consecrated tongue has but one occupation and that is to tell the story of Jesus.

Let us read some words from our Great Physician about the tongue: "Death and life are in the power of the tongue" (Prov. 18:21); yes, for you can say "Yes" to Jesus with it, and alas, you can also say "No" to Him. How is it with your tongue? Does it always say, "Yes, Lord," "Amen Jesus," to all His blessed will? If not, get it trained to do it, and begin today, this very hour. You'll never have a more convenient season.

"He that keepeth His tongue keepeth his life" (Prov. 13:3). "Keep thy tongue" (Ps. 34:13). What does that mean? Have you read the life of Frances Ridley Havergal? If not, I am sure you are all familiar with the great consecration hymn God gave her. I remember being at a very largely attended meeting once where they all voiced their consecration to God by singing that hymn, and I thought what a gift was bestowed by the Holy Ghost on the author in that sacred song:

Take my life and let it be,
Consecrated, Lord, to Thee;
Take my moments, and my days,
Let them flow in ceaseless praise.
Take my voice and let me sing
Always, only, for my King;
Take my lips and let them be,
Filled with messages for Thee.

She has also written a little book, *Kept for the Master's Use,* and that is what is meant, I believe, by keeping your tongue, reserving it for the purpose for which God created it. David's tongue had a name. It was called "Glory"; you will find it in Psalm 30:12: "To the end that my glory may sing praise unto Thee, and not be silent." No use for a lazy tongue. A tongue that is silent toward God is not a healthy tongue, but a "Glory" tongue is the sign of spiritual well- being, and the cause of physical health and vigor, for it is the overflow of a pure heart, filled with the love of Jesus; for "out of the abundance of the heart the mouth speaketh" (Matt. 12:34).

There were some people, you will find them in Numbers 21 who "murmured"; their tongues were not called "Glory" but "Grouch," and we find fatal disease, caused by the bite of fiery serpents, coming upon them, and some of them perished. And they would all have perished had not Moses, in obedience to God's command, lifted up the cross, in type, the brazen serpent upon the pole, so that they might look upon it and live.

We are told in 1 Corinthians 10:10 not to murmur, "as some of them also murmured, and were destroyed of the destroyer." What is your tongue called—Glory or Grouch? Look out for the stings from the old serpent if it is called Grouch, and let me tell you his bites are just as venomous as ever. His virus doesn't improve with keeping.

Does someone say, "Well, to be honest, Dr. Yeomans, I am an awful grumbler, a regular crepe hanger; what am I to do about it? My tongue is called, 'Grouch,' and not, 'Glory.' I may work up a hallelujah or two when I come to meeting and hear the bright singing and the testimonies of those who have overcome through the blood of the Lamb, but when I get home and find a big bill in the letter box, twice as large as I expected it to be, and that the vegetables I ordered for dinner haven't come, and the children have littered up the front porch, the hallelujahs change to old-fashioned grumbles. What am I to do about it? It seems as though I just can't help it, and I want to help it, for I see now it means giving Satan power in my life to destroy me physically as well as spiritually. I can feel the nips of the fiery serpents already. Neuritis pains are beginning in my limbs so I can hardly crawl around."

Now I am glad you said just that, for you can't help it sure enough, but you can make application today to the Supreme Court of Heaven, to have the name of your tongue changed from "Grouch" to "Glory," and it will be granted. And change of name in God's language always means change of nature too, so you will be transformed, by the power of His Grace, from a Groucher to a Glorifier, through Grace from Grouch to Glory.

Put out your tongue! I tell you it is not a bad thing to do sometimes, not in company, that would be very rude indeed, but under the loving eye of your Great Physician. I used to tell my patients to take a look at their tongues sometimes in a hand mirror, and God has furnished us with a looking glass of clearest crystal, without one flaw in it, which instantly reveals the smallest blemish, blot, or spot, which we are to use to view ourselves from His standpoint.

You will find it in the epistle of James 1:22-26, inclusive: "But be ye doers of the word, and not hearers only, deceiving your own selves. For if any be a hearer of the word, and not a doer, he is like unto a man beholding his natural face in a glass: for he beholdeth himself, and straightway forgetteth what manner of man he was. But whoso looketh into the perfect law of liberty, and continueth therein, he being not a forgetful hearer, but a doer of the word, this man shall be blessed in his deed. If any man among you seem to be religious, and bridleth not his tongue, but deceiveth his own heart, this man's religion is vain."

A healthy tongue is a bridled tongue, controlled, directed by the Holy Spirit. That doesn't mean that you are never to speak. A horse is bridled, not in order that he may become inactive, but that his activities may be directed to useful ends. And so with our tongues. There is a religious order among Roman Catholics called the Trappists, who solved the problem of the tongue by turning themselves into dummies.

I remember hearing a little Roman Catholic girl arguing about them with her elder sister. The older girl said that was the very best, and holiest way to live, never to speak.

But the younger one said, "I know it isn't for if God had wanted them dummies, He would have made them dummies."

And she was right; our tongues have most important uses, first to glorify Jesus, and second, to feed the flock of God with the sweet honey and goodly rich milk which are ever to be under them, as it says in the Song of Songs (Song 4:11). We are to be ever ready to impart sweetness and strength, His sweetness and His strength, to all to whom He may send us. And, believe me, you will have no trouble with your own health if your tongue is the kind I have just described.

Put out your tongue. What is it like? Honor bright now. Art thou in health, my brother? Perhaps you say frankly, as we read the Word together, "No, I realize from my examination of my tongue in that looking glass that I am in bad shape. My tongue shows it. What shall I do? Come without a moment's delay to the Great Physician. That's what my patients used to do when they wakened up and found their tongues all swollen up, and black or brown or scarlet, instead of clean pink; sometimes they get so large that they won't stay in the mouth try as hard as you will.

Did you ever hear of a case like that? They would head for my office and say, "Doctor, fix me up." And I would write a formidable prescription and separate them from a substantial sum of their hard-earned cash. Well, if you will call on Jesus, He will give you an alternative that will change you, tongue and all, so that people will hardly know you, and your health will prosper as your soul prospers (3 John 2), and long life will be added to you, and you will see many days, and not have to hunt after elixirs of life, serums, and glandular extracts.

You will find it in Psalm 34:12-14 inclusive, "What man is he that desireth life, and loveth many days, that he may see good? Keep the tongue from evil, and thy lips from speaking guile. Depart from evil and do good; seek peace and pursue it."

Let me tell you a true story of a man whose cruel tongue was changed into a "glory" tongue by the power of God. My sister and I were evangelizing in a rural district, and God was blessing us and crowning our labors with souls saved and bodies healed. The Methodist church, in which we were holding meetings, was packed every night. The good people in the district were very happy over it, but there was one man, a rich and very capable farmer, who was an awful thorn in their sides. He had a terrible tongue; would swear at everybody and everything in sight, his cattle included—he had magnificent stock—and stick the fork into the poor brutes, shy billets of wood at them, and maltreat them in every possible way when his diabolical temper got the better of him.

He had not been inside a church for 20 years, and the people were afraid to call and invite him to the meetings, as they had been obliged to have him arrested more than once for his atrocious cruelty and were not at all sure what kind of a reception he might accord them. But they decided to pray and ask us to go and call, while they prayed. It happened that we had to walk to his house, through some tie-up of vehicles, and the distance was 4½ miles, and the road heavy with new-fallen snow.

As we left the house, someone called out, "Be sure you make him hear. He is as deaf as a post." As we trudged along through the drifts, I said, "I promise you I will make him hear. Thank God for a good pair of lungs. I certainly am not going to take this long walk for nothing."

As we arrived at the house, we were courteously entreated, as Luke says of Paul in Acts, and promptly admitted to a spotless house. I noted in a quick glance about me that everything connected with the farm, buildings, fences, etc., was in apple-pie order. Upon being given chairs, I, remembering my host's terrible affliction, drew mine up quite close to his, much closer than the book of etiquette would sanction. I thought he looked rather surprised, perhaps a shade almost of alarm showed itself on his face, but paying no heed to trifles like that, I proceeded to tell him, bellowing like a bull of Bashan in doing so, of his terrible predicament; how he was lost and undone, without God, and without hope. Then I told him of Jesus, the mighty to save, and invited him to the Savior and also to the meetings. I cannot say that I remember exactly what I said, but I can take my affidavit as to how I said it, and it was at the top of my voice.

He seemed to look startled, which I considered a good sign, and I asked leave to pray, which he granted by a nod of his head, I think. I knelt much nearer to him than etiquette would prescribe, and prayed at the top of my not feeble voice. Then, as we could not seem to get any expression from him or his wife—they appeared stunned—we bade them farewell, again inviting them to the meetings. When we got home the intercessors eagerly enquired as to how we had fared. I said, "Well, there was no outward, visible sign of capitulation, but one thing you may be sure of, I made him hear."

"Why shouldn't you make him hear? He isn't deaf."

"Isn't deaf?" I replied. "Well if he isn't, he is sure I am an escaped lunatic." And I told them the whole story. I think that, praying people though they were, they were really discouraged, but they just kept on praying; there was nothing else to do.

Some nights after, we had a crowded house as usual, and just as we were beginning the song service, Mr. Farmer, with his wife, daughter and son-in-law, walked in and came well toward the front. The congregation were petrified at the sight, and the intercessors praised God. After preaching I gave an invitation for those who were saved through faith in the sacrifice of Calvary to indicate it by standing up for Jesus, and to my amazement, and the amazement of all present, he rose to his feet. I thought he had misunderstood my call, and believed it to be for sinners, so I said, addressing him directly, "If you are saved, you had better tell it out."

He replied directly, almost in a terrified way (I think he believed me to be a woman capable of strong measures), "It's out."

And thank God it was out, and better still, it was in. He was upright, and downright, and in-right and outright and all right. His heart and his tongue were right. His son-in-law said the stock must think they had died and gone to Heaven. His tongue was changed from Grouch to Glory. And Jesus is just the same today. There is nothing too hard for Him to do.

Put out your tongue. Is it all right? Does it bear tales?

> Said Mrs. A to Mrs. B, while roaming up and down, "My husband said to me last night, Smith bought his goods from Brown."
> Said Mrs. B to Mrs. C, while buying a new gown, "The people say, and I suppose, Smith got his goods from Brown."
> Said Mrs. C to Mrs. D, while walking in the town, "It's said, and I believe it's true, Smith took his goods from Brown."
> Said Mrs. D to Mrs. E, and said it with a frown, "Don't say I said it, but it's true, Smith stole his goods from Brown."

These verses contain samples of unhealthy tongues. I believe tale-bearing—now listen, for I am giving you a medical opinion free, gratis, for nothing—is the most fatal occupation, from the standpoint of your health in which you can engage. If I were an advisory physician to an insurance company, I should instruct them to discriminate against chronic talebearers. The Bible says on this point, "The words of a talebearer are as wounds, and they go down into the innermost parts of the belly" (Prov. 18:8). I believe that some of those profound diseases, which baffle the powers of the ablest diagnosticians and prove utterly hopeless so far as any curative treatment goes, originate in this way. Remember, oh, remember, whatever else you forget, that an evil word wounds not only the one against whom it is spoken, but like the boomerang, returns straight to the one who sent it; in popular parlance, "Curses, like chickens, come home to roost."

Put out your tongue. If Miriam had only done that when she was uttering those stinging criticisms of Moses on account of his Ethiopian wife, what a difference it would have made in her history.

Let us pray that inspired petition in the 19th Psalm, remembering that a pure heart, and a tongue cleansed by faith in Jesus' blood, mean physical health and vigor, and longevity, on the authority of God's own Word.

"Let the words of my mouth, and the meditation of my heart be acceptable in Thy sight, O Lord, my strength, and my Redeemer" (Ps. 19:14).

> *Boys, flying kites, haul in their white-winged birds;*
> *You can't do that way when you're flying words.*
> *Careful with fire is good advice, we know;*
> *Careful with words is ten times doubly so.*

CHAPTER 8

MOSES' MEDICINE CHEST

Balm of Gilead, heal my wound,
Make me whole, and strong, and sound.
Thou the medicine I take,
Forth with speed my health doth break;
It is finished.

Moses, by the practically universal verdict of mankind, has been adjudged one of the greatest men of all time, an outstanding figure of the centuries. And, differ as they may on many other subjects, Jews and Gentiles, believers and unbelievers, learned scientists and ordinary individuals, like ourselves, are agreed as to this.

Jurists and legislators extol the wisdom of his laws, physicians admire his methods of sanitation, while his courage, capability, and splendid powers of administration elicit the highest encomiums from all thinking people.

But human verdicts are liable to be reversed by a higher tribunal, for we are informed that some things which are highly esteemed of men are an abomination with God. In the case of Moses, however, there is no fear of such a reversal for the Highest has spoken of him as a servant of God, "faithful in all his house" (Heb. 3:2,5).

In Acts 7:22, we are informed that "Moses was learned in all the wisdom of the Egyptians, and was mighty in words and in deeds." That implies, among other things, that he was a fully qualified Egyptian physician and surgeon. Something of what it meant to possess such qualifications in Egypt in Moses' time we may gather from the report of the distinguished Egyptologist, Dr. James H. Breasted, of Chicago University, upon the Edwin H. Smith papyrus, the property of the New York Historical Society, a very ancient Egyptian document dating back to 1,700 years before Christ, a treatise, and a very elaborate one, on medical science. The manuscript is 15 feet long.

Dr. Breasted tells us that, from the contents of the papyrus, of which he made a translation, it is perfectly evident that the ancient Egyptians were true scientists in their aims and methods, not mere charlatans and magicians, as some people have supposed. He says that the author of the treatise on the Smith papyrus had a profound knowledge of human anatomy, and was also familiar with the circulation of the blood, which was not known to the Western world until 1616 A. D., 3,316 years later, when Dr. William Harvey announced its discovery.

The Hearst papyrus in the University of California, which is of somewhat more recent date than the Smith papyrus, is also an ancient Egyptian treatise on medical science, said to be one of the most wonderful of the kind in existence.

This knowledge was the monopoly of a privileged class among the Egyptians—the priestly caste. The hierarchy had the custody of all these secrets. They were the priests and physicians of Egypt and very influential men. But into all their secrets Moses was initiated.

Some of these secrets scientists of today would be glad to have divulged to them. The Egyptian art of embalming, for instance, is a lost art. The Egyptians believed that the spirit would return to the body, and they, therefore, took infinite pains to preserve the body for the spirit's future use. I do not deny the excellence of their workmanship, but I would not want the best mummy that was ever mummified for a resurrection body. I want one like unto Christ's glorious body.

But see what Moses was, and how he was qualified and equipped after the long years of preparation through which God put him, including a 40-year post-graduate course in the University of the Back Side of the Desert. That was a grand university, and Moses took first-class honors there!

We cannot fail to recognize that Moses was not only equipped spiritually, intellectually, and physically, for the work to which God had called him, but specially prepared medically and surgically to organize the great expedition of which he was the God-appointed leader.

Just think of it—leading upwards of two million people of all ages, sorts, and conditions including old men and old women, tiny newborn infants, young mothers, and children of all ages, out on a most arduous and perilous journey, over land and through sea, to a place where drug stores, or their Egyptian equivalents, were altogether unknown. Using our reason, we would expect to find that Moses, realizing the tremendous responsibility that he was taking upon himself, would see to it that his medicine chest was fully equipped. The Egyptians had all kinds of drugs. There was no shortage of them in Egypt.

Dr. A. T. Buck, author of an authoritative work on medical history, tells us about the complexity of the Egyptian pharmacopeia. He says that they used drugs in the form of powders, potions, inhalations, snuffs, fumigations, injections, and other ways. Also, that they depended much on dietetic measures, and resorted to eliminative treatments much like those used by modern physicians. In short, they were quite scientific in their aims and methods.

So Moses had a copious pharmacopeia from which to make his selections. All he had to do was to put his gigantic drug order into one of the Egyptian wholesale houses far enough ahead to enable them to assemble or manufacture all the remedies he needed. Two things they had in abundance were castor oil and opium, and the ancient Egyptians depended largely on these.

Presumably Moses got everything together. Oh, I am desirous to know exactly what he had in his medicine chest! I want to know what tonics he chose, and what alteratives, digestants, laxatives, and stimulants. I have a very special reason for wanting to know what Moses had in his medicine chest to get the results that he secured. Do you know that they are absolutely unparalleled in history? They have never been duplicated elsewhere. In connection with the physical well-being and general health of the people comprising the expedition under his charge he established a record that has never been approached in any other expedition known to the annals of history.

There is no doubt about this for the Word of God tells us in Psalm 105:37 that "He brought them forth also with silver and gold; and there was not one feeble person among their tribes." Not one feeble person! What a tune to march to! Not one feeble person! Not one feeble person!

He had two million people, perhaps more. We read in Exodus 12:37 that there were over half a million men who marched, and one man stood for a good many children in those days, so that very possibly two million is quite an underestimate.

Think of it! A mighty nation comprising aged people, tiny infants, young mothers, and children of all ages, every one erect and stalwart, every skin clean and clear, every eye bright and shining, every man, woman, and child fit for the day's march.

Not divine healing alone, but divine health-superb, all-round physical well-being, one hundred percent physical efficiency, every organ functioning properly, separately and collectively, all working in perfect harmony and unison toward the end for which the organism was created.

Wasn't that wonderful? O Moses, let us see inside that medicine chest! For, Moses, we know that those people you led out of Egypt were just flesh and blood like us. We know they had real hearts and real lungs and real livers and real gall ducts and real appendices. Everybody in that procession had an appendix, yet everybody had perfect health and vigor.

O Moses, tell us what you had in your medicine chest! For, Moses, the Word of God tells us that those things that happened to the people you shepherded happened to them for an ensample unto us upon whom the ends of the world are come; that God provided some better thing for us who are living in the full radiance of the outpoured Holy Ghost.

And, Moses, sometimes we are afraid we are making but a sorry appearance as compared to your procession, and we know we are marching down the aisles of the ages, and are encompassed by a mighty cloud of witnesses, and reviewed by an innumerable company of angels. O Moses, tell us what you had in your medicine chest!

And Moses says, "Draw near, and I will open my medicine chest and show you its contents. They are for you, for 'whosoever will may come and take of the water of life freely' (Rev. 22:17). The contents of my medicine chest are 'life to those who find it and health to all their flesh' (Prov. 4:22). That takes in every organ of your body, every cell and tissue."

Moses opens his medicine chest, and he has there *one remedy* and only one—only one remedy is needed.

The multiplicity of human remedies is a confession of the absolute failure of man to deal satisfactorily with the problem of disease and sickness. If we had one remedy that could strike at the root of the trouble, a radical cure, there would be no need for a multiplication of remedial agents.

There is such a remedy, but it is not human; it is divine—the blood of Jesus Christ, the incarnate Word of God. "He sent His Word and healed them" (Ps. 107:20). He didn't *try* to heal them; He didn't heal them ninety-nine percent, but *He healed them.*

Moses, accomplished Egyptian physician and surgeon that he was, did not deny the value of Egyptian learning.

You will remember that we are told that Moses declined to be called the son of Pharaoh's daughter, to accept the title of Prince of Egypt, although it might have meant that he would eventually be called Pharaoh Moses, King of Egypt; we are told in God's Word why he did this; it was because he was looking for something better. He had respect unto the recompense of the reward. Moses was long-headed, and he esteemed, estimated, and valued the reproach of Christ as greater riches than all the treasures of Egypt. He did not deny that there were treasures in Egypt. Moses was no fool. But he knew of treasures, richer far than they, which his soul craved.

And so it was with the riches of learning, the treasures of wisdom of the Egyptian scientists. I do not believe that Moses for one moment belittled anything that they had accomplished. I am sure he did not berate his former teachers and colleagues or deny their ability. I am sure that he was not forgetful of the devotion with which they had applied themselves so diligently in their efforts for the benefit of humanity.

But for himself Moses knew something as far above the results of human experiment and learning, as the heavens are high above the earth. And so convinced was he as to this that, responsible as he was for the physical well-being of a mighty nation, he took only one remedy in his medicine chest, and that remedy never failed him. That remedy has never failed the man or woman who has trusted it. It cannot fail for it is the immutable Word of the living God, and the scripture cannot be broken.

In order to be effective, medicine must be taken, and the way to take this divine remedy is to believe God's Word *exactly as it reads*.

It matters not whether the disease is acute or chronic; it does not matter if the whole American Medical Association has pronounced your case hopeless. From the human standpoint, they are no doubt quite correct in their prognosis. But turning to God, and viewing the matter from the divine standpoint, we find that He says, "I am the Lord that healeth thee—who healeth all thy diseases."

The moment you believe this, just as it reads, *in the present tense,* you are healed, for the Lord Jesus Christ said, and still says—for He is the same today, "As thou hast believed, so be it done unto thee" (Matt. 8:13).

God showed Moses a tree! Oh, what precious fruit it bears! Salvation full and free for you and me; for every bit of us:

> *If you only will come to our Christ on the tree*
> *He hath borne all your sickness and you may go free;*
> *The covenant's signed, and the contract is sealed,*
> *If you only will come, you are healed.*

CHAPTER 9

'I WILL—WILT THOU?'

And when your faith is weak
Look to Jesus;
He's never far to seek—
Look to Jesus
He's the author of your faith
And the finisher till death,
For so the Bible saith—
Look to Jesus

The scene of this story is Jerusalem; the occasion, a feast of the Jews which Jesus has come from the city to attend. Among the helpless sufferers in the five porches about the Pool of Bethesda, by the sheep gate, there lay a man. He with the "great multitude of impotent folk, of blind, halt, withered, waiting for the moving of the water" (John 5:3). They felt they must have something outside of themselves to deliver them from their distress. Thus, here we find another type of fallen humanity.

The occupants of all five porches needed help. Five—the number of the senses, the number of man. In his awful misery and abject helplessness, the man of whom we speak is perhaps the most hopeless of them all. His case has become chronic and is of 38 years' standing. Observe his pitiful plight as he sprawls helplessly like some huge jelly fish, his limbs, designed for activity, hanging to his body like bags of soft, useless tissue.

The sight of him appeals to the compassion of the Lord Jesus Christ who addresses to him a question—a question perhaps the last one we would have asked under the circumstances: "Wilt thou be made whole?" (John 5:6). We would say, "Of course we would like to be restored to activity and usefulness." Who wouldn't? It seems cruel to ask him if he desires it.

But note that Jesus didn't ask him if he *would like* to be made whole, if he *desired* restoration of his physical powers. He doesn't ask you either if you would like to be completely delivered from those ailments which so militate against your comfort and usefulness, which hamper you in your work for God, and perhaps even becloud your testimony to Jesus Christ, the same, yesterday, today, and forever.

No, Jesus asked him a far more searching question, and He puts the same question to *you* today, if you are suffering from physical debility. "*Wilt* thou be made whole?" What does that mean?

You say, "Oh, I am willing to be made whole. I am ready to believe it is His will to heal. He says, 'I am the Lord that health thee.'"

But that is not what the Lord asked the impotent man, nor is it what He asks of you. It was not of passive faith He was speaking. Indeed, the Bible teaches that there is no such thing. Faith invariably *acts* along the line of God's Word. "Faith without works is dead" (James 2:26).

It was of active faith—*invincible determination*—that the whole will of God shall be accomplished in every part of us, spirit, soul, and body, that the Lord Jesus spoke.

When we come to the Lord with our burden of sins, and our bondage, sometimes life-long, to evil habits, sinful appetites, and ugly tempers, we don't say, "Well, the Lord may have His way about these things. I see from the Word that it is His will to cleanse me from them, and I am willing. Let Him begin cleaning house as soon as it pleases Him."

No, we say, "'The blood of Jesus Christ...cleanseth from all sin,' (1 John 1:7) and *I will* be clean, purged from all filthiness of the flesh and spirit." And you don't sprawl helplessly around, the prey of evil tempers, impure appetites, and vicious habits. In faith you throw the whole weight of your willpower on God's side, against all these things. And as you do this, the enemy comes in like a flood, bringing all the old temptations to untruth, unkindness, impurity, self-indulgence, or whatever your besetting sins may have been, reminding you that you are constitutionally addicted to this or that, have been all your life, and so must succumb to the temptation.

But you say, "Never. I *will* walk in the Spirit. I *will not* fulfill the lusts of the flesh." And immediately the power of God ratifies your determination, the Holy Spirit lifts up a standard against the forces of darkness, and seals your "I will" and "I will not," and the victory is gained.

It is exactly so with temptations to sickness. We must see, as clear as the sun at noonday, in God's Word, for ourselves, that it is God's will to heal us, and then we must claim it with a courage, strength, and tenacity, into which we throw the whole force of our will and power of being. How dare we do less when His will is so clearly revealed?

I once knew a woman who, for the greater part of her life, had recurrent erysipelas, or so her doctor diagnosed it. It appeared quite frequently at irregular intervals, particularly upon her face. When she got saved, she saw clearly in the Bible that her sickness, as well as her sins, were borne by the Lamb of God on the cross of Calvary, and in faith in the Word, she resisted this recurrent malady. Every now and then the adversary attempted to bring on an attack, pointing out that it was constitutional with her, chronic, incurable, etc. But you know his etceteras as well as I do and don't want to hear any more of them. She always met him with, "It is written," and steadily gained ground in God, so that the most Satan could accomplish was a slight flush on her face that would only last a few hours.

She was brought into a rather large ministry for God of which healing formed an important part, and her house, a fine one, was filled most of the time with people who were seeking to get in touch with the living Christ. She was much used in maternity cases, many little ones coming into the world under her roof, without pain, compassed about by songs of deliverance.

One day when her house was full, and at least one little expectant mother (a minister's wife), in momentary anticipation of the joyful event—there may have been more than one but this particular one I distinctly remember—the sister waked up in the morning with the old enemy, erysipelas, flaming in her face. At once Satan said, "You will have to send that minister's wife to the hospital or you will be liable for manslaughter. You know it is death for her to be exposed to this contagion. And this case, and that case you have in the house. You must do thus and so with them. They must go too."

It was a pretty kettle of fish. But after she had had time to open her Bible, and get her heart fixed on God, she saw through the deception. She replied: "No such thing. The minister's wife won't have to go to the hospital. Those children won't have to move; you are the one who will have to go, and that immediately. I will be made whole. So take your erysipelas with you." And it was according to her faith.

Not many months ago, I saw at a meeting the very little girl. She is a big girl now, who came into the world on that occasion, the minister's daughter. A bonnier specimen it would be hard to find. She has lovely long curls (and I believe we all have a sneaking fondness for long curls on little girls in spite of the vogue for bobbed hair), rosy cheeks, and eyes that shine as though she still remembered the songs of praise and joy that welcomed her advent to this sphere. I promise you that not one germ touched her or her mother.

When Jesus asked the impotent man this question, the man began to talk of the hindrances, in the human and natural, to his deliverance—"I have no man, etc." You don't need any. You don't need anybody, or anything, in the human and natural, whether man, woman, pill, powder, electric current, change of climate, or altitude, for perfect healing if you bring your case to Jesus.

"Rise! Get above all that," said Jesus. "My help cometh from the Lord which made Heaven and earth." First say, "I will," then rise. There is no trouble about rising if you say, "I will" first. You will go up like a balloon.

"Take up thy bed." Carry what carried you. Perhaps your family is carrying you now. Oh, how heavy you are! Carrying you on their prayers, their patience, their pocketbooks. Say, "I will be made whole," rise, and you will take them all up and carry them on your faith. Many and many a time I have seen this done, and so have you.

One day in Oakland, I had a suitcase which was as heavy as lead. I should have been ashamed to have such a heavy one, but people are so kind about giving me books. They are such lovely books and I do love them, and I usually have two or three to slip in at the last moment, and that is how it comes about that my suitcase is so ponderous.

I was taking the train, and I don't know just how I would have managed if a lovely girl who had been healed of spinal complaint—she had been carried about for a long time—hadn't jumped up and carried it.

You will be surprised at what you will carry when you say, "I will be made whole," and rise and take up your bed. There are all sorts of things and people waiting to be toted. You had better get busy.

But there was another word in Jesus' instructions to the impotent man, impotent no longer, and a very important word. It was this, "Walk. Walk!" Move on and out. "Go on unto perfection" (Heb. 6:1). "Speak to the children of Israel, that they go forward" (Ex. 14:15). The devil is behind you, and you must keep on the move if you are to abide in victory, physical and spiritual.

> *Farther on, yet still farther,*
> *Count the milestones one by one,*
> *Jesus will forsake you never,*
> *It is better farther on.*

We *walk* by faith. There is no standing still for believers. Following these instructions, the man "was made" whole. It is all God from beginning to end, start to finish. He was made whole, not one half, two thirds or 99 percent even.

Afterwards Jesus found him in the Temple, a good place to be found. I wish all the people who get healed were found in God's house praising Him. Alas, it is often "Where are the nine?" That is the reason why some people fail to retain their healings.

And Jesus had a final word, a most solemn word, for the impotent man, and it is for us as well: "Sin no more, lest a worse thing come upon thee" (John 5:14).

Scientific investigators are bending over microscopes, test tubes, retorts, X-ray photographs, and I know not what else besides looking for means of preventing disease; millions of dollars are expended annually in the great laboratories of the world for this purpose. But here is the way, the only way, of realizing this ideal of immunity from sickness: "Sin no more." Get rid of sin. Get it out of your life, root and branch; only so can you be free from sickness; for "Sin, when it is finished, bringeth forth death" (James 1:15), and disease is merely the death process, death begun.

How can we get rid of sin? By accepting, and dwelling in, the grace of God in Christ Jesus, for it is written, "Sin shall not have dominion over you: for ye are not under law but under grace" (Rom. 6:14).

CHAPTER 10

THY CHILDREN
LIKE OLIVE PLANTS

Let God's glory fill your soul,
Let His Spirit take control,
Let the tidings of His blessed love
Extend from pole to pole.
Live in the glory place,
Where you see Him face to face,
Then you'll run to teach your children
Salvation, all of grace.

How beautiful that we can by faith and obedience—and obedience follows faith as the night the day—bring covenant blessings upon our children, make of them "olive plants," fed by the oil, vitalized, energized by the Spirit of God, "trees of righteousness, the planting of the Lord, that He might be glorified" (Isa. 61:3).

What more beautiful than "a green olive tree in the house of God" (Ps. 52:8)? What more useful, with its hard, yellow wood, its nourishing and delicious fruit, its golden oil for anointing, lubricating, illuminating? Its very leaf is a symbol of that blessed gift of God bestowed upon us in His Son—Peace—(for He is our Peace). "Great shall be the peace of Thy children" (Isa. 54:13). Peace implies physical as well as spiritual well-being; "in health even as thy soul prospereth," and this is the heritage of our children in the beneficent plan and purpose of our heavenly Father.

Alas, there is a reverse to the medal—another side to this lovely picture. When a rich man dies, we read of his assets, the size of his estate, the value of his various properties, and the item is apt to conclude with a brief statement something like the following:

"The entire amount, with the necessary deductions for legal expenses, and a few trifling legacies to old friends and faithful servants, was left to the only son of the testator," and we are apt to think, if we do not express the thought: "What a lucky chap that young fellow is to have such a noble estate left to him! What splendid opportunities he has to be all, and accomplish all, that his heart could desire."

But did you ever pause to consider that money, realty, stocks, and bonds, valuable securities of any kind, are only part, and by no means the most important part, of what a man hands on to his children, and children's children? There is a spiritual, a moral, an intellectual, and a physical heritage transmitted by every parent to his offspring, the Word of God itself being our authority for the statement.

Supposing a will and testament included all actually bequeathed to those inheriting under it, we can imagine that some would have to read something like this:

"I hereby give and bequeath to my son, John Doe, Roe, or Moe," as the case might be, "the property of which I die possessed," etc., "also spiritual blindness, the result of my persistent Christ rejection, for I loved darkness rather than light because my deeds were evil, a tendency to moral obliquity because I made me crooked paths, to mental confusion and uncertainty for 'there is no wisdom nor understanding nor counsel against the Lord,' and physical deterioration, the result of evil habits and sins. I pass on to him my gout, and other diseases, or a tendency thereto, the result of my gluttony and self-indulgence, and even fouler diseases, or a tendency thereto, being my iniquity visited upon my children, and their children, to the third and fourth generation."

Methinks some of us would not care to accept the legacy if we had to take all it included.

On the other hand, a will might read:

"I give and bequeath to my son, John Doe, Roe, or Moe," as the case might be, "such and such property, real or otherwise, acquired by honest effort under the blessing of God, and the benediction of the Almighty on him for spiritual soundness, moral integrity, mental vigor, and physical health, mine to hand on to him through faith in a covenant-keeping God, whose promises cover not only myself, but my progeny after me." "All these blessings shall come upon thee, and overtake thee, if thou shalt hearken unto the voice of the Lord thy God. Blessed shalt thou be in the city, and blessed shalt thou be in the field. Blessed shall be the fruit of thy body" (Deut. 28:2-4). "By faith Isaac blessed Jacob and Esau concerning things to come. By faith Jacob, when he was dying, blessed both the sons of Joseph" (Heb. 11:20-21).

Joseph, occupying as he was a princely position in Egypt, which doubtless carried with it countless cares and responsibilities, hastened to his father's deathbed, taking both his sons with him, that they might receive this patriarchal benediction, this priceless heritage, which he rightly valued above all the treasures in Egypt.

As this blessing applies to the whole man, spirit, soul, body, possessions, activities of all kinds and relationships (read Deuteronomy 29:1-14), we can undoubtedly claim not only spiritual but physical health for our offspring.

Noah prepared an ark for "the saving of his house" (Heb. 11:7); this ark typifies Christ, who bare our sins and sicknesses, by whose stripes we were healed.

In Exodus 12:3 we read, "A lamb for a house," and the blood of the Passover Lamb meant, among other things, immunity from disease which, in the form of a fatal epidemic, was destroying life in the homes of all who were not sheltered behind it. "Christ our passover is sacrificed for us" (1 Cor. 5:7).

We can even claim the Baptism of the Holy Spirit for our descendants under this covenant. "This is my covenant with them, saith the Lord, My Spirit that is upon thee, and my words which I have put in thy mouth, shall not depart out of the mouth of thy seed, nor out of the mouth of thy seed's seed, saith the Lord." (Isa. 59:21). What an illustration of this the evangelistic activities of the descendants of the late General William Booth furnish.

Don't you think we should "get busy" and secure some of these priceless boons for our children? The resources of Heaven are at our disposal, and we can put those angelic messengers to work delivering good things at our homes if we will requisition the throne in the appointed way, in the name of Jesus, "lifting up holy hands without ... doubting."

On the other hand, we have distinct promises of disaster, including ill health, to the children of those who forsake God, and the Bible abounds with concrete instances of it.

Note Job 5:3-4: "I have seen the foolish taking root" (the fool in the Bible is the one who says in his heart "there is no God," who, in the very core of his being, fails to acknowledge his Creator); "but suddenly I cursed his habitation, his children are far from safety."

How people use flattery these days in society, in business, in the church; alas, even from the pulpit, we hear its cloying and unwholesome sweetness. How sorely we are tempted to say "nice" things even if we have to sacrifice perfect candor to do so! May God deliver us from flattering words! The apostle Paul says: "Neither at any time used we flattering words" (1 Thes. 2:5), and in the 17th chapter of Job, and the 5th verse, we read, "He that speaketh flattery to his friends, even the eyes of his children shall fail."

Have you noticed how many children have to wear glasses these days? Such a thing was unheard of a few years ago.

You remember how God struck David's child by Bathsheba with fatal sickness, sending Nathan, the prophet, to tell him it would surely die because of its father's sin? (2 Sam. 12:14-18). That was a sin unto death (1 John 5:16). Also let us notice the case of the child of Jeroboam, Ahijah, whom God refused to heal on account of his father's sin (1 Kings 14:1-8).

"Come thou and all thy house into the ark" (Gen. 7:1). Bring them in; command your children after you by faith as did our father, Abraham. Remember the Lamb is for the house.

> *Beneath the blood-stained lintel,*
> *I and my children stand;*
> *A messenger of evil is flying through the land;*
> *There is no other refuge from the destroyer's face;*
> *Beneath the blood-stained lintel shall be our hiding place.*

CHAPTER 11

DIVINE HEALING IN THE LORD'S PRAYER

A Savior, what a Savior! He plucked me out of sin, He cleanseth all unrighteousness, And makes me whole and clean. His stripes have healing power, And by them I was healed, Now to redemption's hour, By His Spirit I am sealed.

Our Father which art in heaven, Hallowed be thy name. Thy kingdom come, Thy will be done in earth as it is in heaven. Give us this day our daily bread. And forgive us our debts, as we forgive our debtors. And lead us not into temptation, but deliver us from evil: For thine is the kingdom, and the power, and the glory, forever. Amen. (Matthew 6:9-13)

People often ask me, "Where do you find divine healing in the Bible?" To this I invariably reply, "Where don't I find it?"

The Bible's one theme is Jesus Christ, the Son of God, the Savior of the world. His very name is as ointment (healing and fragrance) poured forth. Wherever you find Jesus you find healing for every disease, balm for every wound, an anodyne for every pain.

Someone has said, "I don't know how to pray for healing"—meaning what form of prayer to use, thinking a form necessary. So, I said, "You can say the Lord's Prayer, can't you?"

"Oh, yes."

"Well, that's pretty strong on healing, isn't it?"

"Why I didn't know there was anything about healing in it."

"Well, let us study it together and see if we can't find something," I replied. And as we did so it opened wider and wider, in connection with the great truth of the Lord for the body.

I just long to have everyone enter those beautiful portals with me and share the precious treasures we have found there. So I am writing this little message.

Our Father which art in Heaven—Matthew 6:9

My earthly father was a physician and surgeon in the United States Army, a veteran who had charge of many different hospitals during, and subsequent to, the Civil War. As a child I always felt that I was much safer than other children, for was not my father a doctor and, in my estimation at least, a wonderful one?

I remember on one occasion, my youngest sister, a child of about three, toddling around, fell and cut her forehead wide open on the carved leg of an old mahogany bedstead. Blood poured from the wound and her face was a sight to behold, while her shrieks, and mine rent the air. But my wonderful father came instantly to our relief.

"What can he do?" I pondered in my childish mind. But he seemed undismayed, and after laying the little thing very tenderly on a couch, made her breathe something from a handkerchief for a moment or two, after which she lay quite still. Then he washed her face gently till it was quite free from blood. But, alas! the deep, awful gash showed even more plainly than before.

"Yes, he can wash her face but he can't mend her." I said in my poor little unbelieving heart. But there was a great surprise in store for me.

A man who had come to assist my father produced a leather case full of bright steel things.

What are they? I wondered and ventured to move a step nearer, for in the excitement I was quite lost sight of, or I would certainly have been told that my room was more desired than my company.

Then my wonderful father disclosed yet more of his amazing capabilities, for taking one of the gleaming things, which I saw must be strangely shaped needles, he proceeded to sew up my sister's face, and what a job he made of it! She looked as good as ever when he was through. Oh, how my confidence in my father was confirmed and extended almost limitlessly, by this experience!

I just felt I couldn't be sick, or have any part of my anatomy seriously damaged, just because I was my father's daughter. He would prove more than equal to any emergency that could possibly arise, and I had a rightful claim to the very best he could do for me, for he was my father.

Do you read the parable? Our Father is God Almighty, our Creator, and our claim upon Him is that of children. You will never urge it in vain for spirit, soul, or body, if you present it in simple, childlike confidence. "Our Father which art in Heaven."

HALLOWED BE THY NAME—MATTHEW 6:9

Pray that His name may be held sacred, given all honor in Heaven and in earth, believed on implicitly. And what is this but a prayer for the manifestation of those things for which that name stands, including, among others, deliverance from disease and physical infirmity?

In Acts 3:16, we read, "His name through faith in his name hath made this man strong, whom ye see and know: yea, the faith which is by him hath given him this perfect soundness in the presence of you all." Faith *in His name* brings perfect soundness.

Thy kingdom come—Matthew 6:10

This is also a prayer for healing and physical well-being, for we read that the increase of His government means the increase of peace, "Of the increase of His government and peace there shall be no end" (Isa. 9:7).

Nothing in the world is more surely inimical to peace than bodily affliction. Even a toothache, or a corn on the little toe, has power to mar our tranquility. But God has promised to keep us in perfect peace if we trust in Him (Isa. 26:3), and that means superb health—health so perfect that we hardly know we have a body except for the things it accomplishes.

I have a friend who has a beautiful Cadillac car and he used to employ it in the Lord's service by taking some of us to our preaching appointments. It purred gently, and rolled as though on velvet, and I could hardly realize that I had been in a car at all except by getting to my destination. I believe that is the way God wants our bodies to function—"in perfect peace."

Thy will be done on earth as it is in Heaven—Matthew 6:10

Here we pray that God's will may be done in earth, even in the clay which composes our mortal bodies, as it is done in Heaven! How much arthritis, catarrh, rheumatism, diabetes, cancer, locomotor ataxia, and all the rest, do you think they have there? How many cases of measles, diphtheria, mumps, and whooping cough? If you can think of any disease they have in Heaven you may have that, but no others, for our Lord Jesus teaches us to pray that God's will may be done on earth as it is done in Heaven.

In Revelation 21:4, we are told, "God shall wipe away all tears from their eyes; and there shall be no more death, neither sorrow, nor crying, neither shall there be any more pain."

GIVE US THIS DAY OUR DAILY BREAD—MATTHEW 6:11

Here again we are praying for physical as well as spiritual blessing. The Lord Jesus Himself speaks of healing as "the children's bread" (Matt. 15:26). So we pray for healing and health when we ask for bread, as well as for material sustenance, and spiritual strength. What good is bread, or food of any kind, to a man whose stomach, and liver, and pancreas, and other digestive organs, are out of kilter? In this petition we ask for perfect digestion, absorption, and distribution for our bread has to be "given" not only into our hands and mouths, but into our stomachs, and through the absorbent system into the blood current, and by means of it to every cell in the tissues that make up our bodies.

AND FORGIVE US OUR DEBTS (OR SINS)—MATTHEW 6:12

In the second chapter of Mark's Gospel Jesus healed the paralytic that the onlookers might know "that the Son of man hath power on earth to forgive sins" (Mark 2:10). God wants people to know that His spiritual gifts to believers are real, and to this end He manifests His power in our bodies in a tangible manner by healing us and making us strong and vigorous. He desires to be the health of our countenance that we may be living epistles, known and read of all men, for He is not willing that any should perish. Your very face is to preach full salvation.

LEAD US NOT INTO TEMPTATION —MATTHEW 6:13

I do not know any temptations that are harder to withstand than those to fear, unbelief, discouragement, and despair, which come with Satan's attacks on our bodies. It is said that the third chapter of Job is the most eloquent of despair to be found in all literature. We are taught to pray, in full submission to the divine will, of course, that we may not be led into temptation.

Deliver us from evil—Matthew 6:13

This petition covers all forms of disease, for the curse entailed upon the Israelites by disobedience to the divine law includes "every sickness, and every plague" (Deut. 28:61). So when we pray, "Deliver us from evil," we are asking for immunity from all sickness and every physical disability. And we are sure of the answer to our petitions, "For thine is the kingdom, and the power, and the glory, for ever. Amen."

CHAPTER 12

TROUBLE—TRUST—TRIUMPH

PSALM 107:1-31

Stand fast in the faith through the darkest night,
Whatever your trouble, fight the good fight.
It may be today, faith will turn to sight—
Stand fast in the faith.

I once owned a beautiful prayer book. It was of the most costly leather and silk and had a silver cross, on purple ribbon, hanging to it. It contained prayers for all occasions it seemed to me: morning and night, seedtime and harvest, joy and sorrow. You had just to look it up in the index and there it was. It was very convenient, and the petitions were couched in the choicest language; but it was mislaid somehow and you don't need to return it, if you should happen to find it; for, since the Comforter came in to abide, there is a prayer and praise book somewhere inside that is ready for any emergency. You don't even have to look in the index—the prayer and praise just roll out.

Once I was present in a church where a new pulpit had been installed and was to be dedicated. There were a number of ministers of experience present, and I said to myself, *I wonder who will officiate. I am glad to witness this ceremony for I have not the least idea how a pulpit should be dedicated and this is my opportunity to learn.*

My reflections were interrupted by the voice of the pastor calling on me to pray the dedicatory prayer. I was dismayed, but that internal prayer and praise book was ready, and the prayer and praise rolled out.

In the Psalms of David, we have a Holy Ghost inspired prayer and praise book by the use of which we can pray and praise until courage and faith will enter our hearts under all circumstances.

Before reading the first 31 verses from Psalm 107, let us note that, while this psalm is separated from the 106th by a doxology, the 106th being the last in Book Four, while the 107th is the first in Book Five, it is really a pendant to the 105th and 106th Psalms, and intimately connected with them.

The theme of the 105th Psalm is God's faithfulness, or God's mercies to the fathers, while the 106th Psalm tells the sad story of man's unfaithfulness to God, or man's failure toward God.

God never fails. Man does nothing else. "Remember His marvelous works," we are exhorted in Psalm 105, but, alas, we are told in Psalm 106:13, "They soon forgat." Oh, let us be careful, lest we, too, forget.

> *God of our fathers, known of old,*
> *Lord of our far-flung battle line,*
> *Beneath whose awful hand we hold*
> *Dominion over palm and pine:*
> *Lord God of Hosts, be with us yet,*
> *Lest we forget!*

But in spite of man's unfaithfulness, God abideth faithful, and we find the prayer of Psalm 106:47, "Save us, O Lord, our God, and gather us from among the heathen," answered in Psalm 107:3, He "gathered them from the east, and from the west, and from the north, and from the south."

In this Psalm that we are studying they are gathered, and are recounting the mercies of God toward them. The Psalm is a sort of general portrayal of God's gracious dealings with mankind, as well as an authentic recital of what has taken place in certain specific cases.

I like to call it *Trouble-Trust-Triumph*, for we have here four pictures showing the vast ocean of human misery in its breadth and variety:

First. Wanderers, hungry, thirsty, fainting, travel-stained souls who have lost their way (verses 1-9).

Second. Captives, bound in affliction and iron, sitting in darkness and the shadow of death (verses 10-16).

Third. Sick folks (verses 17-22).

Fourth. Men in the perils of the deep, storm-tossed (verses 23-32).

Over against each and every one of these desperate situations we have set divine deliverance for all who will trust God. So trouble, that unfailing heritage of every child of humanity— "Man is born unto trouble as the sparks fly upward" (Job 5:7), is changed by trust into triumph.

Let us march boldly onward to the music of our text, *Trouble-Trust-Triumph*, and one day "our feet shall stand within thy gates, O Jerusalem" (Ps. 122:2) and "the toils of the road will seem nothing when we get to the end of the way."

We have all figured in the first group, travelers who have lost the way; but, thank God, some of us can sing, "I was lost but Jesus found me, found the sheep that went astray." Can you? If not, there is good news for you; the Good Shepherd is looking for you. "Come unto Me." Answer His loving call and enter the fold.

Some of us have belonged to the second group and been captives. Perhaps they were remembering their Babylonian bondage in verses 10-16. Well may they praise their faithful God! Well may we praise Him! Thank God, when every door is shut and barred with iron, there is still a way out: "I saw a door opened in Heaven"! (Rev. 4:1). Look up, poor, languishing captive! Jesus breaks every fetter! I have proved it in my own proper person, for He delivered me from the most awful slavery known to man, addiction to the demon drug, Morphine!

Now for the third group, the sick people. What about them? The Psalm tells us a great deal, and we can depend on every word, for "All Scripture is given by inspiration of God" (2 Tim. 3:16).

Let us ask a few questions about them. Why were they sick? Because of hereditary predisposition or undue exposure to hardship? The Bible does not mention these things. It says "because of their transgressions, and because of their iniquities" (Ps. 107:17).

For failing to discern the Lord's body we are told that "many" not a few— "are weak, and sickly ... and many sleep," (1 Cor 11:29) and in this connection we are told that if we would judge ourselves we should not be judged. Remember that it is ourselves that we are to judge, not others.

How sick were they? So sick that all food, even the most dainty, was abhorrent to them; so sick that they drew near to the gates of death.

What will *they* do? What could they do? One thing only; so long as God lent them breath, they could cry unto Him.

I have known what it was to be so weak, so near those mysterious portals which the Bible calls "the gates of death," (Job 38:17) that I had only a gasp or so of breath in me; but, thank God, I used it in crying unto the Lord, and invested that way it has already realized for me 32 years of vigorous health and strength and glad service for my King. Was that a good investment? I once prayed for a man who was so choked up that he couldn't cry unto the Lord with his voice but he talked on his fingers, and God heard and delivered him.

You say, perhaps, "But my case is hopeless." All the more reason to cry unto the Lord, for there is nothing too hard for Him to do.

What did God do when they cried unto Him? What did He send? Rather *Whom* did He send, for the Word is personified here. Did He send a serum, radium, pills, powders, potions? People tell us that He sent all these things. But the Bible says "He sent His Word and *healed them*." As the Word did the work, I can see no need for medicaments and therapies. Certainly there is no mention of them here.

But must we not observe the laws of health? Certainly, and be sure you don't omit the most fundamental and important, such as Psalm 34:12-13, "What man is he that desireth life and loveth many days? ...Keep thy tongue from evil." And Matthew 15:18, "Those things which proceed out of the mouth come forth from the heart; and they defile the man."

We are likely to be more exercised as to what we put into our mouths than as to what we let out of them.

God sent His Word, and He has never recalled Him. His name is not only Jesus, the Savior, but Jehovah-rapha, the Great Physician, the sympathizing Jesus. He is eager to heal you this moment. Cry unto Him, and He will deliver you out of your distresses.

Have you figured in the fourth group, the storm-tossed sailors? Perhaps you reply, "No; dry land is good enough for me." But, after all, is not life's voyage over stormy waters, and have not we all tasted somewhat of its ups and downs? Have we not known what it is to have our souls melted because of trouble?

Well, let us praise the Lord that Jesus still walks the stormy sea and says, "It is I, be not afraid," to all who cry unto Him.

> *He maketh the storm a calm, so that the waves thereof are still. Then are they glad because they be quiet; so He bringeth them unto their desired haven* (Ps. 107:29-30).

> *O Savior, whose almighty word The winds and waves submissive heard, Who walkedst on the foaming deep, And calm amidst its rage did sleep; Oh, hear us when we cry to Thee, For those in peril on the sea.*

Trouble—Trust—Triumph!

CHAPTER 13

LAUGHTER

Child of promise, 'tis enough, Laugh upon your way, Till all others laugh with you, Shout and sing and play. Simply take, what love bestows Fathomless and free, Hallelujah! child of grace! Isaacs, you and me. "God hath made me to laugh so that all that hear will laugh with me."

(Genesis 21:6)

When God has His way with us, He makes us laugh so that all that hear will laugh with us. I do not mean a laugh that is mere sound, guffaw, roar, chuckle, giggle, grin, titter, smile, smirk, snicker, or simper; but real deep, whole-hearted jubilation coming from appropriation of the work accomplished for us when Christ died for our sins, rose for our justification, ascended on high, and shed forth the Holy Ghost, baptizing us into His glorious body, so that this laugh is the overflow of divine life "My cup runneth over" (Ps. 23:5), and the overflow is laughter that laughs.

God makes us to laugh. The enemy generally causes people to weep, wail, lament, sob, whimper, whine, groan, grumble or grouch; but He can make people laugh too, a laugh that is sadder that any groan, the laugh of the fool. You may read about it in Ecclesiastes 7:6, where it is compared to the crackling of thorns under the pot, and described as vanity, that is emptiness, futility, hollowness. Like all scripture comparisons this is perfectly apt, for when the thorns crackle merrily they are perishing, in the very act and article of destruction, and the fool laughs his hollow laugh on the brink of eternal doom.

But God makes people laugh, and this God-given laugh, like the crystal stream that flows from the virgin snows of the everlasting hills, is pure as the Source from whence it emanates—God. There is not one minor strain, one mournful cadence, one lingering regret, one hidden hurt, one subtle sneer, one unholy triumph, in it. Oh, I think a laugh with a sob back of it is the saddest thing in the world. How often I have seen patients going to the operating table with a smile, trying to be "good sports."

But God *makes* us to laugh. You don't have to try to laugh because you think it is your duty. This laugh is the most uncontrollable, irrepressible, irresistible thing you ever experienced.

I wonder if anybody here remember how we used to have our photographs taken long, long, long ago? If not, I will tell you how it was done. They used to adjust a steel bar to your spine, on the top of which was an iron arrangement into which they inserted your head, screwing it in securely so you couldn't escape. You felt as though you were going to be guillotined on the spot, and the black cloth thrown over the camera seemed like the judge's black cap. When you were all set the operator said, "Smile please," in a sepulchral voice. It is just about as ghastly when they say, "Keep smiling"; "The great big grin and the tilted chin are what is needed." "Pack your troubles in an iron chest, lock it, throw the key in the sea, and sit on the lid and laugh." That is the fool's laugh, the crackling of thorns under the pot. No; let God make you laugh, so fill you with Himself, His overflowing love, joy, and ecstasy that you can't help laughing, because you are an incarnate laugh.

Is that too strong? By God's command Abraham called the son God gave him, in whom the promised seed was called, with whom the everlasting covenant was established, "Laughter." "Thou shalt call his name 'Laughter'" (Gen. 17:19). You also are an Isaac, child of Abraham by faith in Jesus Christ (Gal. 3:26, 29). Don't dare to call yourself out of your name. God named you "Laughter." Don't dare to go round looking like grief.

Well may the Isaacs laugh,
Well may the Isaacs laugh;
Heirs of all things, poised for flight,
As they laugh faith turns to sight,
Well may the Isaacs laugh.
See the cradle softly laid for the coming heir,
Everything is all prepared, food, and warmth and care,
See the baby nestle close, wrapped in boundless love,
Learn the lesson—You're that child,
Nurtured from above.
Child of promise, promise born, must be promise fed,
Grasp the promise, 'tis your drink, and your daily bread;
Simply take what love bestows, fathomless and free,
Child of laughter, child of faith, Isaacs you and me.
Child of promise, 'tis enough laugh upon your way,
Till all others laugh with you,
Shout, and sing, and play.
Simply take what love bestows, fathomless and free,
Hallelujah! child of grace, Isaacs, you and me.

So it is not too much to say that we are to be divine laughter incarnate, for we are Isaacs. "He that sitteth in the heavens shall laugh" at anything and everything that would seek to frustrate His purposes and make void His eternal Word; and we, His children, resting securely on His promises, laugh with Him.

God hath made *me* to laugh. All that is *me* is to laugh so that all that hear will laugh with me. The Bible describes man as a trinity spirit, soul, and body (1 Thess. 5:23). Your spirit is to laugh. In Psalm 143:4, the

Psalmist says his spirit is overwhelmed within him. But his spirit must laugh. How is it to be brought about? He remembers the days of old, he meditates on all God's works (verse 5), he muses on the works of God's hands; he stretches out his hands to God (verse 6), and God causes him to hear His loving-kindness, and quickens him; turns his mourning into dancing, takes away his sackcloth, girds him with gladness, gives him beauty for ashes, the oil of joy for mourning, the garment of praise for the spirit of heaviness. "My spirit hath rejoiced in God my Savior" (Luke 1:47).

Is your soul cast down? Are you filled with vague forebodings, nameless fears, carking cares, endless worries? Your soul must laugh. Psalm 42 tells us how David talked to his soul under similar circumstances. "Why art thou cast down, O my soul? ... Hope thou in God: for I shall yet praise Him for the help of His countenance" (verse 5). Oh, how this divine laughter will clear the cobwebs away! God will make you laugh in every faculty and power of your physical being so that all that hear will laugh with you.

Spirit and soul, is there any more to "me"?

The other day I went to the dressmaker to be fitted. It is always an ordeal, and I try to lose myself in meditation as she does her worst. But my senses were suddenly recalled by a sharp jab which caused me to exclaim "Ouch!"

"What's the matter?" from the dressmaker who had just driven a long pin into my shrinking flesh.

"The matter is that that's *me.*" I replied, ungrammatically.

God undertakes to make me, every bit of me, laugh so that all that hear will laugh with me. Oh, for a laugh that will vibrate in the very marrow of our bones today!

You say, "I need a pill; my liver is sluggish, my stomach, intestines, glands—oh, yes, it's my glands, they're responsible for everything these days—are not functioning properly. I need something."

Yes, you need something. You need a great, big, faith-inspired, God-given laugh—a laugh that will clear your brain, steady your heart's action, stir up your liver, house clean your entire system, send living lightnings flashing along your nerve trunks, and make the corpuscles dance in your veins and arteries. This laugh is nothing less than God's omnipotence released in your being by faith.

> *Faith, mighty faith, the promise sees,*
> *And looks to God alone;*
> *Laughs at impossibilities,*
> *And cries, "The work is done."*

God will make you laugh if you will believe His Word without addition or subtraction. Perhaps someone says "I thought you were to speak on the ministry of divine healing." "That's what I am speaking about, for this laugh is contagious, and that is the ministry of divine healing. Catch the laugh."

I can remember when children who had chicken pox, or even measles, used to be sent round as missionaries to give it to other children so they might have it and "get over it." I am by no means recommending this method in connection with diseases, but I do urge you to catch this contagious laugh and then run round so others will catch it. If they really catch it, they'll never get over it.

Do you inquire, "How am I to catch it?" Just believe God and, believing, rejoice, believing, rejoice, believing, rejoice (1 Pet. 1:8). Isn't that simple enough? How did Sarah catch this laugh? What was the joke? She laughed because God spoke a Word that was life from the dead. "Life from the dead is in that Word, 'tis immorality."

Sarah's womb was dead but she received life in that dead organ to conceive seed, to bud, and blossom, and bloom, and produce a seed that multiplied, and multiplies, and shall multiply, as the stars of the heavens, and as the sands of the seashore for multitude. Something to laugh about for sure! "Sing, O barren, thou that didst not bear; break forth into singing and cry aloud, thou that didst not travail with child" (Isa. 54:1).

The healing ministry consists in bringing the quickening Word of God to bear on souls and bodies in which the death process is working—disease is death begun, a death process. With the contagious laugh of triumph over all that opposes itself against God and His will as revealed in His Word, you are to cry, "Ye shall not die but live and declare the works of the Lord." And those who hear will laugh with you.

Surely it is a *laughing matter* that though our sins were red as scarlet they have become as white as snow: it is a *laughing matter* that we, who once were far off, have been brought nigh by the blood of Christ; it is a laughing matter that by grace we are saved, through faith, not of works; it is a *laughing matter* that He is able to keep that which we have committed to Him against that day; it is a *laughing matter* that He is coming again to receive us unto Himself; it is a *laughing matter* that we are going to be forever with the Lord; it is a *laughing matter* that He forgives all our iniquities, and heals all our diseases, acute, chronic, old-fashioned liver complaint and new-fangled ailments that have only just been discovered. Some of these new ones are just old ones dressed up in new and horrific names. Thank God, however horrible their names, they are only diseases after all, and God heals all diseases, so we are safe.

If you are in a dark place, just make the air vibrant with heavenly laughter and you will get into the sunshine if God has to send an earthquake as He did to Paul and Silas at Philippi. They laughed and soon had the jailer and all his family laughing with them. Well may the Isaacs *laugh!*

CHAPTER 14

GREEN HEARTS AND ROSY TRUMPETS OR FAITH GROWS AS IT GOES

Afriend, who like myself was interested in horticulture, once gave me a little piece of black root which she said, if given the proper facilities, would grow and spread and burgeon and bud and blossom and bloom into a mass of green hearts and rosy trumpets.

I planted it and green shoots promptly appeared above the dark earth. But I soon discovered that its law of life was "growing by going," and it had to be allowed to go if it was to grow. It simply jumped around the garden, lawn, veranda, roof, and chimney. It seemed as though the whole place was to be nothing but heart shaped green leaves forming a background for huge pink trumpets. Every step it took it became stronger and the roots struck deeper and increased in grit and toughness. It was the strongest thing! Someone said to me, "They have it in Denmark. It came from there." I wondered if they have anything else in Denmark, for it didn't leave room in my garden for anything else.

I call it the "Faith Plant," (I am in complete ignorance as to its proper botanical nomenclature) because faith, if you let it grow by going, won't leave room for anything but hearts green with the unchanging verdure of eternal life, and rosy trumpets through which to proclaim the praises of Him who has redeemed us by His precious blood.

In Mark 5:21-34, we find this seed planted in a very desert of desolateness, the heart of perhaps the loneliest, saddest, most hopeless woman in Galilee that day. Old, her disease from which she had suffered for twelve years is one of advanced life; not only impoverished but a veritable pauper, dependent upon the bounty of the charitable for her daily bread; the victim of a loathsome disease which constituted ceremonial uncleanness and made her, in the eye of the law, unfit for human companionship. "She had heard of Jesus" (verse 27), and "faith cometh by hearing."

I can imagine her lying on a mat, in some rough outhouse possibly, stirring faintly as the dawn began to change the placid surface of the Lake of Galilee from gray to amethyst, and from amethyst to rose and gold. A new life is moving within her. "She had heard of Jesus." This new life demands expression in activity. It has a "Go" in it which will not be denied.

Perhaps some kind soul hears her moving on her wretched pallet and calls to her, "Lie still, Mother Rebecca; you are too weak to move after the terrible hemorrhage you had yesterday. Wait till my man has his breakfast and I will bring you a piece of bread and a cup of water." But she cannot lie still. Faith is not static but dynamic.

"I know I can't get up but I must," she gasps.

Was she weaker for it? No. *She was going and growing.*

"Why sit we here until we die?" Have you heard of Jesus? Then, in His mighty name, I say unto thee, Arise! If this woman had not risen, she would have perished. She spent her last atom of strength in seeking the Man of Galilee, and as she *"went"* like the ten lepers, she was healed and cleansed.

It seems to me that if we fail to put our willpower back of the measure of faith, He has dealt us, whether that measure be large or small, and move out and on, we are going to suffer serious loss, spiritually and physically, At the Red Sea crossing the command was "Go forward!" "But the Red Sea!" "Never mind that. Keep a going, Moses."

When this woman reaches her objective—*Jesus,* what does she find? That the Master, surrounded by a mighty throng, is on His way to the home of the ruler of the synagogue, Jairus, to minister to his dying daughter. Small chance for her to claim the smallest atom of His attention!

"Oh, roll into the ditch and die!" says the devil.

But her faith has been growing for she has been going step after step, along the dusty highway, battling her way through the ever-increasing crowds, stronger at each step. Now when she finds that the Master's face is turned toward the home of Jairus, and that there is no chance of her getting close enough to see His gracious smile, or win one word of love and compassion from Him, Faith takes a mighty leap and says, "What matters it? A touch, a vital contact is all that is necessary. 'He touched her hand and the fever left her.' If I cannot see and hear Him, I can touch Him in the dark and the work is done."

And she pressed forward through the solid mass of humanity. Did they give way before her? No; but they gave way before Faith. Everybody and everything has to give way before it for it brings God into action, releases omnipotence. "If I may but touch, I shall be made whole." And she touched and something happened. It always does. You can't touch Jesus without something happening. That is an impossibility.

What happened?

"*Dynamite* went forth." Jesus said so. The word translated "virtue" in the authorized version (Mark 5:30) is the Greek *dunamis* or power. "Dynamite" comes from the same root.

Last night I prayed with a woman who had been sick for years and both of us, she and I, were literally struck by heavenly lightning. She fell to the floor prostrate to rise in perfect health, and I tumbled into a convenient chair. Dynamite went forth from Jesus as we obeyed His command, "They shall lay hands on the sick in My name." "The fountain of her blood was dried up." The foul, malignant, probably cancerous, tissue became clean and sound so that the blood vessels retained their contents.

The change took place with lightning rapidity as she touched. "He spoke and it was done. He commanded and it stood fast."

"I couldn't get into the healing line at all!" Neither could she, but she touched and so can you. Those other folks who were in the line didn't get a thing because they didn't touch. They crowded, jammed, pressed, pushed, squeezed, and struggled, but they didn't touch. It takes faith to do that. You can do it anywhere at the tail end of the line, or out of it altogether. "She only touched the hem of His garment as to His side she stole … and straightway she was whole." The feeling came all right, and Jesus felt it too. He loves to heal you.

What did the loneliest saddest most hopeless woman in Galilee gain by that touch of faith?

Sonship ("Daughter"); peace ("Go in peace"); healing ("thy faith hath made thee whole"); preservation ("Be whole of they plague") (See Mark 5:34.) Let us set our faith going so that it may grow!

Some of us may have to seek Christ to save us. Others need to pick up that axe blade in the place where it fell. Others again will have to stop pampering Satan by retailing their symptoms. He enjoys that just as a poodle dog on a satin cushion relishes cream. You are to RESIST Satan instead of assisting him, and he will flee from you. The Bible is true. Others may have to step out by giving largely to the work of God. If God is leading you to give by faith nothing will take the place of it.

I once prayed, "Lord bless me;" and He replied; "Give me something to bless, some venture of faith. I can bless nothing but faith." And I made the venture. It involved what seemed a tremendous sum to me, and He met me and blessed me exceeding abundantly above all I could have asked or thought.

Set your faith moving in God and it will turn the arid wilderness of life into a bower of green hearts and rosy trumpets.

CHAPTER 15

'THIS IS THE REST...AND THIS IS THE REFRESHING'

I t was in the city of Calgary, Alberta, Canada, nestled in the foothills of the stupendous Canadian Rockies, that it happened.

The 23rd of September, 1907, began as all my days began, with prayer, breakfast, then work in the Government office which I had entered after ceasing to practice medicine. I was also holding meetings constantly, for after my marvelous healing from the last stages of morphine addiction I could do no less than tell others of the Great Deliverer I have found. The day began in a commonplace way, but its closing hours found me seated in heavenly places, my soul magnifying the Lord, my spirit rejoicing in God my Savior, and my whole being entranced by such a revelation of the Lord Jesus Christ as I never had expected to enjoy while tabernacling in the flesh.

For that is what the Baptism of the Holy Ghost means to me—a revelation of a real Christ. "He shall glorify Me: for He shall receive of Mine, and shall shew it unto you" (John 16:14).

Ever since that sacred hour my spirit has cried night and day:

> *Oh, sweet wonder!*
> *Jesus, Thou Son of God!*
> *How I adore Thee!*
> *Oh, how I love Thee!*
> *Jesus, Thou Son of God!*

As I emerged from my office at five in the evening, I met an old friend and beloved sister in Christ, Mrs. Lockhart, late of Winnipeg, Canada, now a resident of the Homeland. She greeted me with the words, "I have come on purpose to see you. I have received the Baptism with the Holy Ghost as in Acts 2:4, and you must also receive Him."

I had heard nothing about the Latter Rain outpouring excepting what I had gleaned from some newspaper clippings, but I knew from the Word of God that if they were not really speaking in tongues in Los Angeles they ought to be, in view of Mark 16:17, and other scriptures, so I hastened to a place of prayer with Sister Lockhart and we had a few moments before going to meeting.

For the first time, I heard the unknown tongue—just a sentence as Sister Lockhart prayed—and my only thought was:

"That is God!"

Arrived at the meeting we found it a particularly quiet, not to say dull, one. But there was nothing dull in me. My spirit was all aflame. They handed me a hymn book and I tried to sing, but just then the heavens struck a leak over my head, and the hymn they were singing seemed as lifeless as the Dead March in Saul. I commenced, all unaware, to make some music on my own account. They said afterwards that I was "very noisy" so they had to pronounce the benediction. I didn't know what they pronounced as I seemed almost more in Heaven than on earth.

Arrived at home we two sisters knelt at my bedside and in a moment I was pouring out my soul to God in intercession in the most majestic language I had ever heard.

Surely I found it "The Rest"; after all my many years of praying at last I really prayed; rather, Another prayed through me, prayer that must prevail. It was the most tremendous experience of my life up to that hour.

I had interpretation and gave it aloud. I was praying that my mother also might receive the promise of the Father. She was hundreds of miles from me geographically, and perhaps many more spiritually. A splendid woman, gifted, and conscientious to a fault, but she was conservative to the last degree and often said: "O Lilian, if you could only be less intense how happy it would make me!"

But that prayer had to be answered, and within three weeks from the day it was uttered my mother knelt beside me in Calgary and received the Baptism just I had received it. She was true to her testimony to the day of her departure to be with the Lord.

"The Rest... and...The Refreshing." Oh, what a refreshing! "He that believeth on Me...out of his innermost being shall flow rivers of living water ... this spake He of the Spirit"..."and everything shall live whither the river cometh."

Oh, the blessed dew of the Holy Spirit upon drooping spirit, jaded intellect, and weary heart and brain, nerve and muscle! How it calms and cools and strengthens!

Oh, the springing fountain of inexhaustible vitality which we find within as we acknowledge the quickening presence of the Spirit who raised Christ from the dead!

Oh, the rushing rivers of restless energy bearing us in triumph over every opposing force, and through every barrier, into all the will of God for us, for it is "not by might, nor by power, but by My Spirit, saith the Lord of hosts."

Truly, this is *The Rest...* and this is *The Refreshing!*

He sent His Word and healed.
(Ps. 107: 20)

Lilian B. Yeomans. M.D.

PART 3

CLASSIC TEACHINGS BY DR. YEOMANS

COMPILED FROM TRACTS AND OTHER
PUBLICATIONS, MANY OF WHICH HAVE NOT BEEN
REPUBLISHED SINCE THE 1920S AND 1930S.

'HOW SHALL I CURSE WHOM GOD HATH NOT CURSED?' (LIFE FOR A LOOK)

NUMBERS 23

The startling question of this chapter is asked by one of the most awful and mysterious personages in holy writ, Balaam, the son of Beor, brought from Aram, out of the mountains of the East, by Balak, king of Moab, to curse Jacob and defy Israel (Num. 23:7).

That Balaam was possessed of extraordinary powers is evident from the absolute confidence placed in him by his fellow men as represented by Balak, who said to him: "…for I wot that he whom thou blessest is blessed, and he whom thou cursest is cursed" (Num. 22:6).

The wonderful testimony to God's faithfulness which he uttered, God is not a man, that He should lie; neither the son of man, that He should repent… (Num. 23:19), and the sublime prophecy of the Messiah as the Star and Scepter that issued from his lips when for the third time Satan vainly tried to use his tool to the destruction of Israel, mark him as one singularly gifted of God.

What a tragedy that such splendid powers should have been prostituted to earn the "wages of unrighteousness"! But it is with his confession of absolute inability to accomplish that for which, with great care and effort, he was brought from the mountains of the East to do, that we are concerned.

Three times he tried; no expense was spared; money was poured out like water. No effort was too great. To the high places of Baal, seats of Satan, they betook themselves. Seven altars smoked with sacrifices of bullocks and rams. Balak and the princes of Moab with him stood by the burnt offering. Expectantly the king and his train waited for the awful word that should curse the people of God. At last the seer, prostrated by the prophetic impulse, with wide-open eyes, staring yet blind to things of earth, speaks in solemn accents:

"... Hath he [God] said, and shall he not do it? or hath he spoken, and shall he not make it good? Behold I have received commandment to bless: and he hath blessed; and I cannot reverse it. He hath not beheld iniquity in Jacob, neither hath he seen perverseness in Israel; the Lord his God is with him, and the shout of a king is among them. Surely there is no enchantment against Jacob, neither is there any divination against Israel..." (Num. 23:19-21,23).

In despair Balak implores: "...Neither curse them at all, nor bless them at all" (Num. 23:25). But his plea is in vain. Balaam says, "If Balak would give me his house full of silver and gold, I cannot go beyond the commandment of the Lord, to do either good or bad of mine own mind; but what the Lord saith, that will I speak?" (Num. 24:13).

Then from his controlled lips pour sublimely glorious prophecies of the coming Messianic kingdom: "There shall come a Star out of Jacob, and a Sceptre shall rise out of Israel...Out of Jacob shall come He that shall have dominion" (Num. 24:17,19).

Note that in every instance increased effort to curse only results in augmented blessing.

Had there been iniquity in Israel? Alas, the Bible makes it clear that they had repeatedly failed God.

Did God condone it? Never. He condemned and punished them, but when Satan rose against them to curse them by means of his tool Balaam, He stood like a lion and defended His people. For the Rock had been smitten and abundant life-giving water (type of salvation by grace) had reached the need of the people.

The brazen serpent, type of the cross of Christ, had been lifted up in their midst; and they had received *life for a look.*

Who shall lay anything to the charge of God's elect?

It is God that justifieth (Rom. 8:33).

We read that these things ... happened unto them for examples: and they are written for our admonition, upon whom the ends of the world are come (1 Cor. 10:11). The curse for disobedience to God's commands includes every disease to which humanity is liable. This is explicitly stated in Deuteronomy 28:58-62. Satan comes with all his power and exhausts his resources to curse us with some blighting, blasting, devouring disease; but if we will look in simple faith to the One who was made a curse in our stead, the enemy is inevitably defeated.

He *cannot* curse whom God has not cursed; nay more, his very efforts to do this only result in increased blessing for us. On his own confession we learn this, "Behold, I have received commandment to bless: and he hath blessed; and I cannot reverse it" (Num. 23:20).

If you are threatened with alarming symptoms in your body, *have no fear!* The children of Israel were abiding in their tents, "according to their tribes," when God wrought this mighty deliverance for them. See to it that you are in the circle of His arms, in the center of His will.

If the Holy Spirit shows you that you have strayed, come home to *your tent* by the appointed path of repentance toward God and faith in the Lord Jesus Christ. Then rest securely in the knowledge that Satan *cannot* put disease (part of the curse) upon *you.*

Does someone ask, "But Dr. Yeomans, what about Sister 'So and So,' or Brother 'This or That,' who is suffering at this moment from an awful ailment; and how can you explain the case of a saint who died of a deadly disease?"

There is an answer to every legitimate question in the Bible, a solution to every problem; and I find it in this case in Deuteronomy 29:29: "The secret things belong unto the Lord our God: but those things which are revealed belong unto us and to our children forever, that we may do all the words of this law."

It is clearly *revealed* that Christ hath redeemed us from the curse of the law (Gal. 3:13), including every sickness to which humanity is liable. This truth belongs to us and our children, and we are responsible before God for the use that we make of it. Things that God has not seen fit to reveal to us at this time *are not our property*, and we do well to remember this and refrain from touching them even in thought.

The fact that the prophet Elisha, who raised the dead in his ministry, fell sick "of his sickness whereof he died" (2 Kings 13:14) does not exonerate us from our responsibility in regard to God's provision for our healing and health; neither does it justify us in judging the prophet. If we feel any inclination to do this, it would be well for us to note that when a dead man was put into Elisha's tomb, he was revived and rose to his feet the moment he touched Elisha's bones (2 Kings 13:21). Just so, we are healed the moment our faith *really touches* the sacrificial death of our Lord Jesus Christ on Calvary.

When I was on the very brink of the grave, the holiest person I ever met nearly rolled me in by the fact that she was so ailing and frail. The enemy would ask, "How can *you* hope to be healed when Mrs. 'So and So' always has one foot in the grave and the other on the brink? You know you are not holy like she is and have no hope of ever being her equal spiritually. Explain her condition before you expect restoration to health."

How much precious time I wasted trying to explain Mrs. "So and So's" case. But one day I got desperate and said, "I don't care if every saint on earth dies of disease, the Word of God promises me healing; and I take it, and I have it." I have had it ever since.

I may say that years after I met this lovely saint (I had not seen her for years and did not know if she was on earth or in the glory) in a great department store purchasing a new dress. That didn't look as though she contemplated casting off these earthly cerements. I took courage and approached her, and a fresh surprise waited me. Her terrible illness had caused her to lose all her hair but now her beautiful, abundant silvery locks were a halo of glory around her face.

I stared at them until she said sweetly, "Were you looking at my hair, Lilian?"

"Is it real?" I stammered, forgetting my manners in my astonishment.

"Quite real. God gave it to me in answer to prayer. Do you like it?"

"Like is a feeble word; I love it, I never saw anything more heavenly in the way of hair."

The Bible says, "The hoary head is a crown of glory, if it be found in the way of righteousness" (Prov. 16:31), so perhaps I was not far wrong in calling her hair "heavenly." And while that dear woman was going on from faith to faith until she was able to pray the hair back on her head even in old age, I, at the enemy's behest, was beholding lying vanities and forsaking my own mercy until it nearly cost me my life.

A word to the wise is sufficient.

At the Beautiful Gate—
the Place of Healing

Acts 3:1-16

Apparently, the friends of this unfortunate lame man had done all in their power to aid him. Day after day they washed him, dressed him, fed him, and carried him to the Beautiful Gate of the Temple, where his pitiful plight was sure to appeal to the sympathies of worshipers in that sacred place. They had persevered in this benevolent work for years, for we are told that the man was "above forty years old" at the time of his healing. But let us note that all that human effort could accomplish left him outside of everything worthwhile.

It was a "Beautiful Gate," but he was on the wrong side of it.

A gate is something through which to pass to something beyond: an entrance, a portal, to the supply of your needs, the satisfaction of your longings and desires, the fulfillment of your aspirations. How perfectly the condition of this sufferer typifies the state of unregenerate humanity!

By nature, we are outside the Beautiful Gate, "afar off," without God and without hope, "strangers from the covenants of promise." It doesn't matter how people may cleanse us by reform methods, or how resolutely we may endeavor to cleanse ourselves; how we may be dressed up in culture, morality and refinement; we are still outside the Beautiful Gate. We may be borne along on our own native resolution, or the willpower of others, to the very portal; but we cannot enter; for Jesus has said, "No man cometh unto the Father, but by me" (John 14:6). It takes Jesus to bring you in. And how ready He is to do it! See where He comes, in the persons of two of His representatives, Peter and John, and of them the lame man "asked an alms."

What a poor, imperfect prayer! But a prayer nevertheless; and oh, the power of prayer! He asked, and One has said, "Ask and it shall be given you; seek, and ye shall find; knock, and it shall be opened unto you.... Every one that asketh receiveth" (Matt. 7:7-8). Every one that asketh, *no matter how imperfectly*, receiveth.

Many years ago, I heard a woman address an audience of thousands in one of the great cities of the world. She has been in the homeland for a long time now, and it is not necessary to mention the name by which she was known on this earth, suffice it to say that she bore a title of nobility and had been closely associated with royalty. She was educated, cultivated, accomplished, graceful, and beautiful; owned more castles than she could live in, and had been brought up in a most dignified church, where she was accustomed to sit in cathedrals, with the light pouring from windows of amethyst, ruby, and topaz-stained glass; listen to the sobbing of great organs, and the oratory of famous ecclesiastics, and murmur responses out of a prayer- book to the prayers prescribed by the ritual.

She didn't realize that she was outside the Beautiful Gate till one day when stark, staring, shameful tragedy stalked into her home, and she had to find a living Christ to help her bear her unsupportable burden. Under the shadows of the trees of her ancestral woods, at evening, when the dusk was falling and the stars were beginning to shine, she cried: "O God, let me know that You are!" for truly she was outside everything.

Quick as a flash came the answer, "Act as though I was and thou shalt know that I AM."

So real was the message that she replied, "I'll do it."

Into the house she went to get her Bible and fall upon her knees. In a few moments she found herself inside the Beautiful Gate, brought nigh by the blood of Christ. How astonished people were!

I could not begin to tell you how wines were banished from her home, how prayer meetings took the place of balls and dinner parties, how she forgot to send cards to the dukes and duchesses and how she invited the poor and lowly. Yes, prayer, even a poor and imperfect prayer, if heartfelt, will work wonders.

Now to return to the lame man who is still outside the Beautiful Gate. In answer to his prayer Peter says, "Look on me." It matters everything where you look. The power of a look! It brings what you look for right into your soul and body. It changes you into what you look at. "We, beholding as in a glass the glory of the Lord, are changed into the same image" (see 2 Cor. 3:18). Beholding. the glory of the Lord we are changed into the same image. God says so.

There is life, spiritual life, physical life for a look at the Crucified One.

And the lame man obeyed; he gave heed to them, expecting to receive something of them. Looking, and expecting, he could not be disappointed. Neither can you.

Look, and expect, this moment.

Those who do this are never disappointed.

But right here Peter carefully explains to the man just what he may expect from Peter and John, and that is exactly and precisely nothing. No more and no less. "Silver and gold have I none." "We're bankrupt; so far as I go personally, I couldn't heal you of a wart on your finger, or the smallest corn, on your little toe."

That is what Peter would tell us if he were here this moment, and by actions if not words he said further:

"Nevertheless, look on us and see through us, and in us, Another, who is almighty, whose will it is to heal all who call upon Him! Such as I have give I thee."

"Then you have something?"

"Yes," he could have answered, "I have the name, which conveys the 'all power' of Jesus the Son of God.

"Utterly bankrupt and perfectly helpless in ourselves, we are nevertheless the accredited agents of Omnipotence. In the name of Jesus Christ of Nazareth, rise up and walk."

And the lame man, looking steadfastly with the eye of faith, saw no longer feeble human beings, but ambassadors for God, plenipotentiaries, through whom God is operating. He yields to the kind, warm grasp and lets himself be lifted up.

Immediately, the response to immediate faith is instantaneous—his feet and ankle bones receive strength, "and he leaping up (oh, the buoyancy, the ecstasy of newborn faith!), stood, and walked, and entered with them into the temple."

This is the first recorded miracle of healing in the Holy Ghost dispensation. As that is the era in which we are living, we have a right to expect that God will work, in answer to implicit faith, just as mightily today. And we shall not be disappointed if we cast ourselves upon Him, and trust Him wholly.

Are you outside the Beautiful Gate?

Don't stay there!

Yield to the kind, strong Arm which is held out to lift you up.

'Aeneas, Jesus Christ Cures You...'

Now Peter, as he went to town after town, came down also to God's people at Lud. There he found a man by the name of Eneas, who for eight years had kept his bed, through being paralyzed. Peter said to him, Eneas, Jesus Christ cures you. Rise and make your own bed. He at once rose to his feet.

(Acts 9:32-35, WNT)

Here is a case of healing of a hopeless chronic disease which took place after Christ's ascension.

If the eye of some sufferer from chronic disease is scanning this page let me lovingly entreat him to pray, before reading further, in the words of the psalmist, "Open Thou mine eyes, that I may behold wondrous things out of Thy law."

Can you not in this scripture see Peter hurrying from town to town, ministering everywhere in the "power of His resurrection," reaching Lydda, and being lovingly greeted by the brethren there? It was probably not long before some brother said: "We have a very sad case here. A man by the name of Aeneas has been absolutely bedfast for eight long years. Could you visit him?"

As the apostle stands by that bed of pain, those sad eyes that have looked so long in vain for deliverance, are fixed upon his face. What does Peter do? Nothing. What can he do but fade out of the picture and let the One who has already done it all shine forth in His power and glory—the

One by whose stripes Aeneas was healed already if he would only believe it.

"Aeneas, Jesus Christ cures you." The "messenger" delivers his message, brings the sufferer face to face with Jesus, "who went about doing good and healing all" (Acts 10:38).

One look of faith to the risen One and Aeneas' eyes, sad no longer, flash with superabundant vitality. He rises "immediately." We can't blame him for being in something of a hurry to get up after eight years of helpless recumbency. He makes his own bed. What a luxury after being hauled and mauled around by well-meaning but oftentimes awkward people! Only those who know what it means to lie an inert mass of flesh at the mercy of others can appreciate Aeneas' feelings.

How he enjoyed walking! By merely walking about, letting people see him, he was used to bring about a revival that swept all the people of Lydda and Sharon into the fountain of cleansing.

If the Word of God says, "Jesus Christ maketh thee whole," have we any right to be one half or even three quarters whole? If Peter told Aeneas, "Jesus Christ cures you," are we justified in remaining sick? Or was this wonderful gift only for Aeneas and certain other favorites?

We can find the answer to this query in Luke 4:16-30. Jesus had returned to His hometown. He read as follows from Isaiah 61: "The Spirit of the Lord is upon Me, because He hath anointed Me to preach the gospel to the poor; He hath sent Me to heal the broken-hearted, to preach deliverance to the captives, and recovering of sight to the blind, to set at liberty them that are bruised, to preach the acceptable year of the Lord."

Then closing the book and sitting down, when all eyes are fastened upon Him, He said, "This day is this scripture fulfilled in your ears." In other words, He proclaimed salvation, healing, deliverance, the opening of blind eyes, physical and spiritual, for all who would accept it, then and there. What hindered? One thing only—their failure to acknowledge, accept, believe upon, and submit to the Word of God made flesh, who stood among them offering Himself freely to all.

"He sent His Word and healed them." Naaman humbled himself, believed the message in the mouth of a serving maid, obeyed God and was healed.

The widow of Sarepta believed so thoroughly that at God's command, she took the bread from the mouth of her son who was threatened with death from famine, and she and her son, and her house, were saved from death. If you really believe the promise, you will obey the precept that accompanies it.

"Aeneas, Jesus Christ cures you." Put your name, James, John, Jacob, or whatever it may be, in place of "Aeneas" in this scripture, and believe it.

Your disease will vanish—I say it on the authority of the Word of God.

God says, "I am the Lord that healeth thee" (Ex. 15:26).

"I am the Lord, I change not" (Mal. 3:6).

FREE FROM THE LAW OF SIN AND DEATH

Medicine and law are called the two great "learned professions," and I love to study them both, from the only complete textbook to be found on the subjects, the Bible.

Search every medical library in the world, but you cannot find the cause and cure of every disease that ever afflicted, or will ever afflict, humanity; but this is contained in the Bible.

Transfer your research activities to legal libraries and admire the wisdom of the various legal codes of ancient and modern times, but it is only in the Bible that we find the "perfect law," the law of the Lord which converteth the soul, something which no human legislation can effect (Ps. 19:7).

How reassuring it is to learn from this infallible authority on legal matters that freedom from sin and sickness comes to us by virtue of a law "The law of the Spirit of Life in Christ Jesus hath made me free from the law of sin and death" (Rom. 8:2).

Never shall I forget the glad day when I made this discovery! Rather I should say the glad day when it was revealed to me that the teaching of the Bible in reference to the healing of sickness is just as universal and unchanging as that regarding deliverance from the guilt and power of sin.

We are freed from both by the operation of the law of the Spirit of life in Christ Jesus.

Laws have no favorites. We have only to meet the conditions necessary for their operation and the work is done. When the conditions of faith and repentance are met, a man is freed from the guilt and power of sin just as effectively today as in apostolic times. The blood has never lost its power!

If one asks us, "How can I be sure that these promises of pardon and cleansing refer to me and are effective in my case today?" we reply, "Because Jesus Christ said, 'Him that cometh unto Me I will in no wise cast out' , and 'Lo I am with you even unto the consummation of the age'" (see John 6:37; Matt. 28:20).

But when it comes to sickness, we encounter an altogether different attitude in some who profess to believe God's Word. The promises regarding the healing of disease are held to be special, or particular, rather than universal. They seem to be considered the property of such people as Elijah, Moses, Miriam, Peter, John, Philip, and others like them, and not generally available today. But we find in this scripture (Rom. 8:2) that freedom from the law of sin and death (including the death process which we call disease), comes to us not as some special favor, accorded only to the few, but by the operation of a law.

As said before, "Laws have no favorites," are no respecters of persons. Given the necessary conditions, and the law invariably operates.

Edison accomplished wonders in the realm of electricity. Each night as the shadows fall upon the great Pacific near which I dwell, the shores of the bay are decked for miles and miles with gleaming lights that shine like diamonds against the darkness.

Edison accomplished his wonders not because he was Edison, but because he acquainted himself with the laws governing electricity and obeyed them. The force electricity—existed long prior to his experiments and stood ready to serve anyone who would place themselves under the sway of the laws that govern its operations. These laws are invariable, and the power of electricity was the same as it is today, in ancient days, when men did not obey its laws and utilize its power.

God's law for us is holiness, health, and happiness. In absolute obedience to it, Jesus Christ, the Spotless Lamb, went about healing all that were sick, and diffusing joy and gladness. "These things have I spoken unto you that your joy might be full" (John 15:11). Following in His footsteps, we come under the operation of the "law of the Spirit of life in Christ Jesus" and are free from the law of sin and death. We are lifted above it into a realm where it is inoperative, just as we lift an object and hold it, by the superior force of vital power, above the action of gravitation.

The gateway into this life is Galatians 2:20: "I live; yet not I but Christ liveth in me: and the life which I now live in the flesh I live by the faith of the Son of God, who loved me and gave Himself for me."

The manner of it is—always joyful…unceasing in prayer…in every circumstance… thankful…aloofness from every form of evil.

The result—holiness, happiness, health. "Bodies preserved complete and found blameless at the coming of the Lord Jesus Christ" (1 Thess. 5:16-23 WNT).

"Faithful is he that calleth you who also will do it" (1 Thess. 5:24).

NOTES

1. Gordon P. Gardiner, "Out of Zion ... into All the World," Bread of Life XXXII, no. 1 (January 1983): 6; Dr. Amelia Yeomans ([Canada]: Manitoba Culture, Heritage and Recreation, 1985), 1; "Noted Woman Dies," Calgary Farm and Ranch Review 9, no. 9 (May 5, 1913): 453. "Lilian Yeomans" research file of Gordon P. Gardiner for his book, Out of Zion, located at the FPHC. Henry J. Morgan ed., Canadian Men and Women of the Time: A Handbook of Canadian Biography of Living Characters (Toronto: W. Briggs, 1898), 1108. Her parents named their firstborn Lilian, perhaps in part because of the lilies which grew at that time of year, and Barbara after her maternal grandmother. See: Morgan, 1108.

2. Toronto Mail, May 20, 1880. Cecil Robeck states Augustus took his family to the U.S., but I have been unable to locate evidence for this. See: Cecil M. Robeck, "Yeomans, Lilian Barbara" in The New International Dictionary of Pentecostal and Charismatic Movements, rev. ed., ed. Stanley M. Burgess and Eduard M. van der Maas (Grand Rapids: Zondervan, 2002), 1222. An online biography of Lilian Yeomans life also lists the entire family as moving in 1862, but does not list the citation. See: Healing and Revival, "Out of the Depths I have Cried unto Thee, O Lord," Healing and Revival Press, 2004, accessed, April 30, 2015, http://healingandrevival.com/BioLYeomans.htm.

3. Obituary: Yeomans, Charlotte Amelia, Los Angeles Times, October 31, 1939.

4. Gardiner, 6; Morgan, 1108.

5. Gardiner, 6.

6. Ibid.

7. Kim Mayer, Bentley Historical Library, The University of Michigan, correspondence with Glenn Gohr Assemblies of God Archives, September 12, 1996, which includes information from the necrology file of Amelia Le Sueur Yeomans—Record card completed June 11, 1900 and a form for alumni and former students completed and sent to the alumni office, February 3, 1911. Photocopies in Amelia Yeomans file, FPHC. See also Dr. Amelia Yeomans, 1, which states there were no women medical students in

Canada until 1880.

8. Captain Augustus Asa Yeomans, Assistant Surgeon, died on May 19, 1880 in Toronto, Canada. See: "1881," US Army Military Registers 1789-1969, 266. See also Dr. Amelia Yeomans, 1.

9. Toronto Mail, May 20, 1880. See also Toronto Globe, May 20, 1880.

10. Mayer correspondence; Carlotta Hacker, The Indomitable Lady Doctors (Halifax, Nova Scotia: Formac Publishing Company Ltd., 2001), 89.

11. Amelia Yeomans file, FPHC.; Hacker, 89.

12. Gardiner, 6.

13. Lilian Yeomans file, FPHC.

14. Dr. Amelia Yeomans, 2; Lilian Yeomans file, FPHC.

15. Amelia Yeomans file FPHC. Thomas W. Miller, Canadian Pentecostals: A History of the Pentecostal Assemblies of Canada (Ontario: Full Gospel Publishing House), 73; One historian described the effect of the changes to Winnipeg between 1870 and 1880 in the following terms, "Overcrowding in the city's north end, poverty, unemployment, prostitution and inadequate sewage, housing and medical facilities were only a few of the problems plaguing the new provincial capital." See: Dr. Amelia Yeomans, 2.

16. Dr. Amelia Yeomans, 2; According to Carlotta Hacker, both Dr. Amelia Yeomans and her daughter Lilian were well established in their practice in Winnipeg by 1885. See: Hacker, 70.

17. Amelia Yeomans file, FPHC. See also: "Medical," Winnipeg Manitoba Daily Free Press, February 13, 1884, 1; and May 19, 1886, 1.

18. Winnipeg Manitoba Daily Free Press, April 7, 1886, 2.

19. John Alexander Dowie, "Cheering Words from Zion's Guests," Leaves of Healing: Notes From Zion Home 4, no. 18 (February 26, 1898): 351. See also: Charlotte Amelia (Amy) Yeomans ministerial file, FPHC.

20. Winnipeg Manitoba Daily Free Press, December 22, 1887, 4. Dr. Amelia Yeomans, 2. Amelia was active in multiple social and humanitarian endeavors including the Women's Christian Temperance Movement, the Winnipeg Humane Society (vice president), and was the founder and president of the Manitoba Suffrage Club. See: Morgan, 1108.

21. Lilian B. Yeomans, Healing from Heaven (Springfield, MO: Gospel Publishing House, 1926), 12.

22. Ibid., 12-13.

23. Ibid., 12.

24. Ibid.

25. Lilian B. Yeomans, "Out of the Depths: A Testimony," Evangel Tract No. 917 (Springfield, MO: Gospel Publishing House, [1923?]), 2.

26. Robeck, 1222; Yeomans, "Out of the Depths," Evangel Tract No. 917, 7; Yeomans, Healing from Heaven, 12.

27. Yeomans, Healing from Heaven, 12.

28. Ibid.

29. Ibid., 12-13.

30. Ibid., 13.

31. Ibid.

32. Ibid.

33. Dowie, "Cheering Words," Leaves of Healing, Feb. 26, 1898, 350.

34. Yeomans, Healing from Heaven, 14.

35. Ibid, 15.

36. Ibid.

37. Ibid.

38. John Alexander Dowie, "Cheering Words from Zion's Guests," Leaves of Healing: Notes From Zion Home 4, no. 15 (February 5, 1898): 295.

39. Yeomans, Healing from Heaven, 17.

40. Ibid., 12. For a look at the contemporary Assemblies of God position on the relationship between healing and faith see: "Divine Healing: Adopted by the General Presbytery in session August 9-11, 2010," accessed June 1, 2015, http://ag.org/top/Beliefs/position_papers/pp_downloads/PP_Divine_Healing.pdf.

41. Yeomans, Healing from Heaven, 11.

42. Ibid., 12; Robeck, 1222.

43. Ibid.; Yeomans, "Out of the Depths," Evangel Tract No. 917, 5.

44. Yeomans, Healing from Heaven, 15.

45. Lilian B. Yeomans, "The Bible or Christian Science—Which?" Evangel Tract No. 948 (Springfield, MO: Gospel Publishing House, n.d.), 5.

46. Ibid., 5, 9.

47. Ibid., 9.

48. Ibid., 5, 11.

49. Ibid., 10.

50. Ibid., 5, 6.

51. Ibid., 10.

52. Ibid., 11.

53. Ibid.

54. Ibid.

55. Yeomans, Healing from Heaven, 11.

56. Ibid., 15.

57. Lilian B. Yeomans, "Delivered from the Use of Morphine," Triumphs of Faith 41, no. 9 (September 1921): 201.

58. Yeomans, "Out of the Depths," Evangel Tract No. 917, 6. This testimony was also reprinted in Carrie Judd Montgomery's Triumphs of Faith 32, no.10 (October 1912): 220-226; see also: Yeomans, Healing from Heaven, 16.

59. Yeomans, Healing from Heaven, 12.

60. Ibid.

61. Yeomans, "Out of the Depths," Evangel Tract No. 917, 8.

62. Ibid., 7.

63. Ibid., 8-9. All Scripture quotations drawn from the KJV unless otherwise noted.

64. Ibid., 9.

65. Ibid.

66. Ibid.

67. Ibid.

68. Yeomans, "Delivered from the Use of Morphine," 201.

69. Dowie, "Cheering Words," Leaves of Healing, February 5, 1898, 295. This publication which contained testimonies from the Zion Home's guests, lists both Dr. Lillian (name incorrectly spelled), and her sister, Miss C. A. Yeomans.

70. Dowie, "Cheering Words," Leaves of Healing, February 26, 1898, 350.

71. Ibid., 351.

72. James Opp, The Lord for the Body, (London: McGill-Queen's University Press, 2005), 94.

73. Yeomans noted of her experience, "I doubt if any competent physician would have dared to take it away from me." Dowie, "Cheering Words," Leaves of Healing, February 5, 1898, 295.

74. Yeomans, "Out of the Depths," Evangel Tract No. 917, 10.

75. Dowie, "Cheering Words," Leaves of Healing, February 5, 1898, 295.

76. Dowie, "Cheering Words," Leaves of Healing, February 26, 1898, 351.

77. Yeomans, "Out of the Depths," Evangel Tract No. 917, 11.

78. Ibid.

79. Ibid.

80. Ibid.

81. Ibid.

82. Dowie, "Cheering Words," Leaves of Healing, February 26, 1898, 350; Robeck, 1222.

83. Yeomans, "Out of the Depths," Evangel Tract No. 917, 11-12.

84. Yeomans, Healing from Heaven, 19.

85. Lilian B. Yeomans, "Out of the Depths: A Testimony," Triumphs of Faith 32, no.10 (October 1912): 220-226; Yeomans, Healing from Heaven, 17-19. This is also true of the following reprinted versions of her testimony: Yeomans, "Out of the Depths," Evangel Tract No. 917 (Springfield, MO: Gospel Publishing House, [1923?]). Also edited and published posthumously in the Pentecostal Evangel under that same title (December 26, 1942), 6-7; "The Raven and the Dove: A Personal Experience," Bridal Call 8, no. 5 (October 1924): 25-26; and "Delivered from the Use of Morphine," Triumphs of Faith 41, no. 9 (September 1921): 199-203.

86. Grant Wacker, Chris R. Armstrong, and Jay S. F. Blossom, "John Alexander Dowie: Harbinger of Pentecostal Power," in Portraits of a Generation: Early Pentecostal Leaders, ed. James R. Goff and Grant Wacker (Fayetteville, AR: University of Arkansas Press, 2002), 3-19. It is not clear if Lilian would have seen the leaving out of Dowie's name as a human or Holy Spirit

prompted omission. See: Yeomans, "Out of the Depths," Evangel Tract no 917, 12, where she states, "I was greatly helped in my hour of anguish and sore trial by the prayers and counsels of some of God's people. I had thought to mention the names of some of these, but I am withheld from doing so." This phrase was also included in Yeomans, "Out of the Depths," Triumphs of Faith, 226.

87. Opp, The Lord for the Body, 93, 95.

88. Lilian B. Yeomans, "Not One Feeble Person Among All Their Tribes," The Bridegroom's Messenger 7, no. 148 (January 15, 1914): 4.

89. Ibid. However, this high praise of physicians was not included in a similar recounting of the health of the children of Israel in Lilian B. Yeomans, "Moses' Medicine Chest," Evangel Tract No. 647 (Springfield, MO: Gospel Publishing House, n.d.).

90. Yeomans, "Delivered from the Use of Morphine," 202.

91. Lilian Barbara Yeomans, ministerial file, FPHC. See also: Charlotte Amelia (Amy) Yeomans, ministerial file, FPHC.

92. Yeomans, "Delivered from the Use of Morphine," 202.

93. Ibid., 202-203; Jodie Loutzenhiser, "Lilian Yeomans: To God Be the Glory," Memos 33, no. 4 (Fall 1988): 4.

94. Yeomans, "Delivered from the Use of Morphine," 202; Dowie, "Cheering Words," Leaves of Healing, February 26, 1898, 351

95. Yeomans, "Delivered from the Use of Morphine," 203.

96. Ibid.

97. "Tanis" means "daughter" in Cree. Loutzenhiser, "Lilian Yeomans," 4; Gordon P. Gardiner, Out of Zion into All the World (Shippensburg, PA: Companion Press, 1990), 131.

98. A small reference to a Miss Tanis Miller, listed as Dr. Yeomans' "coworker" is made by the editor of the Pentecostal Evangel. See: "The Miracle Baby," Pentecostal Evangel, July 6, 1940, 4; From the "Lilian Yeomans" research file of Gordon P. Gardiner for his book, "Out of Zion," located at the FPHC.

99. Dr. Amelia Yeomans, 8.

100. Heather Cummings, Bentley Historical Library, The University of Michigan, correspondence with Glenn Gohr, June 17, 1996, and "Record

for General, Catalogue of Alumni and Former Students," February 3, 1911. In the Lilian Yeomans file, FPHC; Census Record (June 25, 1906: Calgary, Alberta, Sub District 21A,) 1, family 8; Loutzenhiser, 4.

101. Grant Wacker, Heaven Below (Cambridge, MA: Harvard University Press, 2003), 175.

102. Amelia Yeomans, "A Home for the Friendless," The Latter Rain Evangel 2, no.1 (October 1909): 10-14; Brainerd (MN) Daily Dispatch, March 23, 1927, 7.

103. Lilian B. Yeomans, "This is THE Rest ... and this is THE Refreshing," Pentecostal Evangel, April 26, 1930, 1.

104. Ibid.

105. Ibid.

106. The birthday of Pentecost in Manitoba was either May 2 or May 3, 1907, depending on which account one takes as primary. Miller, Canadian Pentecostals, 75, 76; Yeomans, "This is THE Rest ...," 1; Gloria G. Kulbeck, What God Hath Wrought: A History of the Pentecostal Assemblies of Canada (Toronto: The Pentecostal Assemblies of Canada, 1958), 139-140.

107. Yeomans, "This is THE Rest ...," 1.

108. Apostolic Messenger 1, no.1 (February & March 1908):4, accessed via IFPHC on April 30, 2015; Yeomans, "This is THE Rest ...," 1.

109. Yeomans, "This is THE Rest ...," 1.

110. Allan A. Swift, correspondence with P.S. Jones, September 24, 1959, and October 16, 1959. PAOC Archives.

111. John H. Watts, "Pentecostal Tabernacle of Calgary: An Historical Sketch," January 19, 1959, PAOC Archives. See also: Kulbeck, 166.

112. Carl Brumback, Suddenly from Heaven (Springfield, MO: Gospel Publishing House, 1961), 134; Gardiner, "Out of Zion ...," Bread of Life, 6.

113. Annie Douglas, A Mother in Israel: The Life Story of Mrs. Annie Douglas and a Tribute by Rev. J. McD. Kerr, Toronto, Canada, ed. G. S. Hunt (Seattle, WA: N.p., [1924?]), 106-107; Yeomans also recalls this experience in her book The Hiding Place (Springfield, MO: Gospel Publishing House, 1940), 4.

114. Douglas, A Mother in Israel, 107-108; Yeomans, The Hiding Place, 4.

115. Lilian Barbara Yeomans, ministerial file. It appears the family may have moved back and forth between San Francisco and Vancouver, British Columbia.

116. Ibid.; Charlotte Amelia (Amy) Yeomans, ministerial file.

117. "Glad Tidings Assembly and Bible Training School, San Francisco Calif," Pentecostal Evangel, Aug 6, 1921, 14.

118. Lilian Barbara Yeomans, ministerial file; Charlotte Amelia (Amy) Yeomans, ministerial file.

119. Carrie Judd Montgomery, "A Letter from the Editor," Triumphs of Faith 40, no.9 (September 1920): 206.

120. James W. Opp, "Balm of Gilead: Faith, Healing, and Medicine in the Life of Dr. Lilian B. Yeomans" (paper presented to the Canadian Society of Church History, Memorial University of Newfoundland, June 3-4, 1997), 5.

121. Lilian Barbara Yeomans, ministerial file. She also notes having served the Southwestern Bible School, Enid, Oklahoma (no date listed).

122. Loutzenhiser, 4; Brainerd (MN) Daily Dispatch, March 23, 1927, 7.

123. Loutzenhiser, 4.

124. See: Carry On L.I.F.E (Los Angeles: Lighthouse of International Foursquare Evangelism, 1931), 71 and 1933, 92. "Although she received much acclaim during her life she was always careful to give God the glory. She knew that she was just the vessel and God was the actual healer." Loutzenhiser, 4.

125. Brainerd (MN) Daily Dispatch, March 23, 1927, 7; A similar note about her preaching occurs in the Alton (IL) Evening Telegraph, June 5, 1926, 3.

126. Lillian Barbara Yeomans, letter to W. T. Gaston, July 30, 1929, Lilian Barbara Yeomans, ministerial file.

127. Ibid.

128. Ibid.

129. Ibid.

130. Matthew Avery Sutton, Aimee Semple McPherson and the Resurrection of Christian America (Cambridge, MA: Harvard University Press, 2007), 41-43, 90-118.

131. Lilian Barbara Yeomans, ministerial file.

132. Ibid.

133. Ibid. This was not the end of the controversy. After visiting an ill Sister McPherson, she noted in a letter to General Council Secretary J. R. Evans, dated September 15, 1930, that "Exception was taken to my action ... and I am informed that an effort is being made to oust me from the District Council." Evans replied that while he had not heard of her particular case, "it was the opinion of the Executive brethren that we could not endorse any of our General Council ministers having anything to do with Angeles [sic] Temple ... we feel it would be very unwise for you to take up work at that school." Though she continued as an Assemblies of God minister until her death in 1942, she was again the subject of scrutiny by the Southern California district as noted in a letter from General Secretary J. Roswell Flower to Yeomans dated June 6, 1938.

134. Lilian B. Yeomans "Poppies Red and Poppies White," Pentecostal Evangel, January 23, 1926, 5; Lilian B. Yeomans, "The Living Dead: Victims of the Narcotic Evil," pamphlet (Springfield, MO: Gospel Publishing House, 1931); The Springfield Leader announces her preaching every night at "8 o'clock" at the Gospel Tabernacle on Boonville and Lynn St. (April 8, 1930, 5), "Subject for Tuesday night: 'How I was delivered from being a drug addict,' & etc."

135. Montgomery, 206. Both Lilian and her sister Charlotte were published in Triumphs of Faith, and the Pentecostal Evangel. Lilian wrote primarily healing articles while Charlotte wrote Spiritual Poems. For examples of Charlotte's poetry see: "The King is on His Way," Pentecostal Evangel, June 24, 1922, and "Laughter" in Triumphs of Faith 40, no. 8 (Aug. 1920): 178.

136. Lilian B. Yeomans, "Divine Healing," Pentecostal Evangel, January 26, 1923, 6.

137. To order a digital or print copy of one of several of Dr. Yeomans books phone 1(800) 641-4310, visit gospelpublishing.com, or write Gospel Publishing House 1445 N. Boonville Ave., Springfield, MO 65802. Most of Dr. Yeomans' books went through several editions and in the process a few underwent name changes, including: Divine Healing Diamonds which became The Great Physician (1961); and The Royal Road to Health-Ville which became Health and Healing (1966). Lilian also compiled a list of her

sister's "Spiritual Songs" or poems under the title Gold of Ophir: Spiritual Songs Given Through Amy Yeomans (1941); original copies of her GPH tracts, often drawn from portions of previously printed articles may be found on file at the FPHC.

138. Opp, The Lord for the Body, 177.

139. See: "Forward" to revised, 1973, edition of Healing from Heaven, 3. Note also: The Royal Road to Health-Ville: Some Simple Talks About Divine Healing.

140. Yeomans, "Delivered from the Use of Morphine," 199.

141. Yeomans, Healing from Heaven, 18; Lilian wrote, "If one asks us, 'How can I be sure that these promises of pardon and cleansing refer to me and are effective in my case today?' we reply, 'Because Jesus Christ said, "Him that cometh unto Me I will in no wise cast out."' " Yeomans, "Free from the Law of Sin and Death," Tract No. 442 (Springfield, MO: Gospel Publishing House, n.d.), 2.

142. Yeomans, Royal Road, 55.

143. Ibid., 56; "Do you ask, 'How can I make the remedy effective in my own case?' by taking it! That is, believe the Word exactly as it reads, in relation to yourself, reading it in the present tense: 'He sends His Word and heals me.' In this way the power of the omnipotent Word of God is released in your physical being, cleansing and quickening every cell, fiber and tissue." Yeomans, "Moses' Medicine Chest," Tract No. 4540 (Springfield, MO: Gospel Publishing House, n.d.), 5-6.

144. Yeomans, "Moses' Medicine Chest," Tract No. 4540, 4.

145. Yeomans, Royal Road, 56.

146. Ibid., 57.

147. Yeomans, "Free from the Law of Sin and Death," 3.

148. Yeomans, The Hiding Place, 16.

149. Lilian B. Yeomans, Manhattan Beach, California, letter to Rev. J. R. Evans, General Secretary, Springfield, Missouri, August 6, 1935, in Lilian Barbara Yeomans, ministerial file.

150. On the 1938 annual Assemblies of God ministers' questionnaire, she replied: "Have not preached as much as in former years [only 75 times (!)] owing to home responsibilities." Lilian Barbara Yeomans, ministerial file.

151. Lilian B. Yeomans, Gold of Ophir: Spiritual Songs Given Through Amy Yeomans (N.P.: Lilian B. Yeomans, 1941), 3.

152. Lilian Barbara Yeomans, ministerial file.

153. Ibid.

154. Ibid.

155. Ibid.

156. Ibid.

157. Ibid.

158. Lilian Barbara Yeomans, ministerial file. cf. Robeck, "Yeomans" who lists the date of her death as December 9.

159. Yeomans, "Out of the Depths," Pentecostal Evangel, 6.

160. Yeomans, "This is THE Rest ...," 1.

161. Loutzenhiser, 4.

YOUR HOUSE OF
FAITH

Sign up for **FREE** Subscription to the
Harrison House digital magazine, and get
excellent content delivered directly to your inbox!
harrisonhouse.com/signup

Sign-up for Messages that Equip You to Walk in the Abundant Life

• Receive biblically-sound and Spirit-filled encouragement to focus on and maintain your faith
• Grow in faith through biblical teachings, prayers, and other spiritual insights
• Connect with a community of believers who share your values and beliefs

Experience Fresh Teachings and Inspiration to Build Your Faith

• Deepen your understanding of God's purpose for your life
• Stay connected and inspired on your faith journey
• Learn how to grow spiritually in your walk with God

In the Right Hands, This Book Will Change Lives!

Most of the people who need this message will not be looking for this book. To change their lives, you need to **put a copy of this book in their hands.**

Our ministry is constantly seeking methods to find the people who need this anointed message to change their lives. **Will you help us reach these people?**

Extend this ministry by sowing 3 books, 5 books, 10 books, or more today, and become a life changer! Your generosity will be part of catalyzing the Great Awakening that many have been prophesying and praying for.